BUFFALO
BEER

BUFFALO BEER

THE HISTORY OF BREWING
IN THE NICKEL CITY

MICHAEL F. RIZZO & ETHAN COX

AMERICAN PALATE

Published by American Palate
A division of The History Press
Charleston, SC 29403
www.historypress.net

Copyright © 2015 by Michael F. Rizzo and Ethan Cox
All rights reserved

First published 2015

ISBN 9781540211156

Library of Congress Control Number: 2014953416

For Steve, Gene, Mike, Al and Neumann, who introduced me to heavy metal and beer.

Dedicated to my wife and sons—Jennifer, Aleister and Phineas—for their love and patience and to David Mik and Stephen R. Powell, for keeping the flame of history alight.

CONTENTS

CONTENTS

PREFACE

I was sixteen years old. It was a typical cold winter night in Buffalo, New York, where I grew up, when one of my new friends, Gene, called me and asked if I wanted to hang out. Of course I did. I was in a new school, a new neighborhood, and he was the first kid who introduced himself to me.

I met him, Steve and Mike at his house. What was the great plan on this cold night? Why, drink beer and hang out under the viaduct. At this point, I had never really had beer and was not really interested, but these guys were going to do it, so I joined them.

Looking back, standing under that viaduct two blocks from my house, drinking a (literally) ice cold Genny, my fingers frozen, shivering in the cold, bullshitting with those guys, was one of the best nights of my young life. It would lead to many years of friendship.

That was my baptism into beer.

Sometime in the late 1990s, I took a multi-week course on homebrewing that was run by Paul Dyster, the owner of Niagara Tradition Home Beer and Wine Supply (and currently mayor of Niagara Falls, New York). One of the guest speakers Paul had was a friend and homebrewer named Tim Herzog who wanted to start his own brewery. Just a few years later, he did—Flying Bison Brewing Company. As for that class, I went on to brew a few batches of beer and even entered one in a competition, taking home third place in a specialty category.

In 2008, I formed a Buffalo history tour company, and by 2011, we had added walking tours of former brewery magnates in United German and French Cemetery in Cheektowaga. The tours were well received, and through them I met Ethan Cox, co-founder and president of Community Beer Works. We had briefly discussed the only other book on Buffalo beer history, Stephen Powell's *Rushing the Growler*, and our desire to rewrite it one day but left it at that.

When I decided I wanted to pursue this project, he was the first and only person I contacted, and he was ready. Ethan has been a great co-author, editing my manuscript, finding inconsistencies in the stories and questioning, as well as applauding, different aspects of the book. In addition, he went way beyond what I anticipated, taking photos and updating the Facebook page for the book months before its release.

There are always people and places that need to be recognized when a project like this is undertaken. First, thank you to Ethan for his commitment to the project. I think we succeeded. Thank you to brewery historian Dave Mik for access to his enormous collection of breweriana and to Chris Groves for the fantastic photography. Thank you once again to Fultonhistory.com for access to newspaper archives. For photos, thank you to Jennifer Reed, *WNY Craft Beer* magazine, Jeff Ware, Matthew McCormick and Buffaloeats. org. If we missed anyone, we apologize.

And as always, thank you to my wonderful wife, Michelle, and son, Gerlando, for losing me at times while I delved into the Internet or went on a two-day writing binge. I love you both tremendously.

MIKE RIZZO, OCTOBER 2014

I have a photograph—amazingly—of the moment I first discovered that Buffalo had this incredibly rich brewing (and malting) history. I was home in Buffalo for Christmas 1999, on a break from studying cognitive psychology at the University of Arizona in Tucson. I was sitting in front of the tree, holding Stephen Powell's *Rushing the Growler* (a copy I still have in much thumbed-through condition), which was a present that year from my mom. I also distinctly remember buying new local beer that year in the form of Blizzard Bock, from the now defunct Buffalo Brewing Company. Even as I was off in the desert studying intently to research interesting questions in human-language processing (and homebrewing like mad), the seeds of a future in Buffalo's brewing industry were being planted. I have to thank my mother, Stephen Powell and Kevin Townsell for that.

In 2006, my wife and I relocated to Buffalo from Chicago and began our family; I took a job teaching at a local, small college. I also immediately got

PREFACE

active in the local homebrewing scene and have met so many great people through it over the years. I can't thank the various members of the Niagara Association of Homebrewers and the owners of Niagara Tradition Home Beer and Wine Supply enough for encouraging my beery passion but also for formalizing my understanding of beer in the form of education and certification. My Beer Judge Certification Program study and testing have added a lot to my evaluative skills.

Additionally, writing for the online (and briefly print) publication *Buffalo Rising* introduced me to many of the generous and entertaining figures in Buffalo's brewing, drinking and restaurant industry, and without those connections, I very much doubt I'd be part of a successful brewing concern or writing this book. In some sense, Newell Nussbaumer is both directly and indirectly responsible for the craft beer and brewing explosion we've seen in Buffalo over the last eight years or so, and I owe him a debt of gratitude for helping me into the industry.

In 2009, when it became clear that I was parting ways with the academic world, my longtime friend Dave Foster and I began exploring businesses that would combine my brewing interests and his restaurant background. Around the same time, I approached a guy I'd met many times on the beery scene, Robert "Rudy" Watkins, about conspiring to form some kind of homebrewing collective with a shared space. Neither project happened, exactly, but together they evolved into Community Beer Works, and along with Greg Tanski; Dan Conley; Chris Smith; Matthew Daumen; and my dad, Joseph Cox, we've had a really incredible run so far with a very promising future ahead. I have to thank those guys for putting up with me, especially as I try to juggle ever more balls at once, this book being one of them.

Mike aptly described, in his own preface, how we came to meet and the genesis of this partnership; I am forever thankful for his reaching out to me for help. There is no way this book would have or could have happened without him—not only did he have the means to reach out to The History Press to initiate the project, but he can also write far better and faster than I, and his research-from-afar skills are impressive. In providing what I could to this endeavor, I met and got to know an incredible researcher and collector, David Mik (and his wife Lori), and I also cannot thank them enough for allowing me and Chris Groves into their house (and Dave's basement museum) for incredible photos and information.

Finally, thanks to my family. I know sometimes I am just about too busy to be a dad, but I hope not quite so. You certainly tolerate a lot, and I love you!

ETHAN COX, OCTOBER 2014

1

"THE WORLD'S FAVORITE BEVERAGE"

T hat's what a 1910 Buffalo newspaper article proclaimed. Beer has been
around for thousands of years, dating at least to ancient Egypt. It was
often thought of as a healthy drink. As per the "celebrated" Dr. Ule: "Beer,
in its perfect condition, is an excellent and healthful beverage, combining in
some measure the virtues of water, of wine and food, as it quenches thirst,
stimulates, cheers and strengthens."[1]

That 1910 article went on to say that "beer contains so small a percentage
of alcohol as to render it harmless when taken in moderation." Yet we know
from history that the world famous Erie Canal terminated in Buffalo in
1825, and Canal Street, which ran parallel to the canal, was deemed the
wickedest street in the world at one time. Crime and alcohol played a big
part in that. Maybe it was more whiskey than beer, but surely beer was also
consumed, possibly contributing to that wicked designation?

Still, beer has been exalted, loved and cherished. Today, who would think
of a sporting event without thinking of beer? American football, a fall/winter
sport, has become intertwined with beer. But in the nineteenth century,
beer was primarily consumed in the warm months, and sales decreased in
the winter. In fact, "the vast majority of the world's best workers are beer
drinkers, and beer drinking nations have long occupied the foremost position
in the progress of the world."[2] That says it all.

What could better exemplify this man-made concoction than a poem by
Thomas Warton, poet lauerate and cigarette and ale lover? Published in
1750, this is "A Panegyric on Oxford Ale":

A circa 1960s Iroquois draft beer can. Note the tab pull on the top. *Photo by Chris Groves, from the collection of Dave Mik.*

Balm of my cares, sweet solace of my toils,
Hail, Juice benignant! O'er the costly cups
Of riot-stirring wine, unwholesome draught,
Let Pride's loose sons prolong the wasteful night;
My sober evening let the tankard bless,
With toast embrown'd, and fragrant nutmeg
  fraught,
While the rich draught with oft-repeated whiffs
Tobacco mild improves. Divine repast!

THE HISTORY OF BREWING IN THE NICKEL CITY

Where no crude surfeit, or intemperate joys
Of lawless Bacchus reign; but o'er my foul
A calm Lethean creeps; in drowsy trance
Each thought subsides, and sweet oblivion wraps
My peaceful brain, as if the leaden rod
Of magic Morpheus o'er mine eyes had shed
Its opiate influence. What tho 'fore ills
Oppress, dire want of chill-dispelling coals
Or cheerful candle (save the make-weight's gleam
Haply remaining) heart-rejoicing Ale
Cheers the fad scene, and every want supplies.[3]

Buffalo was destined to be a city unlike most in the United States. The Erie Canal (which was the greatest engineering feat in the world at the time) stopped at its doorstep, allowing a small village with abundant resources to quickly grow into a bustling city. It would become a dominant manufacturing center during the industrial age right through World War II. It would grow to be the eighth largest city in America by the early twentieth century, with renowned architects leaving their marks across the city.

Two of many industries that Buffalo dominated in the nineteenth century were malt and beer. But with the advent of refrigeration, mega brewers were able to brew and ship beer to Buffalo cheaper than the local brewers could produce it. Prohibition closed most of the local breweries, and those that reopened afterward were constantly battling the mega brewers that oftentimes dumped their products at or below cost just to gain market share. In the end, the mega brewers won.

The most popular year that many history books reference in Buffalo's brewery history was 1863, when 35 breweries were active at one time. But that was just one year. There have been over 140 different breweries in operation in Buffalo at one time or another, some so small that it is nearly impossible to verify their very existences. The authors have attempted to document every one, but some have left too faint historical fingerprints to trace their pasts.

This book is about the men and women who started small businesses and toiled under conditions most of us would never tolerate—eighteen-hour days, extreme heat and cold and dangerous situations—to build companies and collectively hire hundreds of laborers to fill these growing enterprises.

Often, the people involved in these breweries owned large tracts of land around the city and into the suburbs. Almost weekly, there were land

A fantastic photo of the members of the Buffalo Brewers' Association, circa 1878, when the national association held its convention in Buffalo. *Front row, left to right:* George C. Ginther, Philip G. Schaefer, John L. Schwartz, Charles G. Pankow, Philip Stein and John Honecker. *Middle row, left to right:* Jacob F. Kuhn, Oscar P. Rochevot, William F. Duckwitz, Eugene Irr, John Kreitner, William Simon and Christian Trapp. *Back row, left to right:* Julius A. Scheu, Julius Binz, William T. Becker, George Dittly, Edwin G.S. Miller and Frank J. Illig. *Photo by Ethan Cox, from the collection of Dave Mik.*

transactions to and from the men or the breweries, sometimes to increase the size of the breweries or to purchase new saloons; other times, it was land far from the plants that they might have purchased as an investment or possibly traded with another investor.

These brewers were primarily of German heritage; the early settlers were primarily from modern-day Alsace, in France, and Baden, in southern Germany; others were first-generation Americans; and many would become leaders in the community in fraternal, social and political organizations. Many would leave fortunes when they died, including large monuments and mausoleums in the cemeteries. Some built enormous homes and lived lavish lifestyles.

These are the stories of the people and the companies they started or built. But there are stories of deceit, swindles, vast fortunes fought over and lawsuits. These men and women were pioneers and many times others wanted a piece of what they had.

2

IN THE BEGINNING

In 1800, the investors of the Holland Land Company, a Dutch business that had bought millions of acres of land in western New York, sent Joseph Ellicott to begin surveying the land and selling the parcels.

He began his work in what was then a wilderness with very few inhabitants. He created Niagara County, and then the villages of New Amsterdam (Buffalo) and Black Rock were formed. There were fewer than one hundred people living in Black Rock by 1811, but it was beginning to become an important port. It was in this growing port city that Joseph Webb decided to set up the area's first brewery.

Webb advertised in the *Buffalo Gazette*, the first newspaper published in Niagara County, on November 26, 1811, announcing his new establishment.[4] It has been hard to ascertain where Webb came from. He was definitely there until December 31, 1813, the night the British invaded and burned the villages of Black Rock and Buffalo. Like many, Webb probably moved westward to start over. His family appealed to Congress in 1840 for remuneration for their loss. Whatever came of that is inconsequential, as the area's first brewery was gone and it would take several years for Black Rock and Buffalo to rebuild after the devastation.

Across the state, another man was starting out in the brewing business and would one day be among Buffalo's most enduring brewers. John Moffat was born near the town of Moffat, Scotland, in 1766. He decided to try his luck in America and arrived in 1793, settling in Geneva, New

York. It was there that Moffat opened what is thought to be the first brewery in Geneva with Walter Grieve that same year.

Moffat was also an inventor and, in 1803, was issued a patent for a still. By late 1809, he had sold off his property and other holdings in Geneva and moved to Schenectady, New York, where he began another brewery. By 1815, Moffat's Brewery was selling the "best ale" in Schenectady, possibly the only ale at the time.

He continued to perfect his brewing process and opened other breweries in the Albany and Schenectady area, which would eventually lead to the opening of a brewery in Buffalo. But until that time, residents had to do with the "best ale" in Schenectady.

On May 24, 1820, John Moffat and Henry Topping dissolved their partnership, Moffat & Topping, in Schenectady, New York, ending one of Moffat's business interests[5] and paving the way for his role in Buffalo's brewing history.

3
THE ERIE CANAL

In 1821, Erie County was formed from part of Niagara County, with Buffalo as the county seat. The battle between the villages of Buffalo and Black Rock was heating up because the western terminus of the Erie Canal had not yet been decided. Both villages were fighting for that honor, and the commerce that was anticipated to come with it, as the canal was winding its way across New York. When Buffalo finally won that honor (due simply to its elevation) and the canal opened in October 1825, Buffalo began to explode with commerce and trade, growing to be one of the biggest cities in America by the turn of the century.

According to a publication titled the *Emporium* on January 22, 1825, there were two breweries in the village of Buffalo at the time.[6] Who were these men and where were their businesses? The first city directory was not printed until three years later, in 1828, so details are scarce.

Dennis Kane, P. Peacock and Charles D. Relay are the only persons listed as brewers in the 1828 village of Buffalo directory. When these men actually went into business is uncertain. There is no Peacock or Kane in the 1820 or 1830 U.S. census. Relay is in the 1830 census, but when he arrived is unknown.

It is certain that there was a brewery built at Morgan (later renamed South Elmwood Avenue) and Mohawk Streets, and in 1828, the Kane, Peacock & Relay brewery was listed on Niagara and Mohawk Streets, so it might have been next to what became Moffat's Brewery. The earliest Kane, Peacock and Relay would have started in business was after the burning of Buffalo and the rebuilding of the village, so sometime in 1814.

BUFFALO BEER

The Star Brewery was named after John L. Schwartz and partners purchased the defunct Queen City Brewing Company and renamed it. It would later be closed after merging with the Clinton Cooperative Brewing Company. This picture is circa 1897. *Photo from* Souvenir of Buffalo, on Occasion of the 37th Annual Convention at Buffalo, N.Y.

Immigrants of German origin started to arrive in Buffalo in 1821. They would go on to dominate politics, culture, business and beer right up until the world wars. Older history books on Buffalo generally mention that Rudolph Baer was possibly the third German to arrive in Buffalo in 1826. He was originally from Switzerland and landed in America in 1814. He ended up staying in Harrisburg, Pennsylvania, before making the trek north to Buffalo in 1826.

Baer (in some places named Barr) purchased the Cold Springs Hotel at the southeast corner of Main and Ferry Streets, well outside the city limits of the day, from a man named Major Miller. The property included land as well as the tavern. Baer is often mentioned in historic accounts as owning the first brewery in Buffalo, but since it was outside the city limits and he was never listed in a city directory, it might be an exaggeration.

A large spring was centered in what is the intersection of Ferry and Main Streets. It was enclosed by a stone wall and filled a basin twenty-one feet in diameter. This and other springs in the area gave it its name: Cold Springs.[7]

Shortly after settling into his business, Baer built a brewery behind the tavern, utilizing the nearby sparkling and cold spring water to brew what has been called the first "strong beer" in Buffalo. There is debate about what made this beer strong. One historian claimed it was the first cold-brewed lager in Buffalo. Or was it simply a stronger beer than the citizens were used to? According to a passage in Henry K. Smith's book, it might not have been of "high quality."[8]

It is entirely possible that Baer and Kane, Peacock & Relay were those first two breweries listed in the *Emporium*. It was after the Kane, Peacock &

Relay brewery was first listed in the 1828 city directory that John Moffat, of Schenectady's "best ale" fame, and his son James decided it was time to move west. They chose the bustling Great Lakes port village of Buffalo and, in 1828, purchased property at the corner of Morgan and Mohawk Streets, which included the former Kane, Peacock & Relay brewery, a cooper shop built in 1814 and a vacant lot "for a modest sum." Coopers were the men who built the barrels that the beer was stored in. Over the years, the Moffats used the old cooper shop to build ale and liquor barrels.

Although the father-and-son team purchased the property in 1828, they were not listed in the city directory as brewers until 1832. To further confuse matters, as can be seen in a Moffat's Brewery photo, the brewery claims to have been "established [in] 1833." It is possible that after purchasing the property they set out to build a new brewery while James worked on his products.

4
THE 1830s

A Growing Profession

Another one of the very earliest brewers in Buffalo was Jacob Roos. Born in Alsace, France, in 1808, Roos came to America as a young man. By 1830, he was in Buffalo, where he opened his first brewery in "Sandy Town," an area between Church and York Streets, on the Erie Canal towpath. His equipment "one iron kettle; his daily output, one half-barrel of beer; his delivery facilities, one wheel barrow."[9]

By 1832, Buffalo was growing frenetically, and that year, the village was incorporated as a city, leaving behind its modest beginnings. That year, six men were listed as being brewers by trade: John Benson (202 Main Street); James Carr (Crow Street); Robert Douglass (York Street); James McCulloch (Seneca Street); Alexander McCulloch Jr. (Farmer's Hotel); and Charles D. Relay (Seneca Street), whom, the authors believe, sold his brewery on the corner of Morgan and Mohawk Streets to James Moffat in 1828.

Rudolph Baer, who had a brewery in Cold Springs, leased the land and tavern to William Mosher, who, with Warren Granger, constructed an equestrian racetrack on the property. It is said that the track was the first west of the Genesee River. After Mosher's death in 1838, another man took over but died a year later. Then, Augustus and Charles Baer, sons of Rudolph, took charge of the property and the track. The property was leased multiple times, always returned to Charles Baer. This happened over and over until Baer finally sold the property in 1862.[10] Rudolph Baer had died in 1836.

In 1836, just four years after Buffalo was incorporated as a city, no fewer than twelve men listed their professions as brewer. They included the previously mentioned James Moffat and Alexander M'Culloch Jr., as well as Robert Coombs and Michael Benson at the foot of Genesee and Church Streets; John Benson and Anthony Giesz on Main Street above Chippewa Street; Louis Kappler on Main Street opposite the Western Literary and Scientific Academy, or just the Academy; Joseph Laux opposite the Academy; Jacob Roos on Rock Street below Genesee Street; and two Urbans, George and Lewis—who would go on to earn fortunes in the milling industry—at this time located on Main Street opposite the Academy, presumably very near Louis Kappler.

James McLeish, in 1836, opened a brewery at Main and Ferry Streets, still outside the city limits. Apparently, McLeish could see the future and manufactured his own malt from the beginning.[11]

5

THE 1840s

SCIENCE

David M. Kiefer, in a 2001 article in *Today's Chemist*, said, "Until the 19th century, brewing was more of an art than a science. Brewers had little knowledge of or control over the process, so quality varied widely from batch to batch. The introduction of simple instruments such as thermometers, hydrometers, and saccharometers made quality control more certain."[12]

Valentine Hoffman was born in 1806 and arrived in Buffalo in 1832, the year it became incorporated as a city. Jacob F. Schanzlin was born in Baden, Germany, in 1803 and arrived in Buffalo in 1828. The pair would meet while working for Rudolph Baer during the first years of operation at Baer's Cold Springs Hotel at Main and Ferry Streets.[13]

By 1838, Hoffman was ready to explore new territory and had started his own brewery at Main and St. Paul Streets. In 1840, Schanzlin joined him, and the two men ran the brewery for several years. There was a stone building used as both a restaurant and a brewhouse. Most of the early breweries were also saloons, and the beer brewed was sold, for the most part, for consumption on the premises.

Prior to 1827, there was little grain handled in the port of Buffalo. With the opening of the Erie Canal, general freight charges dropped nearly 90 percent, and Buffalo would now take grain from the Midwest and ship it eastward.[14] By 1841, grain receipts in Buffalo had exceeded 2 million bushels per year and were growing. With the advent of the steam-powered grain elevator, invented by Joseph Dart in 1842, Buffalo would become the leading grain port in the world for the next one hundred years.

The Hoffman Tavern and Brewery in the late 1800s. Jacob Schanzlin and Valentine Hoffman were originally partners. *From the* Picture Book of Earlier Buffalo, *published in 1912.*

Jacob Roos, whose small brewery in Sandy Town was growing, decided in 1840 to purchase land on Hickory Street near Broadway, then called Batavia Street, where he would erect a new brewery.

Alsace, France, was a location from which many brewers emigrated. In about 1809, Francis Joseph Jost Sr. was born there. He left for America in 1836, when he was about twenty-seven. He settled in Buffalo, where he would begin working in the brewery of his stepfather, Ignatius (Ignatz) "Joseph" Friedman. Friedman began brewing about 1837 at Oak and Goodell Streets, moving to Oak and Genesee Streets by 1839.[15] The two then moved in 1840 to Oak Street near Tupper Street, where they continued in business. Like other early brewers, Friedman built a brewhouse, dwelling and tavern and lived and worked at the same address.

Friedman's claim to fame was selling his beer for six pence, or 6¼ cents per quart, while everyone else was charging 5 cents.[16] It did not appear his "sixpencer" cost him customers, as his business continued to grow.

The partnership was dissolved in 1849, and Jost set out on his own.[17] Friedman might have continued brewing for a few years, but his history became cloudy after the separation. A listing in the 1850 *Buffalo City Directory* for Francis Friedman, brewer, at 211 Oak Street might be him. The brewery at Oak and Tupper Streets would later become the site of St. Mark's Evangelical Lutheran Church.

As is evident throughout this book, malt was an important part of the brewing process. All the larger breweries produced at least some of their own malt, while malt companies began in earnest as Buffalo came into its own as a grain port. At the same time as breweries were being established, malting grew and eventually became larger than the breweries themselves.

Malt is an important part of the brewing process. It is germinated cereal grains, in this case mainly barley or wheat, that have been soaked in water and then halted from germinating by drying. The process itself is called malting.

The earliest known maltster in Buffalo was James Carr, who worked at Canal and Court Streets in 1840. He is also the same person listed as a brewer in the 1832 city directory.

Buffalo brewing pioneer Philip Born constructed his first brewery in 1840 at 581–83 Genesee Street at the corner of Jefferson Avenue.[18] He was born in 1805 and later married Anna Weppner, sister of Jacob Weppner. Jacob was born in Zell, Rhine-Bavaria, in 1820 and attended local schools. When he was about fourteen, his family traveled to America and settled in the growing city of Buffalo, where his father opened a meat business at which Jacob worked until Philip Born

The remains of one of the small malting companies, the Kleinschmidt Malt House at 193 Pratt Street. *Photo by Michael Rizzo.*

died in 1848. Weppner, now married to Born's niece Emma Lambert, took over management of the Born brewery, renaming it Born & Weppner.

Brewer Jacob F. Schanzlin left his partnership with Valentine Hoffman on Main and St. Paul Streets in 1842 and then purchased a few acres of land at 1847 Main Street and Delavan Avenue. According to one account, Schanzlin's building was constructed in 1840, and he purchased the property in 1849 from Louis Le Couteulx, the first Erie County clerk. Like Hoffman, his home, a saloon and a brewhouse were all on the same property. It was called the "most pretentious brewery and restaurant up to that time."[19] It was a summertime gathering spot for Buffalo's German population where picnics and other entertainment would take place.

Another early brewery was started by Godfrey Heiser and his brother Henry. They opened up in 1845 at 149 Seneca Street near Chicago Street. Godfrey was born in 1799 in Schwalbach, Main-Taunus-Kreis, Hesse, Germany, and came to America in 1819, when he settled in Philadelphia. In 1828, Godfrey took the Erie Canal from Albany and arrived in Buffalo, where he began both a lime business and a pottery business before starting the brewery with his brother Henry.[20]

The 1840s were a time when early German brewers were experimenting and trying to develop enough clientele to keep their small breweries/saloons operating. They almost always lived at the same address, either above or behind the brewery. Philip Scheu was one of those men. He was born in Standenbühl, Germany, about 1797. Scheu opened his first brewery on Main and High Streets, just above St. Louis Church, in 1847.[21]

Although a thriving city by 1847, Buffalo was still centered along the Erie Canal but was slowly growing northward on Main Street. Two years later, with his beer business growing, Philip Scheu built a new brewery just blocks away at 11 High Street at Main Street.[22]

In 1848, Valentine Blatz arrived in Buffalo from Germany (where he had trained at several breweries). He worked for Philip Born in his brewery at 581 Genesee Street (until Born's death) and continued with Anna Born and Jacob Weppner for about a year before heading to Milwaukee, Wisconsin, where he founded the Valentine Blatz Brewing Company. When he died, he was one of Milwaukee's wealthiest citizens.[23]

Albert Ziegele was born in Stuttgart, Baden-Württemberg, Germany, in April 1818. After attending school, he learned the cooper's trade in France and Switzerland, learned the brewing trade "and then turned his attention to the brewing of malt liquors."[24] In October 1849, he came to America and settled in Buffalo, where he found work in Jacob Schanzlin's malt house for two weeks before working in Jacob Scheu's brewery as a laborer for about six months.[25]

6

THE 1850s

EARLY GROWTH

The 1850s were a time of growth for Buffalo. As lake shipping and canal commerce continued to grow, so did the city. Grain elevators continued to fill the city skyline as the German population was growing. This brought more desire for beer and breweries.

John Schüssler was born in Baden-Württemberg, Germany, in 1819 and was in Buffalo by 1849. In 1853, he established his first small brewery on Batavia (later Broadway) Street. Two years later, Schüssler moved to 147 Clinton Street, where he would continue to grow his brewery and be brewing over 1,600 barrels of beer per year by 1863.[26]

In the early '50s, Abel T. Blackmar, Edwin Gilbert, Joseph D. Roberts, John G. Meidenbauer, John M. Weigand and James McLeish were engaged in the malting business.[27]

Jacob Scheu was born in a Rhineland village near Bavaria in 1814. He apprenticed in a bakery and, in early 1837, traveled to America and went directly to Buffalo. Scheu knew no one and could not find work, so he crossed the border into Canada, where he worked for a farmer through the harvest season. He worked odd jobs, including as a patent medicine peddler in Canada, where he made a small fortune and then returned to Buffalo. After settling in Buffalo, Scheu opened a lumberyard in 1839 at 155 Genesee Street. Scheu added builder and architect to his resume and operated the business for twelve years.

One of the buildings he constructed was a brewery for a cousin on Genesee and Spring Streets. The cousin, though, did not have the business acumen that Scheu did, so he handed the brewery over to Scheu, probably as payment for the construction cost. Scheu immediately enlarged the brewery and commenced business about 1850, moving his residence there also.[28] There were now two Scheus in the brewing business in Buffalo.

Many of Buffalo's breweries started on a small scale, with some brewing only for on-site consumption and others starting small until they built their businesses up. It was in 1853 that Franz Xavier Kaltenbach and Jacob Haefelin opened a small brewery at 25 Lutheran Alley (now Archie Street) on the corner of Walnut Street and named it Kaltenbach & Haefelin.

Kaltenbach was born in 1821 in Baden-Württemberg, Germany. He arrived in America in 1848 and settled in Michigan, where he worked as a tanner. He moved to Buffalo in 1849 and continued as a tanner before joining Haefelin in the brewery business in 1853. Through hard work, they were able to produce about two hundred barrels of beer in their first year.[29]

Gottlieb Bodemer was born in Baden-Württemberg, Germany, in 1810. He had arrived in Buffalo by 1840 and, according to Albert Ziegele Sr. in his 1908 handwritten autobiography, began construction of a brewery on Genesee and Fillmore Streets. His residence was at 298 Genesee Street.

Albert Ziegele Sr. spent about six months working under Jacob Scheu and then ventured to Chicago and Milwaukee looking for better opportunities. After realizing Buffalo was in a better position than Chicago at the time, he returned and rented the brewery that Gottlieb Bodemer was constructing and brewed "upper-fermented beer," also known as ale.[30] This type of beer was ready for sale in small kegs in eight days.

Magnus Beck would one day become one of the largest brewers in Buffalo. He was born in Osterhofen, Bavaria, Germany, in 1819. When he was seventeen, he began an apprenticeship in a brewery in Germany, eventually fulfilling several different apprenticeships in different breweries. It was in 1850 that Beck came to America and went to Buffalo, where he accepted a position as foreman at Heiser Brothers' Brewery on Seneca Street.

Francis Joseph Jost had settled in Buffalo in 1836 and opened one of Buffalo's earliest breweries on Oak Street near Tupper Street in 1840 with his stepfather, Joseph Friedman. The partnership ended in 1849, and Jost built a new brewery at 419–29 Broadway at the corner of Pratt Street in 1850.[31] His goal was to produce "bottom-fermented," or lager beer—still, according to A.F. Marthens, "comparatively an unknown beverage."[32]

Buffalo's changing demographics introduced this new beer to the city. Lager, a derivative of the German word *lagern*, which means "to store," was made by "the bottom-fermentation method...to give it a milder taste and

A glass beer bottle from one of the lesser-known brewers, Alois Muelbauer, circa 1910. *Photo by Chris Groves, from the collection of Dave Mik.*

clearer appearance."[33] Lager was slower and harder to produce, so brewers were not able to see immediate financial gain from it.

The Roths were a smaller, relatively unknown group of Buffalo brewers. Starting in 1851, Lorenz Roth was a brewer at Main and North Streets. In 1855, Maximilian Roth (born in Bavaria in 1823) is listed as also having a brewery. In 1860, Max and Michael L. (Lorenz's son) are listed in the Buffalo city directory as brewers; in the 1861 directory, Michael was listed as a brewer for Max.[34]

By 1868, Max was located at 222 Sycamore Street, and Jacob was now listed as a brewer. In addition, there were now three Roth-owned saloons and three Roths working as coopers.

Max seems to have done well, as his real estate was valued at $12,000 ($221,000 in 2013 dollars) in 1870.[35] By 1890, Max was no longer listed. Lorenz died in 1857 (and is buried in United German and French Cemetery in Cheektowaga), and another Lorenz owned a saloon at 802 Broadway but by 1895 was no longer listed, while Adam Roth was listed as a beer brewer. By 1903, George Roth was listed as a maltster, and Adam was no longer listed.

After working as the foreman at Heiser Brothers' Brewery on Seneca Street, starting in 1850 and lasting two years, Magnus Beck moved to the Kaltenbach & Haefelin brewery on Lutheran and Batavia Streets, where he was made brewmaster.[36]

The Hoefner (often spelled Haefner) brothers arrived in Buffalo in 1848 from Bavaria, Germany. Their father, George, had been a brewer in Bavaria and might have done the same in Buffalo had he not died a year after arriving. His sons, Michael (born in 1824) and Alois, though, would eventually take up the same business in Buffalo. Alois was in business as a brewer in 1852 at Spruce Street at the corner of Cherry Street and about a year later moved to Spruce and Genesee Streets. His brother Michael was in business with him by 1854.[37]

Albert Ziegele was slowly building his business, and although it was a rough and slow start, he marched on. He opened a small store and saloon, which his wife helped run. Ziegele was persistent, and by the second year, he was able to secure some paying customers from the Hydraulics area of Buffalo to Dunkirk, New York (about forty-six miles away), where he personally delivered kegs of beer, even in the dead of winter.[38]

By early 1853, Ziegele had purchased a lot on Main Street, where he dug a deep beer cellar. Underground it was cooler, and the beer was able to stay fresh longer. That winter, he brewed what might be the first lager beer in Buffalo. After digging the cellar, he was convinced to build a house over it, and a new twenty-foot-deep cellar was added behind it where he held his kegs. Ziegele kept large barrels in the cellar and would bring the beer from the brewery in smaller kegs and transfer it by hose to the larger barrels in the cellar, where it could then be stored.[39]

Interior of the new Flying Bison Brewing Company at 840 Seneca Street. Pictured is its twenty-barrel Criveller brewhouse. *Photo by Ethan Cox.*

Valentine Hoffman had been brewing beer since 1838 in the brewery located at his home on Main Street just beyond St. Paul Street. By 1853, Hugh Boyle and Charles W. Gibbons had hired him to produce beer for their Boyle & Gibbons Star Brewery around the corner at 36 St. Paul Street.[40] Hoffman continued brewing for himself and Boyle and Gibbons until 1856 or 1857. At that time, he discontinued his brewery and brewed solely for Boyle and Gibbons until his death in 1861.[41] He is buried in Forest Lawn Cemetery in Buffalo.

Hugh Boyle was also a distiller, along with being an ale producer. In 1863, Boyle alone brewed 820 barrels of ale. But by 1871, production was down to 125 barrels, and he sold only 67 barrels of his ale.[42]

The early years of malting were by no means easy work, and in 1903, maltster Christian G. Voltz explained how work was done in those first years of Buffalo malt houses. "Work," he says, "was commenced at five o'clock in the morning, with an hour each for breakfast and dinner, and continued until six o'clock p.m. At eight o'clock we were required to return and do the necessary floor and kiln work, lasting until nine-thirty or ten o'clock.

"The malt house of those days was a different affair from the modern one. Of course, only floor malting was then in use. The barley was received in bags and was brought into the malt house by a hand hoisting apparatus. The water was pumped by hand from deep wells into the steep-tubs, and the green malt was hoisted from the growing floors in oaken tubs, holding about four bushels, with rope tackle. From the kilns to the bins the malt was rolled in the same oaken buckets or tubs.

"Except the furnace, the kiln was constructed entirely of wood, the floor laid on hemlock joists, being composed of one-inch maple strips, and beveled on the under side so as to form openings through which the hot air might penetrate and circulate through the green malt."[43]

Frederick Albrecht was born about 1823 in Germany. In about 1854, he built a brewery at 815 Batavia (Broadway) Street in Buffalo. It was one of the "most complete and best arranged," with a capacity of fifty-five barrels of lager beer per day and cellars so large they could hold four thousand to five thousand barrels of beer. There was also a malt house attached to the brewery.[44] His address would be one of the most popular for brewers over the years.

7

SOME OF THE BIGGEST BEGIN

Magnus Beck had been in America for five years, first working for Godfrey Heiser and then as brewmaster at the Kaltenbach & Haefelin brewery on Lutheran and Batavia Streets. In 1855, he partnered with Jacob Baumgartner and purchased Joseph Friedman's (Francis J. Jost's stepfather) brewery on Oak Street near Tupper Street, where the partners began brewing.[45]

By 1855, Albert Ziegele had constructed a new brewery and left the one he had leased from Gottlieb Bodemer for the previous five years. The new brewery, although rather small, was able to produce two thousand barrels the first year. With persistence, he continued to brew, transfer to the cellar down the street, sell and deliver the beer himself. About this time, he wanted a truck to carry the beer, so he hired a local wagon maker. The wagon maker had no idea how to build it, so Ziegele drew him a picture of what he wanted and the wagon was built.[46]

William W. Sloan was born in July 1831 in Tannybrake, Ireland. He arrived in the United States in 1845. In 1856, he purchased the Gilman & Barton Brewery[47] from Matthew S. Gilman and James H. Barton, an unknown brewery pair. The brewery was located in the Hydraulics neighborhood on Steuben Street near Van Rensselaer Street. By 1857, he was also operating Hydraulic Brewery at 698 Carroll Street, and by 1860, the first location had closed. In 1863, Sloan produced 2,238 barrels of beer.

George Rochevot was born in Rheinpfalz, Bavaria, in 1832. He learned the art of brewing in Mannheim, Baden-Württemberg, Germany, and afterward worked in France in what was one of the "great brewing centers

The remains of Rochevot Brewery at Spring and Cherry Streets. The Rochevot family would fight over the brewery after brewery founder George Rochevot died in 1897. *Photo by Michael Rizzo.*

of Continental Europe."[48] After becoming a master brewer, Rochevot turned his sights on America, arriving in 1854 at just twenty-two years old. After making his way to Buffalo, he worked as a foreman for several breweries before traveling to Chicago, St. Louis and Cincinnati to gain further experience.[49] But for Rochevot, Buffalo was his ultimate destination. He returned three years later in December 1857 and opened his first brewery at the corner of Spring and Cherry Streets, an address that would become a veritable incubator for breweries over the years.

James McLeish, who had operated one of Buffalo's first brewery and malt businesses in 1836 at Main and Ferry Streets, was also running a distillery by 1857. He decided that the malt business was superior, so he joined with another maltster, Abel T. Blackmar, to open a malt house on the property and discontinued brewing.[50]

In 1857, John G. White of Albany and Thomas Clarke of Buffalo started a distilling business in Buffalo. The next year, they turned a cowshed into a malt house and opened for business. The original malt house was built in south Buffalo, near the Red Jacket reservation.[51]

Charles Gerber was born in October 1818 in Kestenholz, Alsace, France. He moved to Baden, Germany, at a young age and later learned the butcher trade in Switzerland. All these locations were in the same general area—southern Germany, northern Switzerland and eastern France. Gerber immigrated to America, arriving in 1842 in Buffalo, where he started in the butcher business at 821 Main Street and Burton Alley. Gerber was involved in Democratic Party politics almost from the time he arrived in Buffalo, and meetings were held at his home as early as 1851.[52] In 1858, he hung up his cleaver and apron to start a brewery in the same building in which his butcher shop had been.

In 1858, James Moffat decided it was time to expand his brewery. He filed plans with the city to construct a new and extensive building, with 125 feet of frontage on Mohawk Street and 180 feet on Morgan Street. It would be three stories high and cost $20,000 ($575,000). The new brewery would have a 15,000-barrel capacity. "There is a large cask which is placed in the cellar, the dimensions of which are immense," 33 feet in circumference and capable of holding 250 barrels of ale.[53]

Gottlieb Bodemer had leased the brewery he built in 1850 on Genesee Street and Fillmore Avenue to Albert Ziegele for five years. In about 1857, Bodemer finally entered the brewing business at that location. Although the brewery was small, he was able to hone his craft and make a decent living at it. By 1863, he was brewing about forty-five barrels a month.

About two miles away, John Schüssler was having some success with his brewery at 147 Emslie Street between Clinton and Eagle Streets, where he erected a two-story, fifty- by one-hundred-foot brewery at a cost of $2,500 ($71,200).

Jacob Rheinhart (or Reinhardt in the 1859 *Buffalo City Directory*) was another small brewer located on Best Street at the corner of Jefferson Avenue. The brewery was eighty-four by fifty-four feet and cost $6,000 ($171,000) to build. It was unique in that Rheinhart built a sewer extension that cost $4,000 ($114,000).[54] There were other Reinhardts listed as brewers dating back to 1853, but none seems to have had Jacob's staying power.

In July 1831, another pioneer brewer, Joseph Lambert Haberstro, was born in Buffalo. After getting a common school education, he learned the trade of gunsmithing with his father, who was a native of Alsace, France. He later went into the mercantile business and married Barbara Scheu, daughter of Philip Scheu. In 1858, he embarked on a career in the brewing industry, purchasing the brewery that his father-in-law had started in 1850 at 11 High Street near Main Street and renaming it J.L. Haberstro & Company Brewery. This made him the first native-born brewer in Buffalo.[55]

The Knobloch brothers would, in a short time, become involved with Haberstro in his brewing enterprise. By 1857, John and Charles Knobloch

J. L. HABERSTRO,

LAGERBEER - BREWER,
Cor. Main and High Sts.,   **BUFFALO, N. Y.**

Salesman's card from J.L. Haberstro Brewery on High and Main Streets, circa 1870s. Haberstro would go on to be elected sheriff of Erie County. *Photo by Chris Groves, from the collection of Dave Mik.*

were listed as brewers at High Street near Main Street; they lived at the same location. By 1861, Charles had partnered with Haberstro, and John was employed there.[56]

Other listings over the years include the Haberstro & Knobloch Brewery, located at the corner of Main and North Streets. At the same time, J.L. Haberstro and Company Brewery is still listed in the city directory at High Street near Main Street. Directory listings were often incomplete or inaccurate, especially when it came to spellings. Haberstro and Knobloch would be listed together, separately and together again until about 1869.

By at least 1855, Jacob Roos's son George was involved in the family brewery at 95 Roos Alley (now Iroquois Place) near Pratt Street. By 1859, George had taken over operation of the brewery started by his father. The business was growing dramatically year by year, helped by the burgeoning German population, over 75,000 strong, 50,000 being first-generation Americans. Jacob Roos was doing quite well himself, with his brick home on Roos Alley valued at $3,000 ($83,400) in 1855. He had two servants and six people living with him who worked at the brewery.[57]

George Weber was born in Luxemburg in 1829. By 1859, Weber was in Buffalo and had teamed with Charles Gerber to form the Gerber & Weber

Brewery, located at 585 Main Street.[58] The partnership lasted only a short time before the two separated and ran their own breweries.

The decade ended with the growing Hoefner Brothers Brewery moving, in 1858, from its location on Spruce Street near Genesee Street to a new location on Michigan Street at the corner of High Street.

Another brother, Anselm, began potash manufacturing on Monroe Street in 1852 and, in 1854, moved to 162–70 Van Rensselaer Street in the Hydraulics area, where he started manufacturing candles and soap with his three sons. The company, American Star Soap, would grow to be one of the largest in Buffalo, manufacturing twenty-eight brands of laundry soaps, toilet soaps and more, with a branch office in Baltimore, Maryland.[59]

8
THE 1860s

BUSINESS PEAKS

B ased on historic record, it is generally believed that James Moffat ran the Buffalo brewery bearing his name at Mohawk and Morgan Streets, although it is his father, John, who is acknowledged as the owner until 1860. John Moffat's sons, James and Henry C., were in the hide and tanning business but ultimately joined their father in the brewery.

David Haas built a new brewery on the corner of Spring and Cherry Streets in 1860. This brewery was in addition to the George Rochevot Brewery that was also on that corner. By 1863, Haas was producing 432 barrels of beer per year. His output would continue to rise over the years.

The malt industry in Buffalo grew larger than the brewing industry. Buffalo's grain port proved to be a vital advantage against other cities. In 1860, Anthony Schaefer formed a malt house, which was taken over the following year by his brothers Gustavus A. and Henry L. Schaefer, both natives of Germany who arrived in Buffalo at young ages. Gustavus was born in Germany in February 1843, came to America with his parents and settled in Buffalo. When he was old enough, he secured a clerk's job. In 1857, Gustavus was a clerk for White's Bank and then worked as a clerk in a grain and flour business. After working for several firms, in 1861, he and his brother Henry L. formed Schaefer & Brother at 42 and 44 Lloyd Street.[60]

In the '60s, Abel T. Blackmar (former partner of James McLeish), Joseph D. Roberts, Burdette A. Lynde, Thomas Clarke, the McLeish brothers, William A. Sloan and others were all engaged in the malt business.[61]

Gerhard Lang, a native of Deggendorf, Bavaria, Germany, was born in 1834 and came to Buffalo in 1848. In 1860, Lang, either bringing experience or money, became a partner in the brewery of Born & Weppner on Genesee Street.

The partnership of Magnus Beck and Jacob Baumgartner had been running a brewery since 1855 at 209 Oak Street near Tupper Street. In 1860, the partnership dissolved, and Beck continued at the same location while Baumgartner built a new brewery on Exchange Street at the corner of Van Rensselaer Street. Beck then purchased land and began constructing a new brewery at 467 North Division Street.[62]

Solomon Scheu was born in January 1822 near Standenbühl, Bavaria. In the spring of 1839, after a forty-nine-day boat trip, he arrived in New York. He had spent about five years in New York City working as a baker when his older brother Jacob invited him to visit Buffalo. Solomon accepted and arrived in the winter of 1844, three years before Jacob would open a brewery.[63] Solomon worked for his older brother in the lumber business and then found bakery work, finally opening his own bakery in 1846. He successfully sold the business after three years, then started a grocery business and then a saloon. In 1860, Solomon purchased the Frontier Canada Malt House on Hudson and Fourth Streets and got into the malting business. At the onset, he was producing about 25,000 bushels per year.[64] But for Solomon, the call of politics was strong and took him away from his business many times over the years.

According to the 1855 New York State census, Jacob F. Schanzlin's home on Main Street near Delavan Avenue was worth $6,000 ($164,000), and he had twenty people registered as living at the address. Eight of the people listed were servants, including thirty-eight-year-old German native Anton Muschall, who was also a cooper. Muschall (his name was spelled numerous ways) was a brewer for Albert Ziegele in 1861, and by 1862, he struck out on his own. In 1863, Muschall and Martin Abert were brewing at 565 Main Street and making 609 barrels of beer per year.[65] Subsequently, Muschall would continue on his own for several years.

Michael Hoefner, half of the Hoefner Brothers Brewery on High Street at the corner of Michigan Street, died in November 1861 in a horrible railway accident.

Brewer Gerhard Lang married deceased brewer Philip Born's eldest daughter, Barbara, in 1862. He bought out Jacob Weppner's share in the brewery that his wife's mother, also named Barbara Born, was operating with Weppner at 581 Genesee and Jefferson Streets. He renamed the brewery

Born & Lang. It is believed that Weppner then retired from active business, but he is listed as a brewer throughout the 1860s.[66] Where he worked is unknown, but he did start another business later.

Sometimes, stories that are passed down from one generation to the next are accurate and there are enough other sources to verify them. The story of malt dealer George Fisher was not one of those. All accounts said Fisher was born in France in 1820 and moved to America with his family in 1830, settling in Buffalo. There is not much reason to dispute that part of the story. But that is where the story gets murky. Legend and multiple old books say that Fisher established a malt house in Buffalo in 1862. But the 1864 city directory lists George as a flour dealer in J&G Fisher & Company, with John and Charles Fisher living at 74 West Genesee Street. Their brother Jacob P. is listed as a maltster. The 1867 city directory provides some further details: Fisher Brothers & Company is listed for the first time, with George and Jacob Fisher and Philip Houck as owners, but not under the maltster listing. George is still listed as a flour dealer with Fisher & Zench at 74 West Genesee Street.

It might have been that Jacob started in the malt business, and while George was a grain dealer, he saw his brother's business was fast growing, so they started working together until they formed Fisher Brothers & Company. By 1865, they had an annual capacity of thirty thousand bushels.[67]

While the story of the Fisher brothers is unclear, the same year they supposedly formed their business, in the fall of 1861, Charles Gould Curtiss and Lyman L. Curtiss definitely founded the Curtiss & Company Malt House at 359 Lakefront Boulevard. The plant was originally the Buffalo Cotton Factory before they converted it. The original malting plant was a floor house, meaning all the grain had to be turned by hand, with an annual capacity of about fifty thousand bushels.[68] Charles was born in Utica, New York, in 1827 and moved to Buffalo by 1858, when he was part of the firm Willard & Curtiss, a produce merchant company.

John Baker Manning was born in July 1833 in Albany, New York; his father was of Irish descent. At an early age, Manning wanted to know politicians and became a page in the New York State Assembly and then the state senate. In 1860, he became a newspaper reporter in Albany. Manning then set his sights on another field: the malt business. In about 1862, Manning started a small malting business in Albany, which produced a few hundred bushels of malt per year. At the same time, he started a commission business for the sale of Canadian produce.[69] After some research, Manning saw Buffalo as the ideal location to establish new businesses and moved. He started two new businesses in Buffalo: a produce and commission merchant and a gentlemen's furnishings store. One source says Manning purchased, in 1863, the malt house on Terrace Street, which had a capacity of eighty thousand bushels per year.[70]

Another maltster, Christian G. Voltz, was born in July 1845 in Appenweier, Baden-Württemberg, Germany. In 1851, he arrived in Buffalo, and by 1862, he was working in the malt house owned by John G. Meidenbauer at 992 Michigan Street. Meidenbauer had previously been employed in James McLeish's malt house.[71]

Alois Schaefer was born in Baden-Württemberg, Germany, in 1836. He came to America as a young man and learned the brewing trade, founding Schaefer Brewery in 1868 at 1037 Main Street at the corner of North Street.[72]

As the brewing trade grew locally and nationally, brewer Albert Ziegele attended the second annual United States Brewers' Association Convention in Philadelphia in February 1863. He was the first Buffalo brewer to represent the area in the national organization, and Buffalo would eventually host a number of its conferences.

In 1864, Godfrey Heiser Jr. and Jacob Holser took over running the brewery that Heiser's father had started in 1845. It was not a long affair, and it closed in 1871. Junior then went into the shoe business, and Heiser Sr. became a maltster at 209 East Seneca Street.

Brewers had to continually invest in their breweries to stay up with the times. With the use of icehouses, and later refrigerated storage, they were able to keep their beer fresh longer; otherwise, they were forced to brew seasonally.

It was in 1864 that French chemist and microbiologist Louis Pasteur discovered that airborne microorganisms could contaminate liquids such as beer and milk. He developed a process, which is still used today, that helped brewers keep their beer from spoiling as quickly: pasteurization. The process involved heating the beer to specific temperature, which killed any living microbes without changing the taste of the beer.

By 1864, Charles F. Schuh was listed as a brewer in the city directory. Schuh was born in Baden-Württemberg, Germany, in 1835 and came to America in 1854, when he was nineteen.[73] By 1868, he was living in Buffalo and working as a brewer.

It was about 1850 when Franz Xavier Kaltenbach partnered with Jacob Haeflin to form Kaltenbach & Haefelin at Lutheran and Batavia Streets. In 1860, Kaltenbach took over as sole owner of the brewery and renamed it F.X.

Kaltenbach Brewery. It's likely that he bought out his partner.

By 1865, the McLeish Malt House at Ferry and Main Streets was one of Buffalo's larger concerns, but its founders, Abel T. Blackmar and James McLeish, were ready to put down their shovels. The malt business was turned over to McLeish's three sons—Archibald, James Jr., and C.G. The company would grow to produce 200,000 bushels of malt a year by 1884 and employ fifty men.[74]

There were a lot of minor players in Buffalo's brewing history. One was Michael Schamel, who was born in 1833 in Bavaria, Germany. When he was twenty-four, Schamel arrived in New York City, ready to take on the new land. In about 1824, Anton Messner (also known as Anthony) was born in France. Like Schamel, he eventually made his way to America. Messner arrived in Buffalo around early 1852, when he started brewing beer on Hickory Street near Batavia Street. Although he moved several times, Messner stayed in same general area.

A pre-Prohibition bottle, dating from about 1885, from the Ziegele Brewing Company. Albert Ziegele was a pioneer and can take credit for many firsts in Buffalo brewing. *Photo by Chris Groves, from the collection of Dave Mik.*

Schamel stayed in New York City for about two years, but by 1860, he was in Buffalo, living with wealthy brewer John Schüssler at Schüssler's home on Batavia Street. Schüssler's real estate in 1860 was valued at $6,000 ($173,000), and he had $3,000 ($86,700) in personal goods.[75]

It appears that, in late 1863, Messner joined Jacob Baumgartner at his brewery at Exchange and Van Renssalaer Streets. By 1864, Michael Schamel

and Anton Messner began working together at 1093 Genesee Street, where they operated the Messner & Schamel brewery.[76] It is possible the operation was also a restaurant or tavern.

Jacob Baumgartner was born in Baden-Württemberg, Germany, in 1827. He arrived in America in 1850 and, by 1863, was living in Buffalo. An early partner of Magnus Beck, he would continue as a brewer in Buffalo until his early death in 1878 at fifty-one years old.[77]

By 1864, Scheu Brewery on Genesee and Spring Streets, was producing close to three thousand barrels of beer per year. Jacob Scheu's son Jacob Jr. had joined him and was now working at the brewery.

In 1866, the Scheus had outgrown their brewery and sought a location for a new building. They found land at 1088 Niagara Street along the Erie Canal, which had sat idle for years, and purchased it. They constructed one of the largest breweries in the city, with large cellars blasted out of the rock. The entire facility covered four acres and had a capacity of fifty thousand barrels of beer per year. Shortly after, Jacob Sr. also moved his residence to Niagara Street.[78]

Cretien (Christian) Weyand was born in Lorraine, France, in May 1826. After a common school education, Weyand left for America, landing in New York City in 1847, when he was twenty-one years old. After a short stay, he traveled to Buffalo, where he secured a job as a cobbler. After several years, he started his own shop. For Weyand, though, brewing must have been a passion. In 1866, Weyand and John Schetter opened the Weyand & Company brewery at 793 Main Street.[79] Apparently aiming to be more than the typical saloon brewery, in the beginning, the brewery had a capacity of around 1,500 barrels of beer per year. This made it a mid-sized brewer compared to other Buffalo brewers.

Abel T. Blackmar, formerly partnered with James McLeish, had a new six-story malt house built for himself on Perry Street near Washington Street in 1866. Disaster would strike the malt house years later (see chapter 10). Blackmar was also president of Third National Bank in Buffalo.[80]

Another brewery joined the fray in 1866—Clarke & Johnson, a brewery located at 4 Batavia Street. John P. Clarke and Edwin W. Johnson took out large ads in the *Buffalo City Directory* touting their ales, London porter and stout, which were "strongly recommended by Henry Ward Beecher." They also hired a "celebrated English Brewer from London."[81] Nothing else was ever heard of them.

It was in 1867 that John Martin Luippold Sr. joined with William Voetsch Sr. to open Voetsch & Company at 298 Emslie Street.[82] Voetsch

An ad for the Christian Weyand Brewing Company, circa 1890. *Photo from* Buffalo Illustrated: Commerce, Trade and Industries of Buffalo.

was born in Germany in 1838 and Luippold in Baden-Württemberg, Germany, in 1831. Luippold was in Buffalo by 1853, and Voetsch came to America in 1856 and eventually made his way to Buffalo, probably via the Erie Canal, where the two met.

The brewery had a frontage of 210 feet on Emslie Street, running 217 feet through to Watson Street. It was roughly a square-shaped complex with a large courtyard in the center. The buildings included a brewhouse, stock house and racking and washing rooms. It brewed only one beer, old stock lager, "the quality of which is surpassed by none."

Francis Joseph (F.J.) Jost Sr. opened his new brewery on the corner of Pratt Street and Broadway in 1850. The brewery was producing about two thousand barrels of beer per year. F.J. successfully carried on the business until 1867, when he retired and left the business in the capable hands of his son Francis J. Jost Jr.[83]

One of the pioneer brewers in Buffalo, Jacob Roos, died on November 27, 1867, at fifty-nine years old.[84] He had built a successful brewery that was producing close to five thousand barrels of beer per year. Roos is buried in Forest Lawn Cemetery in Buffalo.

Ice was a commodity that, until the 1860s, had not been a necessity for many and was cost prohibitive for the average man. Breweries, though, began to see the usefulness of using ice to keep their products at a uniform temperature. Alexander J. Briggs and James L. Moore started the Buffalo Ice Company in about 1867. By 1880, they had five warehouses (with storage for over fifty thousand tons of ice). It was the largest concern of its kind between Chicago and New York and accounted for two-thirds of Buffalo's ice business.[85] It was voluntarily dissolved in 1899.

In 1867, John Baker Manning, a successful commission merchant and malt house owner, shut down his produce and commission business to concentrate on his growing malt concern.[86]

The malt house partnership of John G. White and Thomas Clarke in 1868 erected the Niagara grain-elevator on Niagara Street at the foot of Lafayette Avenue—then said to be the largest elevator in the world—and a malt house with a capacity of about 200,000 bushels. The two men were also partners in Clarke, Townsend & Company with George W. Townsend and Cyrus Clarke.[87] The Niagara Malting Company was formed, and White managed the concern until 1876, when the partnership was dissolved.

Alois Schaefer was successfully growing his brewery at 1037 Main Street when he purchased land on Lakeview Street and Porter Avenue in 1868, where he erected the Schaefer Brewery and moved all operations there.

The national organization of brewers became important after a tax on every barrel of beer was proposed by the United States government to help cover the cost of the Civil War. Local associations sprang up around the country, and annual conventions were hosted in different cities each year. Elaborate dinners, tours of breweries and, of course, meetings to discuss the politics of the nation were conducted. All the early meetings, both in Buffalo and at the national level, were conducted in German, since most of the members were native speakers of German. But as the industry grew, so did English-speaking members and convention presenters. At the twelfth annual convention of the United States Brewers' Association, held in New York in June 1872, the policy of holding the convention in German one year and in English the following year was adopted.[88]

Buffalo hosted its first United States Brewers' Association Convention on July 8, 1868, it being the eighth annual meeting. One of the big discussion points at the convention was the Internal Revenue Service's decision that any beer drank while employees were working in a brewery would not be taxable, unless it was used as an inducement to work or to pay lower wages.[89] The convention, as most, was a success, and Buffalo was able to showcase its growing beer industry, one of the largest in the country.

THE HISTORY OF BREWING IN THE NICKEL CITY

It was in August 1868 that Frederick Albrecht rented out his brewery on Batavia Street and headed off to Colden, New York, leaving his wife and children in Buffalo. Once there, he secured work with Martin Miller in Miller's brewery. On November 23, 1868, Miller, Albrecht and three other employees, including Miller's son, sat in the brewery and got drunk. It was late on a Sunday, and after two of them left, the others eventually retired to their rooms above the brewery.

About six o'clock on Monday morning, William Miller returned to the brewery and found the door ajar. Upon entering, he found Albrecht on the floor, barely alive, his head smashed in. None of the others sleeping upstairs claimed to know what had happened or to have heard anything. The coroner's inquest determined that Albrecht was probably murdered, but no one was ever accused of or charged for the crime.[90]

The firm of Lang & Gottman was the start-up that had rented Albrecht's brewery from him at 815 Batavia Street in 1868. But it was not run by Gerhard Lang, it was run by George Friedrich Lang and Henry Gottman.[91] The firm appears to have lasted only a couple years, but Lang continued as a brewer in the employ of others.

By 1868, George Weber, who had run a brewery at 652 Batavia Street, had passed away. His wife, Dorothea, was listed in the 1868 directory as the owner. Interestingly, the 1869 directory listed George and Dorothea, as well as Conrad Gebauer, as the proprietors of G. Weber & Company.[92] The brewery was sold two years later.

John Moffat had two sons who went into the tannery business in 1869. James Jr. and Henry C. Moffat established two tanneries, one in Buffalo, where they tanned about 200,000 sheepskins per year, and one in Alden, New York, where they tanned about 50,000 sides of upper calfskin. Sales were upward of $200,000 ($4,630,000) by 1880, and the Buffalo factory was the second largest of its kind in western New York.[93]

After John Moffat died in about 1869, the brewery on Mohawk and Morgan Streets was leased to the partnership of Arthur W. Fox and Horace Williams, which ran the brewery as Fox & Williams, brewing cream, stock, amber and pale ales and porters.

The Independence Day celebration of 1869 featured a parade with fantastic wagons decorated for the event. Buffalo's principal brewers made a fine showing, including Jacob Roos, Jacob Schanzlin, Heiser & Holzer, Joseph L. Haberstro, David Haas, John G. Bickel (a newcomer who ran a hotel at 610 Genesee Street and was brewing in 1869), Magnus Beck, Rudolph Schlegel (another newcomer who ran a restaurant at 7 West Genesee Street) and Fox & Williams. Someone dressed as King Gambrinus, the patron saint of beer, rode in the first "chariot."[94]

In October 1833, John Kam was born in Pleystein in the Oberpfalz, Bavaria, Germany. After attending school, he studied the malt and brewing trade and, for three years, worked in the brewery of Count Max of Bavaria (possibly Count von Holnstein, who had a brewery at Thalhausen) and several other breweries.[95]

In October 1855, Kam immigrated to America and arrived in Buffalo, where he found employment in Jacob Scheu's brewery at Genesee and Spring Streets. He worked in the Scheu Brewery for five years, the last two as brewmaster, before setting out on his own. Although he had already spent some years in breweries and was a master brewer, John Kam initially decided to become a baker.[96]

Kam opened his bakery on the corner of Genesee and Spring Streets in 1860 and successfully ran it until 1869. At that time, he ventured back into the world of brewing and built a malt house next to his bakery. He ultimately sold the bakery to concentrate on the malt business.[97]

Between 1869 and 1870, Moffat's Brewery on Morgan and Mohawk Streets sold 13,497 barrels of beer. James Moffat was listed in one directory

Resurgence Brewing at 1250 Niagara Street is one of Buffalo's newest breweries. Founded by Jeff Ware, this is an interior view of the brewhouse. *Photo by Matthew McCormick.*

as a "dealer in beer, ale, soap, candles and potashes." Brewers often used hardwoods to heat their brew, which resulted in a lot of ash, so they ran sideline businesses, such as soap and candle making, that could provide extra income during the slow winter months.[98]

9
THE 1870s

RECONFIGURATION

B uffalo had supposedly peaked with thirty-five breweries in 1863, but there were thirty-eight operating in 1875.[99] About half of them were very small, producing fewer than one thousand barrels of beer per year each, but some were already established and were still growing. By the start of the next decade, some had closed, others had started and a handful had continued their growth.

By 1870, Joseph Garies had partnered with John Knobloch to form Garies & Knobloch at 397 Oak Street.[100] Knobloch had previously worked at Haberstro & Knobloch. The partnership was in existence until 1873, when they parted ways.

John M. Luippold Sr. and William Voetsch Sr. had been partners in the Voetsch & Company brewery at 298 Emslie Street since 1867, when they decided, in 1870, to dissolve their partnership. Luippold continued the operation on Emslie Street, renaming it the John M. Luippold Brewing Company. Voetsch's home was at 12 West Bennett Street, near Clinton Street. He started a new brewery there.[101]

Joel Wheeler and his son A.J. began malting in Buffalo in 1870 in their malt house at 283 Perry Street. The capacity of their first house was 125,000 bushels per year.[102]

According to Internal Revenue Service books, in 1871, the breweries of Buffalo consumed in their beer production 330,000 bushels of barley, 162,000 bushels of malt, 400,000 pounds of hops, 2,500 pounds of cornmeal and 204,589 pounds of sugar.[103]

George Rochevot was building a successful brewery on Spring and Cherry Streets. He brewed 5,071 barrels of beer between 1869 and 1870, but he was ready to embark on the next stage of his business. In 1871, he purchased land on Jefferson Avenue, where he built a new brewery. The new brewery would stand at 1003 Jefferson Avenue and would continue to grow under his able leadership.[104]

One of Buffalo's most successful brewmasters arrived in America in 1870. William Simon was born in Renchen, Baden-Württemberg, Germany, in May 1853, the son of a brewmaster. He received a public school education and then went to work in his father's brewery. When he was seventeen, he left for America after his parents disapproved of his choice of wife. A brewer in Brooklyn sponsored Simon, who went to work in a cooperage in Morrisania (South Bronx), New York, before moving to Williamsburg, New York. He worked for several breweries over the course of six years and then left for East Boston, Massachusetts, where he became foreman of the Conrad Decker Brewery.[105]

After ten years in business, the firm of Schaefer & Brother, Gustavus and Henry, located at 42 and 44 Lloyd Street, decided to change the business they were in. At first handling seed and grains, in 1871, it concentrated on handling barley exclusively and, according to Smith in *History of the City of Buffalo*, "assumed control of a heavy malting interest."[106]

It is unknown what happened to the Lang & Gottman company that was brewing beer at the former Frederick Albrecht Brewery on Batavia Street, which it had rented in 1868. In December 1871, John J. Holser took over the brewery that had been "lying idle during the past three or four years."[107] Holser added an icehouse to the brewery to store an additional two thousand barrels of lager. The malt house was rented to another party, but Holser, who apparently ran a brewery on Seneca Street prior to renting Albrecht's brewery, was brewing fifty barrels a day by mid-December, and everything was looking rosy.[108]

William W. Sloan was operating Hydraulic Brewery at 698 Carroll Street, and by 1869, he had added malting to his brewery operation. In 1871, he made 1,586 barrels of ale and sold 1,630 barrels of ale per year. By the late 1870s, he had discontinued the beer side of the business and continued only as a maltster.[109]

Another early brewer, Gottlieb Bodemer, who was sixty-one years old in 1871, retired from active business and closed his brewery on Genesee Street, which had previously been rented to Albert Ziegele in the 1850s.

With increasing raw material costs and "certain restrictions that were being inaugurated by dependent trades,"[110] brewers were losing money "every day they operated." After meeting to discuss their options, the owners of Buffalo's breweries decided to band together to control their costs as well as to regulate what they charged for their beer. In late 1872, the first organizational meeting of the Buffalo Brewers' Association was held. At that meeting, they agreed to admit hop dealers, maltsters and other related businesses into the organization.[111] It was not be long before their employees realized that by organizing they, too, could wield some power over their employers.

Henry M. Diehl was born in Weinolsheim, Germany, in 1825. When he was seventeen, he came to America, and although he was trained as a tailor, he became a cooper. In 1872, after years of working as a cooper and seeing his barrels filled with beer, Diehl set out to start a malt business and opened his first malt house at Georgia Street and Front Avenue. His first year in business was 1873, and that year, he produced ten thousand bushels of malt. The business, though small at the time, would grow much over the coming years.[112] Diehl ran two more malt houses over time: the Union Malt House at 402 Niagara Street at Maryland Street (originally owned by Burdette A. Lynde) and another at 500 Franklin Street near Allen Street (where a section of the building still stands).

Michael Schamel and Anton Messner had been partnered since 1864 at 1093 Genesee Street, where they were brewing beer. Philip Schamel, possibly Michael's brother, was also employed at the brewery. All three might have lived at that address.

At this time, another man came into the picture. Jacob Friedrich Kuhn was born on May 6, 1830, in Eschelbach, Germany. When he was fourteen years old, he came to America with his family and settled in Buffalo. Kuhn served as assistant Internal Revenue Service assessor for eight years. Kuhn then purchased the former George Weber Brewery at 652 Batavia Street (Broadway) for $15,000 ($291,000) in April 1872. Michael Schamel left his partnership with Anton Messner and partnered with Kuhn to start a new brewery there. They constructed a new brewery under the auspices of J.F. Kuhn & Company with the goal of producing extra-fine lager beer and named their plant the Union Brewery. Kuhn and Schamel's partnership did not last long. Schamel was bought out in 1873, a year into their partnership.[113] Kuhn employed five men and did between $30,000 and $35,000 ($705,000 and $823,000) annually in sales.[114]

Anton Messner had several occupations after the brewery, including being a hotelkeeper in Gardenville (West Seneca, New York), and he was a maltster as late as 1886.[115]

THE HISTORY OF BREWING IN THE NICKEL CITY

In 1872, John Kam, who had started in the malt business in 1869, erected a new malt house that was three stories high. The growth of the industry is very apparent when total malt house capacity in Buffalo from 1871 to 1872 and 1872 to 1873 is compared. Four new malt houses were built in 1872, and at least two were upgraded. The total malting capacity in Buffalo was about 1,000,000 bushels in 1872 and went up to over 1,400,000 in 1873.[116]

Anton (Anthony) Muschall had been brewing beer at 565 Main Street since 1862. By 1866, he had moved to 106 Burton Alley near Boston Alley. His business was rather brisk, and in 1871, he brewed 2,823 barrels and sold 2,468 barrels of beer.[117] Unfortunately, he died in 1872, but his wife, Fredericka, continued operating the brewery until she remarried. Fredericka, who was thirty-three and had several children, married Andrew Driskel. He was a native of Austria; she was a native of Prussia. Driskel arrived in America in 1863, and in 1873, he was running a saloon in Buffalo.[118] By 1873, he was listed as a brewer, but Fredericka was still listed as the owner of the brewery at 106 Burton Alley.

Although the Muschall/Driskel business was most likely a combination saloon-brewery, with the Driskels' home on the same premises, it had impressive sales numbers. There is nothing to indicate the business sold its beer to other saloons, but by 1879, it had produced 3,183 barrels of beer. This was nearly as much as Kuhn, Haberstro and Jost had produced.[119] If this was all just sold at their saloon, it was a very busy location. Fredericka Muschall Driskel died in 1894 at fifty-three years old. Andrew continued the business until at least 1906, and he died in November 1912 at seventy-one years old.[120]

In January 1873, the first formal meeting of the Buffalo Brewers' Association was held above Donald Bain's brewers' supplies store at 557 Main Street in Buffalo. Gerhard Lang was elected the first president, Magnus Beck the vice-president, Francis J. Jost Sr. the treasurer and Jacob F. Kuhn the secretary.[121]

Donald Bain ran one of the more successful ancillary brewery businesses in Buffalo. Bain began as a hops dealer in 1862. In 1868, partnered with Michael F. Shaler, Bain founded Bain & Shaler, dealers in hops and brewers' supplies. The business grew until 1875, when Shaler died. Bain continued on his own. He specialized in hops and brewers' instruments and materials, with his business trading as far as New England and Ohio.[122]

John Schüssler, now in his second brewery after outgrowing the first on Batavia Street, was again experiencing growing pains. In 1873, he expanded and remodeled the brewery at 147 Emslie Street and added a malt house.[123]

A John Schüssler bottle, dating from the 1890s. The Schüssler brewery would be purchased by William Simon in 1894. *Photo by Chris Groves, from the collection of Dave Mik.*

The Weyand & Company brewery at 789 Main Street had been open since 1866; it was run by Christian Weyand and his partner John Schetter. From the beginning, it was Weyand's goal to "manufacture a healthful beverage, which for purity and general excellence could not be surpassed."[124] In 1873, the partnership dissolved; Weyand bought out Schetter and continued the business alone. Since inception, the small plant was constantly being updated as funds became available, and by 1873, the company was producing over 4,400 barrels of beer a year and still growing.[125] Weyand's brew was considered the best quality because just malt and hops—no corn or rice adjuncts—were used.

With one malt house under his control, John Baker Manning built what would be his largest malt house in Buffalo in 1873, the Frontier Canada Malt House at the foot of Auburn Avenue near the Erie Canal and adjacent to White and Clarke's operation. After an expansion in 1881, it was nine stories tall, with a capacity of 920,000 bushels of malt. Two grain elevators were connected to the malt house, with a capacity of 175,000 bushels each. The massive malt concern employed eighty men.[126]

John J. Holser was running the (former Albrecht) brewery at 815 Batavia Street since December 1871. Unfortunately, it did not work out, and he went bankrupt. In April 1873, the brewery and its contents were auctioned off.[127]

In 1873, the Charles G. Curtiss malt house at 359 Lakefront Boulevard was sold to A. McPherson, who ran it as a malt house for two more years.[128]

The partnership of Fox and Williams started, along with their brewery at Mohawk and Morgan Streets, a vinegar venture known as A.W. Fox & Company. In January 1874, seeing the need for vast amounts of sugar in their vinegar business, they started the Buffalo Grape Sugar Company in a building at the foot of Court Street and the Erie Canal.[129] Williams was the inventor and superintendent of the works while Fox was the businessman. They needed cash to infuse into their business, which brought them into contact with one of Buffalo's elite. William Hamlin, son of Cicero J. Hamlin, became involved, loaning the partners the needed money, holding all their shares and their brewery as collateral and charging them 1 percent per month. Williams held 66 shares, Fox had 102 shares and Hamlin owned 32 shares.

Unfortunately, Arthur W. Fox died from complications after being run over by a train in August 1874.[130] Because he was in debt, his estate was insolvent, leaving his partner Horace Williams holding all the debt. Cicero J. Hamlin, who had life insurance policies on both men, took over Fox's debts and became president of the firm, providing the financing Williams needed to keep the Buffalo Grape Sugar Company afloat.[131] Williams, who was young, was convinced by the wealthy businessman to let him take care of his shares of stock, about $30,000 ($633,000) worth, which he did.

The sugar business grew; it opened two additional plants and generated millions. Williams, who had helped found the business, was relegated to an employee under Hamlin, making $5,000 ($120,000) per year. He grew desperate and sometimes disappeared for days. In 1880, after complaining to Cicero J. Hamlin for his fair share, he was brushed off. Hamlin finally gave him twenty-three shares of stock. Williams left the business and sold his shares to John L. Alberger for $200,000 ($4,700,000), under the condition that they sue Hamlin and split the settlement if they won.[132]

After a long, well-publicized trial in 1880, Alberger won over $333,221 ($7,790,000) with $247,125 ($5,810,000) in interest.[133] After all that, Cicero J. Hamlin closed the company in 1883 because he said the city charged too much for water. Hamlin, using his experience from the Buffalo Grape Sugar Company, formed the American Glucose Company, which was an immensely profitable company for the Hamlin family.

Jacob F. Kuhn became the sole owner of the Union Brewery in 1873 or 1874.

In 1874, Joseph L. Haberstro partnered with Charles F. Schuh in the Haberstro & Schuh Ale Brewery, located at 20, 22 and 24 Batavia Street, which lasted several years. By 1878, the business was called Scobell & Schuh Ale Brewery, as Schuh had partnered with George Scobell.[134]

A convention was held in Niagara Falls on September 2, 1874, that resulted in the formation of the Maltsters' National Association. Burdette A. Lynde was elected the first president and A.J. Wheeler the corresponding secretary, both of Buffalo. It appears that the association survived only three years before disbanding.[135]

After retiring from management of the Born brewery in 1864, Jacob Weppner, after a ten year absence, decided to begin a malting business at 938 Jefferson Avenue in 1874.[136]

The Albert Ziegele Brewing Company, at 831–41 Main Street, now had the capacity to brew forty thousand barrels annually. The brewery was located on both sides of Washington Street, with a frontage of 116 feet on Main Street; the brewery and an icehouse on the west side; and a malt house, icehouse and barn on the east side. Even though they were capable of producing forty-five thousand bushels of malt yearly, it was not enough to cover the brewery's own needs.[137]

On November 5, 1874, the partnership of Shoemaker and Noble purchased the former Fox and Williams brewery set up shop at 128 Niagara Street. Edson D. Shoemaker was the former superintendent of the brewery. While he and Charles B. Noble produced over 5,100 barrels of beer in 1879, it was not enough to keep the brewery afloat. In August 1880, the brewery and all the machinery were sold at auction to satisfy a chattel mortgage.[138]

John Schüssler added an icehouse to his growing brewery on Emslie Street in 1875, just two years after expanding and adding a malt house. By the early 1880s, he would employ twenty-five men.[139]

The Christian Weyand Brewery at 793 Main Street, founded by Christian Weyand, was growing considerably. In 1875, a $75,000 ($1,640,000) remodel was undertaken at the brewery. Like most brewery owners, Weyand lived at the same address.[140]

Flames were discovered in the brewery of Christian Dier on Van Rensselaer and Exchange Streets at two o'clock in the morning on January 14, 1876. The fire started under a beer kettle in the center of the brewery and quickly spread, causing $7,000 ($155,000) in damage to the structure, beer and hops. The Dier family lived in front of the brewery and escaped unharmed, but one man was badly burned trying to gain entrance to the building. Insurance covered $5,000 ($110,000) of the damage,[141] but Dier was unable to recover from the loss and went bankrupt the next month, selling off most of his personal property to satisfy debts.

In April 1879, Shoemaker, Fox and Williams were charged with allowing kegs of beer to leave their brewery without Internal Revenue Service stamps on them, ostensibly to avoid paying the burdensome taxes.[142] Since both of these companies were no longer in business and Arthur W. Fox was deceased, it is unclear who was charged and when the charge was from.

Detail of a pre-Prohibition bottle from the Kaltenbach Brewing Company, founded by F.X. Kaltenbach at Lutheran and Batavia Streets. This bottle is likely from the 1880s. *Photo by Chris Groves, from the collection of Dave Mik.*

Francis Xavier Kaltenbach, who had been operating a brewery on Lutheran Alley since 1850, moved to 438 East Eagle Street in 1876, when he started a new brewery. Sales in 1863 were 2,992 barrels of beer, which increased to 10,860 in 1869–1870, and by 1879, he was brewing 18,140 barrels of beer and employed twenty-five men.[143]

The brewery started by David Haas on Cherry and Spring Streets had grown considerably since its advent in 1860. He was now producing over three thousand barrels per year, and his sons had joined him in the business. When a terrible explosion and fire struck the brewery on January 23, 1877, it was devastating. A boiler located in the rear of the brewery exploded, blowing a portion of the building apart. Both of Haas's sons were missing after the explosion. Frederick Herman Haas was found in the rubble and regained consciousness but had been badly injured. His brother, Gustavus, was found dead in the brewery. The Haas home, adjoining the brewery, was not damaged. After a coroner's inquest in February 1877, it was determined that a defective boiler caused the explosion.[144] Haas would rebuild and continue the operation but for less than ten years.

The Fisher Brothers & Company malt house at 283 West Genesee Street, founded in 1862 by George Fisher, added to its facility in 1871 and again in 1877. Its capacity increased to 250,000 bushels.[145]

After spending years in the employ of John G. Meidenbauer, Christian G. Voltz partnered with his brother, John S., in 1877 to start their own malting business. They leased a building on Georgia and Sixth Streets.[146]

George J. Meyer was born in Buffalo in April 1864. In about 1877, after his parochial school education and attendance at Canisius College, Meyer began to work for the Buffalo malting firm Charles G. Curtiss Company at 71 Main Street as a clerk. Meyer spent the next twenty-nine years learning every aspect of the business and rising through the ranks.[147]

Francis Joseph Jost Jr. took over his father's brewery at 419–29 Broadway in 1867. The brewery was now producing close to 3,800 barrels of beer per year when Jost Jr. died suddenly in April 1877. Jost Sr., now sixty-eight years old, came out of retirement to run the brewery.[148]

The John M. Luippold Brewing Company at 298 Emslie Street had been in operation since 1867. Luippold's sons, John Jr. and George, were also involved in the business. In 1873, Matthias Voetsch (possibly William Voetsch Sr.'s brother) was still employed by Luippold and would continue working for him until at least 1880. With business increasing, Luippold felt it was time to update the facility, so the buildings were rebuilt in 1878.[149]

Gustav Fleischmann was born in 1849 in Vienna, Austria. His brothers were already in America when he set sail for New York at sixteen. He worked as a stonecutter in New York before heading, in 1869, to Cincinnati, where his brothers Charles and Max were making yeast and distilling spirits as Gaff, Fleischmann & Company.[150]

After a time, Gustav was interested in stepping out on his own and, nine years later, in 1878, headed to the bustling grain port of Buffalo. There he first worked for his brothers' firm, Gaff, Fleischmann & Company selling yeast. In 1879, Gustav met Edward N. Cook, an experienced distiller, and with financial backing from his brothers, they purchased a shut-down distillery at Pratt and William Streets. There they opened E.N. Cook & Company, with their offices at 32 Main Street.[151]

William E. Kreiner was born in 1857 in Buffalo. After attending school, he worked in his father's shoe store. In 1878, he partnered with Peter Lehr, who had been a brewmaster and foreman at William W. Sloan's brewery at 698 Carroll Street in 1860.[152] The partners formed the Kreiner & Lehr malt company and built their first malt house at 467 Spring Street in 1878 and added another in 1920 at 50 Elk Street. An addition was added in 1936, and it would later be known as the Buffalo Malting Corporation.[153] Kreiner married his partner's daughter, Louisa.

John Moffat's son Henry C. decided to take a crack at the brewery business in 1878 with William Service. They restarted the brewery founded by Henry C.'s grandfather John Moffat Sr. at Mohawk Street at the corner of Morgan Street. The new brewery, known as Moffat & Service Brewery, was next door to Shoemaker & Noble. Their first year in business, 1879, they produced 6,426 barrels of ale.

On October 1, 1879, Albert Ziegele Sr. retired from the brewery he had founded. He left several capable men in charge: his sons, Albert Jr. and William, as well as his son-in-law, Herman Grau. To prepare his sons, Ziegele had sent them to study at the College of Applied Sciences in Stuttgart, Baden-Württemberg, Germany. William was in charge of brewing, while Albert ran the finances and Herman supervised the cellars and ran shipping. The cellars were now large enough to hold fourteen thousand barrels of lager, and Ziegele Sr. had installed the first ammonia cooling system in Buffalo. The brewery employed twenty-four men, and there were five wagons and teams available for shipping to and from the brewery. The malt house was capable of malting eighty thousand bushels per year.[154]

In 1879, John Kam, who had started in the malt business in 1869, erected a larger malt house on Pratt and Genesee Streets. With a total malting capacity of 100,000 bushels, he employed sixteen men.[155]

The brewery of Francis J. Jost Sr. on the corner of Pratt Street and Broadway was back in the hands of the founder after his son died in 1877. The brewery was producing nearly four thousand barrels of beer per year when the elder Jost died at seventy years old in mid-January 1879.[156] He is buried in the United German and French Cemetery in Cheektowaga. The brewery was sold, and a new company, Jost Brewing Company, was incorporated by Joseph Berlin and Edward Kretz. The brewery was now forty by one hundred feet, had two icehouses capable of holding two hundred cords of ice each, had a brewing capacity of twelve thousand barrels per year and employed twelve men. The brewery increased production from about four thousand barrels to eight thousand barrels in 1879, and according to A.F. Marthens, its lager beer was considered "equal, if not superior, to any manufactured in Western New York."[157]

Solomon Scheu finished serving a term as mayor of Buffalo in 1879 and returned to his growing malt business. He opened several more malt houses and leased the Niagara Malt House on Ohio Street (apparently from

BUFFALO BEER

From the souvenir of the Brewers' Association meeting in Buffalo in 1878, a collection of Buffalo brewers: F.J. Jost, Gerhard Lang, Magnus Beck and Jacob F. Kuhn. *Photo by Ethan Cox, from the collection of Dave Mik.*

Thomas Clarke) for several years. He also opened the Scheu Brothers Malt House in Lancaster, New York, with his brothers William and Jacob. By 1882, they were producing 400,000 to 500,000 bushels per year.[158]

Julius Binz was born in Baden-Württemberg, Germany, in 1847. When he was twenty-two, he came to America and settled in Buffalo. Binz lived on the city's East Side, where he ran a grocery store and saloon before purchasing the former Frederick Albrecht brewery at 815 Batavia Street in 1879. There he had a long and prosperous career.[159]

George C. Ginther was born in Buffalo in December 1855. He attended parochial school and then set out as a bookkeeper for the New York Central Railroad. Afterward, he worked for the Ziegele Brewing Company until about 1879, when he was made manager of the Magnus Beck Brewing Company at 407 North Division Street near Spring Street.[160] He later became treasurer of the New York State Brewers' Association.

After gaining valuable experience working in both East Boston, Massachusetts, and New York City, William Simon went to Buffalo, where Gerhard Lang, founder of the Lang Brewery, was looking for someone to help with a problem he was having at his brewery. According to Andrew A. Michalak, "Lang was looking for a competent brewmaster"[161] due to spoilage somewhere in his production process. When Lang heard about Simon, he hired Simon to be brewmaster and superintendent of the brewery. After examining the situation, Simon suggested that Lang tear out the entire system and discard all beer stock, which Lang did.[162] Simon had earned the respect of his new employer and more confidence, which he would use to build his own brewery in a few short years.

10
THE 1880s

FIRES, UNIONS AND GROWTH

B y 1880, the malt house operated by the Gerhard Lang Brewery at 581 Genesee Street covered nearly three acres and employed ten men when Gerhard Lang purchased the former Cobb Farm at the corner of Best and Jefferson Streets to build what might have been the most beautiful brewery in Buffalo: the Park Brewery.[163]

A group that wanted to supply product only to its members established a different type of brewery in Buffalo in 1880. On February 20, 1880, the Buffalo Cooperative Brewing Company was formed after it purchased the former Hoefner Brothers Brewery on High and Michigan Streets. Jacob Manhardt was elected president of the firm, Peter Mergenhagen the vice-president, Oswald Banghard the secretary and Conrad Schuler the treasurer. The capacity of the brewery was ten thousand barrels per year. Several others, including John Honecker and Adrian Metz, were involved in the incorporation. Grover Cleveland, when he was an attorney in Buffalo, was an early investor in the brewery, as well as attorney for the Buffalo Brewers' Association.[164] Mergenhagen had run a hotel for fifty years when this opportunity arose and he took it. The brewery was the first cooperative one in Buffalo, where only member retailers could purchase the brewery's beer.

On May 7, 1880, Jacob Schanzlin's brewery at 1847 Main Street suffered a large fire, but the surrounding area was saved.[165] This was probably the time that Schanzlin decided to retire; he had started working for Rudolph Baer back in 1828. For one of the relatively unknown brewers in Buffalo,

An artist's rendition of Gerhard Lang's famous Park Brewery at Jefferson and Best Streets. The completed brewery was very much like this according to photographic evidence. *Photo from* Illustrated Buffalo: The Queen City of the Lakes.

he sold quite a lot of beer. In 1863, he produced 4,897 barrels of beer, and in 1871, he sold 5,009 barrels of beer—more than all but the largest brewers in Buffalo. By 1879, he had sold only 2,824 barrels of beer per year. After the fire, it was probably too much for him to handle. His son ran the business for four more years. In 1884, the Schanzlin brewery was shut down once and for all.

Buffalo would again host the United States Brewers' Association Convention on June 2 and 3, 1880. It was the twentieth annual convention. Robert Portner of Alexandria, Virginia, was elected president.[166] His nephew Carl Strangmann would later work for him and become an important brewery executive in Buffalo.

Fisher Brothers & Company were now proprietors of two four-story malt houses: the Genesee Malt House, located at 285 West Genesee Street, and the City Malt House, located on the Erie Canal at the foot of Carolina Street. They employed nineteen men, and sales, by 1880, were between $100,000 and $150,000 ($2,320,000 and $3,480,000) annually, with total capacity of 200,000 bushels per year.[167]

While the Fisher brothers' sales were growing, the Voltz brothers were also experiencing a sales growth at their malt business. In 1880, they erected a new six-story building at 1710–14 Niagara Street, bringing their malting capacity to 115,000 bushels per year.[168] Around 1884, they changed the business name to the International Malt House.

Schaefer & Brother had been in business since 1861 with Gustavus and Henry operating a growing malt house that they had begun in 1871. In 1880, they built a new malt house on the corner of Seventh and Jersey Streets in Buffalo. The house had four malting floors, a capacity of 100,000 bushels per season (a season being eight months in Buffalo), a cellar, a storage floor and elevator attached to the building.[169]

Sometime in 1880, Henry Diehl purchased the Union Malt House from Burdette A. Lynde. The malt house had been built in 1873 at 400 Niagara Street near Maryland Street. Lynde would go on to other work not related to malting.

The Queen City Malt House, formerly owned by Abel T. Blackmar but at the time by George W. Tifft (of Tifft Farm), was completely destroyed on December 17, 1880, after a horrific fire tore through the Birge Wallpaper Factory next door on Perry Street near Washington Street. Fifteen people died at the Birge factory, and damage to the malt house cost at least $50,000 ($1,160,000). It was rebuilt.[170]

The 1880 census stated that there was $1,859,975 ($43,100,000) invested in the malting enterprises in Buffalo, with $1,636,020 ($37,900,00) in product. The malting concerns were big business in Buffalo.

About a year after the Buffalo Cooperative Brewing Company was formed at the former Alois Hoefner Brewery on Michigan and High Streets, the corporation decided to upgrade and built a new brewery. The company employed twenty men.[171]

Another venture decided to try its luck at the cooperative business model. In 1881, William Voetsch Sr. changed his brewery at 10 West Bennett Street into the Clinton Cooperative Brewing Company.[172] Like other cooperative breweries, only member saloons (often owned by the brewery), could purchase the product. Voetsch was the superintendent of the brewery.

In May 1881, a smell must have been emanating from the icehouse of Jacob Schanzlin's brewery on Main Street and Delavan Avenue that attracted attention. Inside, John Frank, a missing ex-alderman was found, the rope around his neck rotting and his hanging body decomposing. Over two weeks earlier, Frank had gone on a drinking binge, neglected work and then disappeared until he was found in the icehouse. According to news reports, "Family difficulties and hard drinking" contributed to his state of mind and ultimately his demise.[173] Shortly after this, however, Schanzlin's brewery closed. In 1883, the city pushed to purchase the property for $8,000 ($192,000) to build a new school, but after

The gravestone of Magnus Beck in Forest Lawn Cemetery. As with many of Buffalo's nineteenth-century brewers, Beck died a wealthy man, as indicated both by the size of his memorial and its location in a prestigious cemetery. *Photo by Ethan Cox.*

receiving one hundred letters against the idea, it was rejected in September 1883.[174] It was privately purchased in 1888 to be used for a crematory, but that project was also quashed.

Charles G. Pankow was born near Feldberg, Mecklenburg-Strelitz, Germany, in 1851. When he was thirteen years old, he came to America and began working in a bakery. When he was twenty-nine years old, he opened a grocery and saloon at 257 William Street and, in 1885, moved to the corner of William and Pratt Streets. Pankow also served as a Buffalo city alderman during this time. It was in 1882 that Pankow turned some of his attention to the brewing industry. He purchased a share in Voetsch's Clinton Cooperative Brewing Company.

John White managed the Niagara Malting Company until 1876, when he joined with his son, John C., and John W. Crafts to create White & Crafts and built the Lake View Malt House at the corner of Lake View Avenue and Jersey Street.[175] With business increasing, they built a new house in 1882, adjacent to the current, to bring their malting capacity to 225,000 bushels per year and continue Buffalo's dominance in this industry.[176]

According to a write-up in the 1897 convention program, it was said that almost as soon as Magnus Beck embarked on running his own brewery with "untiring energy and ability,"[177] he built the Magnus Beck brewery into one of the more prominent breweries in Buffalo. In his personal life, Beck married in 1851. His wife died in 1873, causing him great sorrow, but he was able to continue on until his own death in May 1883. The convention program said that Beck was known as "a kind and loving father, and tried and true, generous and liberal-minded friend and benefactor."

After his death, Beck's estate, headed by his son-in-law and executor Adam J. Benzing, carried on running the brewery. At the time, the brewery at 467 North Division Street was three stories high, included a malt house, had a brewing capacity of forty thousand barrels of beer per year and employed forty men. Benzing was born in Baden-Württemberg, Germany, and owned an interest in the brewery. He married Beck's daughter Caroline.[178]

George F. Stein was born in Germany in August 1856. After studying brewing in Bavaria, he made the long voyage to America and settled in Buffalo. His first job was under William Simon, who was brewmaster at Gerhard Lang Brewery at that time. This would lead Stein to spend many years in the brewing industry.[179]

The Roos brewery at 95 Roos Street had produced 4,920 barrels of beer in 1863, and by 1883, it was producing over 10,000 barrels of beer per year. It employed forty-seven men, and the malt house connected with the brewery produced 55,000 bushels of malt per year.[180]

By 1883, the John Kam Malting Company was expanding, adding a second malt house on Pratt Street to join the one it ran on Pratt and Genesee Streets. The total malting capacity was 100,000 bushels per year, and the company employed sixteen men.[181]

In 1883, the Clinton Cooperative Brewing Company, founded by William Voetsch Sr., had been turned into a stock company. William Voetsch Jr., who had been involved with the brewery since leaving school, retired from the business and started a liquor store. He would enter politics and run for Buffalo alderman in 1891.[182]

In November 1883, a fire destroyed the malt house of Julius Binz at 815 Broadway, causing an $11,000 loss ($264,000).[183]

The Arthur W. Fox family had lost their father in an unfortunate train accident, and his partner, Horace Williams, had been swindled out of his share of the Buffalo Grape Sugar Company by majority stockholder Chauncey J. Hamlin in 1874. This didn't sit well with Fox's son Arthur G. Fox, and in early January 1884, he sued Buffalo Grape Sugar Company to recover the eighty-six shares of stock his father had owned in the company, as well as earnings dating back to 1874, which amounted to about $3 million ($72,400,000).[184]

By 1884, there were three different Charles Schuhs involved in the brewery industry, and Charles F. was superintendent of the Luippold Brewery on Emslie Street. Charles F. had previously been involved in an ale brewery with Joseph L. Haberstro and George Scobell.[185] He would move to Niagara Falls by the 1890s and would continue as a brewer.

The Buffalo Ice Company, which was formed in 1867, was incorporated in 1884 with $150,000 ($3,620,000) capital.[186]

Edwin G.S. Miller was born in Buffalo in March 1854. After his education was completed, Miller became a bookkeeper. Two years later, he took the same position for George Urban & Sons flour mills. His hard work earned him a partnership in 1874.

In 1884, Gerhard Lang was looking for a "capable and competent" manager, and coincidentally, Miller was his son-in-law, so he was hired. At the time, the brewery was putting out forty thousand barrels of beer annually. The entire facility at Best Street and Jefferson Avenue covered thirty-four acres and employed fifty men in the brewery.[187]

The International Brewing Company was incorporated in 1884 with capital stock of $200,000 ($4,830,000) to purchase the Scheu Brewery at

1088 Niagara Street. August Beck was president, Philip Bissinger was vice-president, Paul Werner was secretary and Philip Bachert was treasurer.[188] The company's most popular beers would become Stock Lager and Hof-Brau, but they also brewed ale and porter.

In 1884, John Kam, who started in the malt business in 1869 and had erected a much larger house, expanded the malt house by the addition of three stories. This made a seven-story building, 125 by 160 feet.[189]

There were two essential ingredients that beer manufacturers used that Buffalo and New York State in general excelled in growing for many years: hops and barley. Buffalo was the central point "in a remarkable barley-growing district" that extended over the Canadian border.[190]

Edwin G.S. Miller, Gerhard Lang's son-in-law, was made manager of the brewery and increased sales from forty thousand barrels to ninety-nine thousand barrels per year in eight years. He was later made president of the brewery and died a wealthy man. *Photo from* Men of New York.

Godfrey Heiser began brewing in 1845 with his brother Henry. Godfrey died in January 1885 at eighty-five years old and is buried in the family plot in Forest Lawn Cemetery in Buffalo, not far from President Millard Fillmore. Heiser's sister Elizabeth married Christian Hormel, whose grandson George would later found the Hormel Foods Company.[191]

By 1885, the Albert Ziegele Brewing Company had sold eighty-one thousand barrels of beer per year, making it the second largest brewery in Buffalo. It was second only to Gerhard Lang's brewery.[192]

The son of Alois Schaefer, Philip G., was born in Buffalo in May 1862. He attended parochial school and then Canisius College and finally Bryant & Stratton Business College. After he finished his studies, he entered his father's brewery, Schaefer Brewery, as a bookkeeper and collector. The Schaefer Brewery on Lake View Avenue and Porter Avenue was brewing about twenty thousand barrels of beer per year by late December 1885. Alois, now ready for retirement, sold the brewery for $120,000 ($2,960,000)

The Lake View Brewing Company on Lake View Avenue, circa 1897. Founded as the Schaefer Brewery in 1885 by Alois Schaefer, it was sold and renamed Lake View. *Photo from Souvenir of Buffalo, on Occasion of the 37th Annual Convention at Buffalo, N.Y.*

to a new group that renamed the brewery the Lake View Brewing Company. George Sandrock was named president, Henry W. Brendel the secretary and T.J. Mahoney the treasurer. Philip G. Schaefer stayed on as general manager of the new firm.[193]

George Sandrock was born in 1838 in Buffalo. He would become a flour merchant and sit on the board of the Grain Commission. By 1880, he was president of the Buffalo Board of Trade (John Baker Manning was vice-president).[194]

In 1885, brewery founder Joseph L. Haberstro decided to step off the stage and retired from brewing to become an insurance agent and notary public. The following year, the German-American Brewing Company was organized with capital stock of $150,000 ($3,780,000). It purchased the J.L. Haberstro & Company at 11 High Street to operate in.[195]

Early breweries were often run as sole proprietorships out of convenience. Sometimes, as the businesses grew or were sold by founders, stock companies were formed to take over and run the companies.

Charles Gerber had been brewing at 821 Main Street and Burton Alley since 1859. His sales had steadily grown from 1,524 barrels of beer in 1863 to 11,245 barrels in 1879, making his business nearly as large as Magnus Beck's and several others. This might have been one

An artist's rendition of Magnus Beck Brewing Company at North Division and Spring Streets. After the founder's death in 1884, the company was restructured as a stock company and his son Edward Beck was chosen as the first president. *Photo from* Souvenir of Buffalo, on Occasion of the 37th Annual Convention at Buffalo, N.Y.

of the reasons it was decided, in January 1886, to transfer ownership of the brewery to the Empire Brewing Company for $120,000 ($3,070,000) after assigning a mortgage to Abraham D. Miller.[196]

In June 1886, the brewery owned by Julius Binz at 815 Broadway struck natural gas at sixty feet, enough to run the brewery.[197] Binz then rebuilt his entire brewery, possibly to accommodate the newly found fuel.

Two years after the death of its founder, the Magnus Beck brewery at North Division and Spring Streets was reorganized in October 1886 as a stock company with $265,000 ($6,670,000) capital. Magnus Beck's son Edward Beck was chosen as the first president of Magnus Beck Brewing Company.[198]

Charles Lamy was raised on a farm in Eden, New York, and when old enough, he moved to Buffalo to work in a grocery store. In 1874, he opened his own store on Elk Street in Buffalo, and after eight years, he purchased the building and had a large business. Lamy invested in real estate and the Magnus Beck Brewing Company when it went public in 1886. He was one of the largest shareholders and served as president of the firm for nearly four years. During his tenure, a new brewery was erected at a cost of almost

$250,000 ($6,510,000). Lamy, who was elected a New York state senator in 1893, sold his stock in 1895 and retired from the business.[199]

Unions had become a stirring presence in Buffalo by the 1880s. They were formed to protect the workers, who were being taken advantage of by the brewery owners. "They were compelled to work 14, 16 and 18 hour days" with three different rates of pay. So in 1886, Brewers' Union Number Seven was formed. It was affiliated with the national organization.[200] The local would become Number Four by 1895. Additional unions covering other aspects of the industry were also forming.

The F.J. Jost Brewery, which was started in 1850, was put up for sale in March 1886 after the then current owners had taken over the property on a debt. Jost Sr. had died in 1879, and Jost Jr. had died in 1877. Organized as the Jost Brewing Company by Joseph Berlin and Edward Kretz in 1879, the legal aid for the sale said the brewery "will be sold at a very low figure."[201]

Prominent Buffalo brewer and German citizen Jacob Scheu retired in 1886 after over thirty-five years in the brewery business.[202] His brewery—then known as the International Brewing Company on Niagara Street—was still going strong.

Six local businessmen formed the Frontier Elevator Company on June 23, 1886. The capital for the company was authorized at $400,000 ($10,200,000). The founders were from two groups: John Davidson, a ship owner; Edward N. Cook; and Gustav Fleischmann were from E.N. Cook & Company, and John A. Campbell, Stephen Ratcliffe Sr. and Stephen Ratcliffe Jr. were all grain merchants in the firm of Campbell & Ratcliffe. By the time the elevator was completed, it was the largest in Buffalo, with a storage capacity of 4.75 million bushels of grain.[203]

Like the brewery workers, the maltsters organized in 1887 and formed Maltsters' Union Local Fifty-Nine.

The Gerhard Lang Brewery, the largest in Buffalo but still a relatively small operation compared to other manufacturing concerns in the bustling city, employed 110 people in 1887 and distributed as far as Virginia.[204]

Business was good for the F.X. Kaltenbach Brewery at 458 East Eagle Street by 1887, so much so that it was purchased from founder Francis X. Kaltenbach and his junior partner, William Miller, and incorporated with capital stock of $175,000 ($4,360,000). The Kaltenbach Brewing Company's new officers were B.F. Gentsch, president; Philip D. Stein, vice-president; Charles L. Fink, treasurer; and William Miller, who stayed on as secretary. The new owners renamed the brewery Excelsior Brewery. The capacity at the brewery was forty thousand barrels of beer per year, but they were selling only about twenty-one thousand barrels.[205] The most popular beer line they sold was Excelsior Beer—which, according to their own ads, was "rich, smooth, bright and sparkling." Kaltenbach's son, Frank X., continued to work at the brewery for a time.

David Haas sold his brewery at Spring and Cherry Streets to a group that renamed it Columbia Brewing Company in February 1887. The president was Zelmer L.H. Loepere, the vice-president was William Eigenbrod, the secretary was August E. Rother and the treasurer was Fred Danager.[206]

Julius Binz's brewery at 815 Broadway was still growing. With the natural gas discovered on the property, manufacturing costs must have gone down, and in 1887–88, the brewery produced 13,250 barrels of beer. In 1887, Binz incorporated, and the name was changed to Broadway Brewing and Malting Company, with $300,000 ($7,470,000) capital.

After being in business for twenty years, the East Buffalo Brewing Company was formed to take control of the John M. Luippold Brewing Company at 298 Emslie Street. With $150,000 ($3,740,000) in capital, attorney Henry W. Brendel became the new president, with William T. Becker as vice-president, John C. Schenk as secretary and manager and George Wesp as treasurer.

The year 1887 was one of change in the Buffalo brewing scene, with many breweries either attacked by fires or changing hands. In June 1887, the Buffalo Cooperative Brewing Company on High and Michigan Streets

John Luippold was in business for about twenty years when the East Buffalo Brewing Company was formed to purchase the business. It was open until Prohibition. This picture is circa 1897. *Photo from* Souvenir of Buffalo, on Occasion of the 37th Annual Convention at Buffalo, N.Y.

suffered a "disastrous" fire that caused $30,000 ($747,000) damage. Because the damage was so bad, the directors decided it would be best to demolish the old buildings and start from scratch, which they did. A modern brewery was built on the site, and the brewing capacity increased to 100,000 barrels per year.[207]

A fire at the Gerhard Lang Brewery malt house on July 21, 1887, was quite destructive, destroying the house, two dwellings and sixty-five thousand bushels of grain. There was $80,000 ($2,020,000) in damage, but insurance covered it all.[208]

The Columbia Brewing Company at Spring and Cherry Streets, which had just formed in February, went up in smoke early in the morning on August 13, 1887. The fire might have started in the engine room and spread throughout the building. Damages were estimated to be $35,000 ($884,000) with one thousand bushels of malt suffering water damage.[209]

Beer coopers were an important aspect of beer production in the nineteenth century. They built and repaired the wooden barrels used to store and ship beer across the city or county, both to retailers and independent bottlers. In mid-August 1887, the beer coopers from several shops went on strike, demanding higher wages from their employers. The thirty-four men organized into a trade union and sent an application to the Knights of Labor to be represented.[210]

The Knights of Labor had started in Philadelphia in 1869, and by 1886, they had 700,000 members. By mid-September, the coopers were still on strike, the owners agreeing to a raise but refusing to put it in writing. At the same time, inmates at Erie County Penitentiary began making barrels for less than the shops were charging.[211]

Alois Schaefer, founder of the Lake View Brewing Company, died in early March 1887 at fifty years old. He is buried in the United German and French Cemetery in Cheektowaga. After his death, his widow contested the will, saying he was not of sound mind when he executed it.[212]

At two o'clock in the morning on November 16, 1887, a fire broke out in the malt houses of the Ziegele Brewing Company on Washington Street between Burton Alley and Virginia Street. It was a devastating fire that spread rapidly. The brewery plant, icehouses and a full malt elevator of eighty-five thousand bushels of grain were destroyed, causing $150,000 ($3,740,000) in damage, of which insurance covered only about $100,000 ($2,490,000). Instead of giving up, Ziegele reorganized the brewery into a stock company, with $200,000 ($4,980,000) stock, and rebuilt the brewery from the ground up.[213]

Moffat & Service Brewery, run by Henry C. Moffat on Mohawk and Morgan Streets, sold only 5,675 barrels of beer between 1887 and 1888,

The headstone of Alois Schaefer, founder of the Lake View Brewery, in the United German and French Cemetery, Cheektowaga, New York. *Photo by Michael Rizzo.*

although the brewery had a capacity of 20,000 barrels annually. It employed fifteen men and was capitalized with $100,000 ($2,490,000). The only possible explanation for the lack of production, as mentioned by Powell in his book, is a catastrophic event such as a fire.

The year 1888 started out horribly for the Christian Weyand Brewery on Main Street. In about 1868, Christian Weyand had rented a beer cellar several miles up Main Street from his brewery on Delavan Avenue. On January 24, 1888, former Erie County sheriff William W. Lawson was at the Weyand beer cellars on Delavan Avenue when he fell down a flight of stairs and was instantaneously killed. Lawson had been sheriff from 1880 to 1882 and had served one term in the New York state assembly.[214]

A new building for the Charles G. Curtiss Company was erected on Niagara and Albany Streets in 1888, with a combination of floor and pneumatic malting systems. In addition to the six growing compartments of the floor system malting house, there were ten Galland-Henning drums and two floors of Tilden drums.[215]

On May 1, 1888, a news article said a lockout by the brewery owners was made after a "mandate issued by the International Brewers' Union"[216] that the Brewers' Union Local 7 should insist on increased pay by that date.

The Charles G. Curtiss malting company, circa 1903, located at Niagara and Albany Streets. *Photo from* One Hundred Years of Brewing.

The men had been paid the night before, and the owners insisted they had enough beer for at least a month. Joseph L. Haberstro stated, "I know of no class of labor that is so well favored as they are. The poorest man in a brewery gets $12."[217] Several breweries intended on taking men from the malt houses and using them in the breweries. The brewers then went on strike, which lasted until the end of the month, when, according to the news article, the "men gave up the contest and returned to work."[218]

Brewmaster and superintendent of the Gerhard Lang Brewery, William Simon, had been employed at the brewery for about eight years when he became ill with typhoid fever and traveled back to his homeland of Germany in May 1888 for three months' recuperation.[219]

The founder of John Schüssler Brewing Company died in May 1888 and is buried in the United German and French Cemetery in Cheektowaga. When William Simon returned to Buffalo, instead of returning to the Gerhard Lang Brewery, he became partners with Susan Schüssler, widow of the late John Schüssler, and took charge of the John Schüssler Brewing Company. When Simon took over, sales were 16,877 barrels of beer per year.[220]

The Columbia Brewing Company (formerly run by David Haas) filed amended incorporation papers on August 2, 1888, with $75,000 ($1,890,000)

A souvenir pin from the annual meeting of the Wine, Liquor and Beer Dealers Association, held in Buffalo in 1888. *Photo by Chris Groves, from the collection of Dave Mik.*

in capital stock. The incorporators included current owner August E. Rother, William Shoemacher, Louis A. Lombard, Henry Jerge and several others.[221]

On November 23, 1888, former Buffalo mayor and owner of the Frontier Canada Malt House on Hudson and Fourth Streets, Solomon Scheu, died after a week's illness. Scheu had entered politics after his saloon became a meeting place for local politicians. He served as Buffalo city alderman and receiver of taxes for four years. Unfortunately, during his tenure, a bank—into which he had deposited money for the city as receiver of taxes—failed, leaving him personally responsible. Eighteen years later, he paid the deficiency plus interest. He also served six years as a state prison inspector before being elected mayor in 1877, serving in 1878 and 1879. Scheu was a personal friend of President Grover Cleveland up until the time of his death, and Cleveland sent condolences to Scheu's widow.[222] He is buried in Forest Lawn Cemetery.

His son Augustus F. Scheu entered the business immediately after graduation from the Buffalo Normal School (a training school for teachers). When his father died, Augustus took over management of the company for the estate.[223]

Herman Grau, born in Prussia in 1845 and the son-in-law of Albert Ziegele Sr., worked as a brewer and for Ziegele for at least seventeen years before taking his knowledge of the brewing trade and moving to Sacramento, California. It was 1890 when Grau, now forty-five years old, started the

Buffalo Brewing Company, which would become one of the largest breweries west of the Mississippi.[224] After retiring, Albert Ziegele Sr. would spend his winters in Sacramento and return to Buffalo for the summers.

The year did not end any better than it had started for the brewing and malting industry in Buffalo. Henry Diehl's Union Malt House on Niagara Street near Maryland Street exploded and then collapsed on December 6, 1888, killing one and burying several under the debris. There were cries for better building regulations and inspections after an investigation determined that, after several building additions, there were thin walls and defective timbers that could not handle the weight of the additions, leading to the collapse.[225] Questioned by reporters on the night of the accident, Diehl said the damages were between $5,000 and $10,000 ($126,000 and $253,000), and he had so many questions of his own that "I haven't even had time to take a glass of beer."[226]

The Broadway Brewing and Malting Company elected new officers in December 1888. George Bork was president of the firm, Stephen Reimann was vice-president, Joseph P. Schattner was secretary and attorney and founder Julius Binz was treasurer and manager.[227]

The former treasurer of International Brewing Company, Franz Knobloch, and Henry Juenling were charged with larceny in 1889 for misappropriating $3,250.85 ($83,700) from the brewery.[228]

Two prominent brewery-related unions were formed in 1889: the Beer Drivers Union Local Sixteen and Coopers Union Local Ninety-three.

Columbia Brewing Company (formerly run by David Haas) at Spring and Cherry Streets became Queen City Brewing Company on August 17, 1889, when it was incorporated with $75,000 ($1,960,000) stock. Charles Effer was president, William C. Peters was secretary and George J. Zillig was manager of the brewery. On November 7, 1890, Irlbacher and Davis sold their combined 141 shares in Queen City Brewing Company to Herman Frost. In January 1892, David Haas, the former owner, was permitted to sell the property.[229]

The aptly named Phoenix Brewery on Washington Street, formerly Ziegele's brewery, had risen from the ashes, "larger and handsomer" than before the fire. It was formally opened on June 6, 1889, with frontage on Washington Street over 200 feet and a depth of 125 feet and five stories high. J. Adam Lautz was president, Charles Bischop was vice-president, Albert Ziegele Jr. was treasurer and Jacob Dilcher was secretary and general manager.[230] The office was located at Virginia and Washington Streets. (The building is still located there; a plaque on the wall denotes the brewery, and as of this writing, the building is being developed into residential property.)

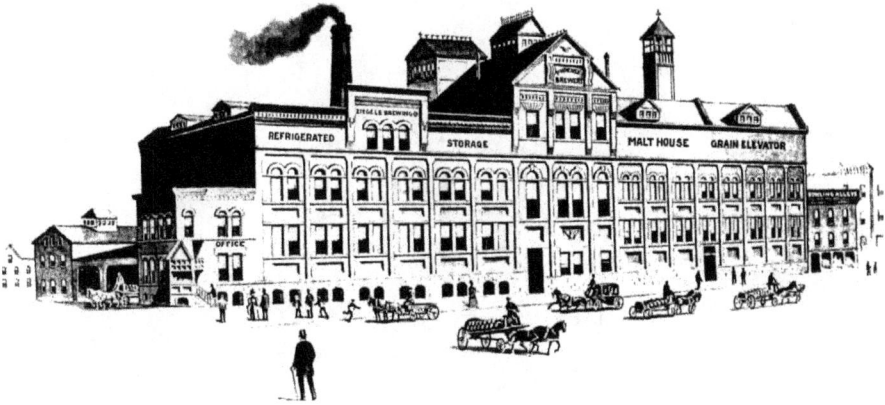

The Ziegele brewery, circa 1897. Founded by Albert Ziegele, the brewery was destroyed in a fire and rebuilt in 1889 and renamed Phoenix Brewery. *Photo from* Souvenir of Buffalo, on Occasion of the 37th Annual Convention at Buffalo, N.Y.

John Kam was one of the largest maltsters in Buffalo by this time. In 1889, the John Kam Malting Company was incorporated, with the founder of the business as president and treasurer. His son Joseph, who was on the board of the German-American Bank and owned the Exchange Elevator Company, was secretary. Kam's eldest son, Henry, was also an executive in the company. The company was operating two malt houses, one at the foot of Hertel Avenue and one leased from another company, which had a combined capacity of 600,000 bushels annually. All of its malt was floor made (turned by hand); no drums were used. Kam's youngest son, John Jr., was born in Buffalo in 1871 and attended Canisius College, afterward joining the firm and, after incorporation, being made general manager. In 1896, he married brewery owner William Simon's daughter Louise.[231]

11

THE 1890s

END OF A CENTURY

In the 1890s, the nineteenth century was winding down and the number of breweries in Buffalo was shrinking. At the same time, those that were still in business were producing more than ever before. Although there were half as many breweries operating in the Queen City in 1894 as there were in 1863 (eighteen versus thirty-five), the breweries produced 600,000 barrels, or 1,200,000 kegs, of beer.[232]

Christian Weyand had been operating his brewery at 793 Main Street since 1866 and was producing about 25,000 barrels of beer per year when, advancing in age, he decided it was time to reorganize the business. It's possible that the death of the former sheriff at his brewery in 1888 swayed his mind. On May 1, 1890, the company was reorganized into a stock company, Christian Weyand Brewing Company, with Weyand as president and his son John A. named vice-president and general manager and another son Charles M. named secretary and treasurer. Both sons were born in Buffalo and had worked for the company since graduating from Bryant & Stratton Business College.[233] The company's primary beverage was Weyand's Lager, which, according to the company, was a prize-winning beer.

It was a warm winter in 1893–94 in Buffalo, so much so that there was not any ice to harvest, and the breweries were big users of ice. Most of the large breweries were either installing ice-making machines or looking to purchase ice from other sources.[234]

The search for more efficient and cheaper ways to illuminate or heat the brewery plants was something else business owners were constantly looking

The Christian Weyand Brewing Company was a very popular brewery on Washington Street. Its founder died in 1898. Today, the location of the brewery is the former *Buffalo Courier-Express* building and is now the home of the Catholic Diocese. Note the cold storage facility on the right. This picture is circa 1897. *Photo from* Souvenir of Buffalo, on Occasion of the 37th Annual Convention at Buffalo, N.Y.

for. Several of them decided to dig wells on their property to search for natural gas. One of the first to find gas was Julius Binz, who found it in 1886. George Rochevot and Gerhard Lang were also successful in finding natural gas on their properties.

Seeing the success other breweries were having, in April 1890, the German-American Brewing Company built a derrick on its property at Main and Highs Streets to take a stab at finding gas on its property. But the bigger story was that Binz and fellow brewers Rochevot and Lang, along with George Hottinger, had bigger plans and purchased twenty thousand feet of pipe to distribute the gas across the East Side and formed Erie County Natural Gas Fuel Company in October 1889. A survey of homeowners found, in two days, one hundred people willing to pay for the fuel.

At the Gerhard Lang Brewery, the company dug eight wells and struck gas in at least three of them. At Rochevot's, one well had enough pressure to supply gas to eight hundred or nine hundred homes. The Erie County Natural Gas Fuel Company's gas field, though, ran out of enough volume to supply the customers it had by 1896, so they leased their pipes to the Buffalo Natural Gas Fuel Company.[235] In 1920, the Iroquois Natural Gas Company (later National Fuel Gas) purchased the stock of Erie County Natural Gas Fuel Company, thus ending its existence.[236]

By 1888, the Empire Brewing Company at 821 Main Street employed fifteen men and had a capacity of ten thousand barrels per year. It installed a new ice machine in the brewery in April 1890. In filing its 1890 annual report, the company stated it had $275,000 ($7,160,000) capital stock with $100,000 ($2,600,000) paid in and half in debts.[237]

In mid-November 1890, a fantastic fire swept the Wells grain elevator in Buffalo, destroying the elevator and leaving $500,000 ($13,000,000) in damage. The estate of Chandler J. Wells, a former mayor of Buffalo, owned the elevator.[238]

One of Buffalo's most powerful, but maybe not most popular, citizens became involved in the brewing industry in 1890. William J. Connors had turned a saloon left to him by his parents into a multimillion-dollar shipping enterprise, with control of all Great Lakes freight. He purchased three Buffalo newspapers, eventually merging them into the *Buffalo Courier-Express*. He was a ruthless businessman who controlled the docks on Buffalo's waterfront until a strike forced him to give up one of his businesses.

In 1890, Connors invested in the Roos brewery on Pratt Street. The brewery was producing about twenty thousand barrels of beer per year. Connors disposed of his interest after a year, and it appears that John Kreitner purchased the controlling interest in the brewery and renamed it the Roos Cooperative Brewing Company.[239] Kreitner—involved in contracting, theatrical and saloon businesses—served as treasurer.

Collusion was not an issue that concerned the brewers when they made decisions. That was the case in late October 1890, when the Buffalo Brewers' Association announced that due to the rise in raw material cost and duty on European hops, the cost of a barrel of beer would rise to $7.00 ($182) from $5.00 ($132) and there would be no discounts. Previously, there was a 10 percent discount for cash-paying customers, and as was mentioned in a news article, often the delivery "driver most allus would buy a round for the house."[240] This was also discontinued. There were eighteen breweries involved. Today, this would be considered price fixing and is illegal.

On December 29, 1890, the Lockport branch of Buffalo Cooperative Brewing Company burned to the ground. The loss was about $1,500 ($39,600) and the contents were partially insured. John B. Naisineth owned the building.[241]

Since 1868, the Christian Weyand Brewing Company had used its beer cellar, several miles up Main Street from the brewery, to store the beer for several months before bringing the beer back to the brewery and chilling in the icehouse until it was sold. At that time, it would pay tax on the beer. But in January 1891, the Internal Revenue Service objected to the practice, saying the company should have been paying taxes when the beer was transferred to the cellar. Company president John A. Weyand went to

Washington, D.C., and New York City to plead his case.[242] The final outcome is unknown.

The Charles G. Curtiss Company on Niagara and Albany Streets was expanded to add a drum system in 1891, bringing its capacity to nearly 1,000,000 bushels.[243]

Speaking of drum systems, maltster John Baker Manning installed a Galland-Henning Pneumatic Malting Drum Company system in 1891,

The original east wall of the Christian Weyand Brewing Company's cold storage facility, which was incorporated into the modern Trico plant when it was found to be too expensive to demolish. *Photo by Michael Rizzo.*

which allowed him to increase his malting capacity to 1,500,000 bushels of malt per year.[244]

At three o'clock in the afternoon on March 14, 1891, an explosion was heard, and then flames enveloped the Christian Weyand Brewing Company at 793 Main Street. It was believed spontaneous combustion of malt and dust caused the explosion, which required three alarms from the Buffalo Fire department. Twenty minutes after the fire began, the wooden tower on top of the brewery came crashing down. It was estimated that damages were $100,000 ($2,640,000), but the company planned to rebuild.[245]

In 1891, the brewers and maltsters combined to form Brewers' Union Local Four. That same year, the employees of Gerhard Lang Brewery, who were all union holdouts, finally unionized.

In late August 1891, a group organized a co-partnership with the purpose of brewing standard lager in Buffalo. With considerable years' experience, the group, led by Eugene Irr—with Conrad Hammer, Peter Reinlaender, Frederick Mersmann and Conrad Klemm—had a company but no brewery. After searching the city, they found that Jacob Kuhn's Union Brewery at 642–52 Broadway was for sale, and they immediately purchased it. Union Brewery had a capacity of just four thousand barrels, and according to a souvenir convention program, by this time, it had seen better days, "the casks and kegs badly worn." The building also needed repairing, but there were extensive cellars and a large property. The brewery was renamed Gambrinus Brewing Company, after the patron saint of beer. The convention program further stated, "As soon as the new beer was distributed, every one who had a taste of it praised its excellence in purity and strength."[246]

Eugene Irr was born in Alsace, France, in 1843 and, after his education, came to America in 1869. Once in America, he stayed with an uncle in Williamsville, New York, for a short time and then moved to Buffalo, where he worked for several lumber companies. In 1880, Irr secured worked as a collector for Francis X. Kaltenbach and later worked for George Rochevot and Gerhard Lang, all brewers. After he helped form Gambrinus Brewing Company, he worked as manager and secretary of the firm.

In September 1891, the Broadway Brewing and Malting Company at 815 Broadway purchased the John O. Meyer Malt House at Eagle and Emslie Streets for $35,000 ($924,000), expanding its malting capabilities.[247]

The George Rochevot Brewery at 1033 Jefferson Street had been expanded several times since its construction in 1871. Rochevot decided it was time to incorporate the business, and in 1892, he did just that, creating Lion Brewery. George would be the first president; his wife, Caroline, was vice-president; and his

THE HISTORY OF BREWING IN THE NICKEL CITY

George Rochevot formed the Lion Brewery in 1892 from his Rochevot Brewery. At the time of this picture, circa 1897, Rochevot had died, and the brewery was causing many family struggles. *Photo from* Souvenir of Buffalo, on Occasion of the 37th Annual Convention at Buffalo, N.Y.

son Oscar P. was secretary of the company, which was capitalized with $100,000 ($2,600,000). The plant was now 121,695 square feet, fitted with modern refrigerating machines and sprinkler system and as fireproof as possible.[248]

The Queen City Brewing Company on Spring and Cherry Streets was sold at foreclosure in January 1892 to maltster John Baker Manning for $59,300 ($1,540,000). At the time, Manning held a $15,000 ($390,000) judgment against the brewery for unpaid malt, and former owner of the brewery David Haas held a second mortgage on the property.[249]

Colonel John Leo Schwartz was born in Buffalo in 1859, his father arriving from Germany in 1836. He was a member of the first class of Canisius College, graduating at fifteen and entering the business of his father. When his father died in 1878, he began working in the coal business, establishing his own coal and wood business in 1880. After a successful twelve years, Schwartz sold the business to his brothers and embarked in a new direction. In early 1893, Schwartz partnered with Edward A. Diebolt, John S. Kellner and Joseph Phillips to purchase the defunct Queen City Brewing Company at Spring and Cherry Streets from John Baker Manning. Schwartz renamed it Star Brewing Company.[250] At the time, the brewery had an annual output of four thousand barrels of beer per year.

John G. White, partner in the White & Crafts malting business, died in January 1892. His son John C. replaced him and bought out his partner John W. Crafts in 1894 after Crafts retired.[251]

A tour group assembled before the obelisk marking the grave of Gerhard Lang in the United German and French Cemetery, Cheektowaga, New York. Lang built one of the most ornate breweries in Buffalo. *Photo by Michael Rizzo.*

Gerhard Lang had brought his son-in-law Edwin G.S. Miller into the fold as manager of the brewery in 1884. When Lang died an early death (at fifty-seven years old) in July 1892, Miller became president of the brewery. In Lang's obituary, it said that under Miller's skilled "goal-oriented leadership," the brewery went from producing forty thousand barrels of beer per year to nearly ninety-nine thousand barrels in just eight years. Lang died at his residence at 704 Main Street from stomach cancer and was buried in the family plot in the United German and French Cemetery under a beautiful, and possibly the tallest, obelisk in the cemetery.[252]

It was in March 1893 that Rochester, New York investors Leonard Burgweger and J.W. Niederpruner, purchased the Ziegele Brewing Company on Washington Street. Then, with John Kreitner, who owned the controlling interest in the Roos Cooperative Brewing Company, formed the Iroquois Brewing Company and purchased the brewery and its good will. George Roos still retained a share but no longer a controlling interest.[253] The men planned on doubling the daily output of the Ziegele Brewing Company from three hundred barrels to six hundred barrels per day. Niederpruner—who started his career in Buffalo before moving to Rochester, where he was treasurer of the Bartholomay Brewing Company—was treasurer of the new company. Kreitner, the vice-president, was a former alderman in Buffalo, and Burgweger—a one-time foreman and superintendent of Bartholomay Brewing in Rochester and breweries in Chicago and Kansas City—became president. With $250,000 ($6,580,000) capital stock, the group razed the Roos buildings and built the enormous Iroquois plant with frontage on Pratt Street leading to Broadway to become the most modern brewery in Buffalo. The brewery had a malt house with a 150,000-bushel capacity and a 200,000-barrel-per-year output, as well as a 40,000-barrel fermenting room. The new owners planned to be operational and selling beer by May 1, 1894.[254]

By mid-January 1893, Charles Gerber's Empire Brewing Company at 821 Main Street was in financial straits and closed its doors. Noted brewery attorney Robert F. Schelling represented the brewery. By November, the company was bankrupt, and its brewery was foreclosed.[255]

Just two years previous, Conrad Hammer and others had formed Gambrinus Brewing Company. Hammer, through eight years' hard work for Joseph L. Haberstro at the German-American Brewing Company and then at the Gambrinus brewery, decided to move on. His son-in-law, George F. Stein, partnered with Hammer and Frank J. Illig (who was born in December 1853 in Buffalo and had served as civil service commissioner and police commissioner in Buffalo) and formed the Germania Brewing Company at 1615–21 Broadway at the corner of Bailey Avenue in 1893.[256] The brewery had a brewing capacity of fifteen thousand barrels per year.

In September 1857, Simon Seibert was born in Buffalo, where he received a public school education. After graduating from Bryant & Stratton Business College, he became a clerk in his father's coal office and then worked in several other fields before being hired by the Magnus Beck Brewing Company in 1893 as a traveling salesman. By this time, the Beck brewery was producing over forty thousand barrels of beer per year.[257]

Nationally, German was the language of brewing. When the German population first began to surge in 1851, an attempt was made to teach German in Buffalo Public Schools, but it was turned down. By 1873, the sentiment, and number of Germans, had changed, and with the hiring of six German teachers, classes began. By 1893, over sixteen thousand of the thirty-nine thousand students in Buffalo schools were of German heritage.[258] With two German newspapers in Buffalo, along with the German Insurance Company and the German-American Bank, the German population was educated and involved in all aspects of political and social activities.

The headstone of J. Adam Lautz, the founder of several large businesses in Buffalo. He also served as president of Ziegele Brewing Company. *Photo by Michael Rizzo.*

On September 1, 1893, the partnership of E.N. Cook & Company was dissolved, and a new company, run just by Gustav Fleischmann, was formed as the Buffalo Distilling Company. The firm would use numerous brand names on its products, including Continuous, Diamond Old Tom Gin, Maple Gin, Old Colonial Rye Malt, Old Mahogany, Silver Barrel, Silver Medal, Superior Old Tom Gin, Golden Grain Whiskey and Four-Cee Canadian.[259]

After just a year in business, Germania Brewing Company on Broadway and Bailey Avenue was converted into a stock company in 1894 with a capitalization of $10,000 ($275,000). Conrad Hammer owned one-third interest and served as vice-president and superintendent, and the Illig brothers, Frank J. and Joseph, controlled the other shares. The company ranked ninth in sales out of the eighteen breweries in production in Buffalo at the time.[260]

J. Adam Lautz, business director and former president of Ziegele Brewing Company, died in August 1894. He was born in Dieburg, Germany, in 1840, and when he was thirteen, he came to America with his parents. They settled in Buffalo. After his education, he volunteered for duty in the Civil War and was involved in multiple skirmishes. After the war, Lautz returned to Buffalo, where his father had been running a candle and soap manufacturing business.

The firm would grow to be Lautz Brothers & Company, a huge concern that was sold in 1898, not long after his death. Lautz was a partner in Niagara Starch Works with his brother Charles, Niagara Stamping & Tool Works and director of Citizen's Bank. He was also president of the German Young Men's Association for many years, co-founder of the Orpheus and was chairman of the building committee for St. Louis Church.[261] The Orpheus and Saengerbund were very popular German singing societies. Lautz is buried in the United German and French Cemetery in Cheektowaga.

On October 1, 1894, brewmaster, superintendent and partner in the John Schüssler Brewing Company, William Simon, purchased the brewery from Susan Schüssler, though under the sale agreement, he would continue using the Schüssler name for six years. The brewery would be known as the John

William Simon's most popular beer was Simon Pure. This serving tray is circa the 1950s. *Photo by Chris Groves, from the collection of Dave Mik.*

Schüssler Brewing Company, with William Simon as proprietor. In 1896, William Simon trademarked his logo, a winged hop, which would become synonymous with the Simon Pure brand for generations of Buffalonians. By 1898, the brewery would be producing almost 100,000 barrels of beer a year.[262]

Pabst Brewing Company established a distribution site at 141 Washington Street in Buffalo in 1895, the first of many inroads from the ever-expanding national companies. At the same time, Buffalo breweries were also expanding their distribution outside the state.

Many of the owners of Buffalo's breweries and malt houses enjoyed tremendous wealth as a result of their hard work. Albert Ziegele Sr., for example, had real estate worth over $100,000 ($2,820,000) and $25,000 ($705,000) in personal property.[263] Ziegele managed

> *a charming place of some six or seven acres near the park, where he resides, and in the cultivation of which, and its adornment, he has spent considerable time, labor and money. The grapery here is perhaps the finest in Buffalo, and the grounds are laid out with taste and discernment. Should Mr. Ziegele ever consent to throw this place open to the public, it would form one of the most delightful resorts about this city. Here, however, he entertains his friends and dispenses his hospitality with a liberal hand. The natural scenery is not surpassed in this section of the country; the growth of original forest trees, a natural ravine covered with grass and well shaded, giving a romantic aspect to the grounds, which, with the artificial steps, terraces, fountain, (etc.), render the place, as a whole, worthy of the highest commendations. Built in the sidehill here, and entirely under the surface, is a Lager Beer cellar of large capacity, over which Mr. Ziegele, ever considerate of his friends (of whom he has hosts), as lately erected a building, perhaps one hundred and twenty-five feet long by about fifty feet wide, more than half of which is devoted to a spacious hall, where picnic parties may enjoy themselves to accompanying music, and avail themselves also of the recreation and diversion of the grounds by a permit from the proprietor. There is no doubt but this lovely spot, with its flower-gardens and pleasing scenery, is destined to become a favorite spot in our city, and reflects the greatest credit upon its projector.[264]*

In 1895, William J. Connors, who would later found the *Buffalo Courier-Express* and one-time owner of the Roos Brewing Company on Pratt Street, purchased a large interest in the Magnus Beck Brewing Company, unseating the Beck family from their longtime leadership roles in the business. Connors was elected president of the brewery and during his tenure increased output by one-third.[265]

That same year, the German-American Brewing Company added a fourteen-story addition to its facility. High Street is the highest point in the city, and the brewery was the tallest in Buffalo, allowing for fantastic views from the roof where you could see the spray of Niagara Falls. For a mere fifteen cents, the rooftop beer garden "up in the sky at Main and High" was a favorite gathering place for local Germans. It also laid claim to one of the highest-class restaurants in Buffalo, as well as bowling alleys and clubhouse of the Buffalo Orpheus.[266]

In late March 1896, Abel T. Blackmar, a former maltster and bank president, died in Buffalo. Blackmar was eighty-one at the time of his death, and according to family records, he is buried in Ohio.[267]

A delegation of brewers, including Edwin G.S. Miller, Charles G. Pankow, John L. Schwartz, William Simon and John Becker, visited Buffalo mayor Edgar B. Jewett in March 1896 and asked him to visit New York governor Levi P. Morton and urge him to veto the Raines Excise Bill. The bill would collect taxes on alcohol and split them between the state and counties, but the biggest obstacle was that it prohibited the sale of alcohol on Sunday, except in hotels that served meals. Unfortunately for the saloon business, the bill passed into law in March 1896. Some saloons found a way around the law by putting a few beds in rooms, putting bricks between a couple slices of bread and leaving them on the saloon tables and calling themselves hotels. The result of the new law by 1902 would be 1,000 fewer saloons in Buffalo and 2,400 fewer in Erie County than there were in 1896.[268] With 1,500 people employed in the Buffalo breweries, malt houses and related business, though, Buffalo was definitely still one of the top producers in the country.

The Christian Weyand Brewing Company at 793 Main Street was nearly at capacity, so between 1896 and 1897, the company made extensive renovations to expand the facility. The bottling department, Weyand & Weigel Bottling Works at 814 Main Street, was started by William J. Weigel and John A. Weyand in 1883, son-in-law and son of Christian, respectively. The bottlers shipped Weyand's beer across the United States and Canada.[269]

It was just three years after forming that the Germania Brewing Company was bursting at the seams. By 1896, the brewery had doubled its capacity to thirty thousand barrels of beer per year.[270]

Francis X. Kaltenbach, the founder of F.X. Kaltenbach Brewery, died in late January 1897. He had amassed a fortune, lived at 458 Eagle Street and left an estate of $360,000 ($10,300,000) in real estate and personal property. He is buried in the United German and French Cemetery in Cheektowaga.

The Lion Brewery at 1033 Jefferson Avenue was established in 1857 by George Rochevot. In 1892, the business was incorporated, with Rochevot at the helm. In late January 1897, Rochevot, sixty-five, died suddenly, and the estate continued to operate the brewery. His wife, Caroline, was elevated to president, his daughter Matilda A. Mesinger became vice-president and his son Oscar P. continued in his position as secretary of the corporation. Rochevot had served as Buffalo city alderman and for many years was treasurer of the Buffalo Brewers' Association. At the time of his death, he was a director of Citizen's Bank of Buffalo and was a Mason. He is buried in Forest Lawn Cemetery. Rochevot's estate, valued at $1,000,000 ($28,600,000), would soon cause the family to be torn apart, never to be whole again.[271]

Buffalo would again host the United States Brewers' Association Convention on June 9 and 10, 1897. Later that same month, a group of maltsters met in Chicago and reorganized a national association that had disbanded in the early 1880s.[272]

As we have seen, fires were common and often costly. After being in business just over seven years, Buffalo Cooperative Brewing Company on Michigan and High Streets suffered a serious loss due to a fire in June 1897. The brewing plant was nearly completely destroyed by the fire, so the company tore down the buildings and rebuilt a state-of-the-art fireproof facility, or so it thought.[273]

A new national malt conglomerate was established in September 1897 when the American Malting Company was formed after it purchased twenty of the largest malt companies in the country, including the Charles G. Curtiss Company of Buffalo. The company was organized with $30,000,000 ($857,000,000) and $15,000,000 ($428,000,000) in stock.[274] Alexander M. Curtiss of Buffalo was the company's first president, which would have a profound effect on him in several years.

In October 1897, Peter Lehr of Kreiner & Lehr malt house died at seventy-seven years old. He is buried in Forest Lawn Cemetery.

In late November 1897, smoke was seen billowing out from the Binz malt house at Eagle and Watson Streets; it was a "black cloud as big as the city of Cleveland."[275] A crowd of five thousand stood by in the drizzling rain waiting for the building to collapse, but the crowd was saddened to find out it was only an overheated dry kiln that started a small fire that burned seven hundred to eight hundred bushels of oats and was more smoke than fire.[276]

Pre-Prohibition beer bottles from Buffalo Cooperative Brewing, Consumer's Brewing Company and Lake View Brewing Company. *Photo by Chris Groves, from the collection of Dave Mik.*

The following April, the maltster organization that had formed in June 1897 disbanded after realizing many of the members had sold out to the American Malting Company. In September 1898, a meeting of independent maltsters convened in Buffalo to form a new organization, and John C. White of Buffalo was named the president.[277]

Sometimes lightning does strike twice and not always in a good way. For the second time in a just over a year, the Buffalo Cooperative Brewing Company at the corner of High and Michigan Streets suffered a devastating loss due to a fire. In early July 1898, the 1897 rebuilt fireproof brewery plant was relatively unscathed, but the rest of the buildings were destroyed when a three-alarm fire started in the barrel room. The damage to machinery and stock was estimated at $150,000 ($4,280,000). Thirty thousand barrels of beer were saved but forty-five thousand barrels were in production. Insurance covered the loss.[278]

The John Schüssler Brewery, which was owned and being run by William Simon, had increased sales from 16,877 barrels of beer per year in 1888 to 55,000 barrels in 1898. The company's malt division was producing 80,000 bushels of malt per year. Breweries of this time "were generally supported in their immediate neighborhoods," which would be the Clinton-Emslie area of the East Side. Does that mean the neighborhood drank a lot of beer? It was a predominantly Polish neighborhood, so most likely. Yet Simon's reputation was such that his beer was sold across the city. Some other reasons for the large increase in sales were Simon's business acumen and knowing his customer. Literally—William Simon wanted to personally know every customer. He also used choice grades of barley malt and hops. His determination and "boundless energy" helped to guide the business.

Simon's son-in-law Joseph G. Schaff had begun working at the brewery in 1891. His "keen foresight and great executive ability"[279] contributed to success during that period of growth. While Simon was the brains and brewmaster, Schaff handled the accounts and other bureaucratic minutiae.

Breweries came and went so when the People's Brewing Company was incorporated on July 14, 1898, by Joseph E. Barnard, former county treasurer George Baltz, Charles R. Roessler, Anthony Bogacki, John Patrzykowski, James M. Rozan, Lyndon D. Wood, August Beck, Emil Krampitz, John P. Sullivan and public works commissioner Martin Maher, it was no surprise. The men planned to refit the former Roessler Carriage Works on Broadway and the Belt Line tracks. The company was capitalized with $130,000 ($3,710,000) and expected to be up and running in three months. It still hadn't begun production by April 1899, but its plans had grown. New stockholders in the company included Buffalo mayor Conrad Diehl and Erie County clerk Otto H. Wende. The corporation now had plans to build a new addition to the plant and install the latest brewing machinery, powered by electricity, giving the brewery a 100,000-barrels-per-year capacity. In May, it announced plans to increase the capital stock to $200,000 ($5,710,000) and add a seven-story fireproof brewhouse.[280]

In early August 1898, Christian Weyand, founder of the Christian Weyand Brewing Company, died in Buffalo. He had lived in a beautiful home at 1152 Main Street just north of Summer Street and left an estate of over $120,000 ($3,430,000) and an impressive stone statue in the United German and French Cemetery in Cheektowaga. His brewery continued to be one of the largest in Buffalo.[281]

The U.S. Maltsters' Association held its first convention in Buffalo on September 6 and 7, 1898, at the Iroquois Hotel on Main Street. Joseph Kam, one of the sons of maltster John Kam, was on the executive board of the association at the time.[282]

In the fall of 1898, the Queen City Malt House at the foot of Washington Street was purchased by Charles and Frederick Sietz of Pennsylvania, who operated it as the Seitz Malting Company.[283]

Gustavus A. Schaefer, who, with his brother Henry L., ran the Schaefer Malt House at Seventh and Jersey Streets, died on May 28, 1899. He left a $65,000 ($1,860,000) estate to his wife and daughter.[284] He is buried in Forest Lawn Cemetery.

The Christian Weyand Brewing Company had been incorporated in 1890 after the founder sought retirement. In late June 1899, Buffalo maltster Christian G. Voltz, during an interview with a *Buffalo Express* newspaper reporter, said that all Buffalo brewers made "impure" beer; they used corn instead of quality malt because it was cheaper, which started a firestorm and battle of words. "If anything else is used, the product, is not beer, whatever the brewers may call it," Voltz told a reporter.[285] He said that every brewer used some, if not all, corn. He said the New York barley was of no value and because inferior western United States–grown hops were being used instead of New York–grown hops, those industries were collapsing. Voltz was apparently an agitator and, in 1900, would be attacked by Buffalo city clerk Charles Susdorf and Alderman James Franklin after his unruly behavior during a paving hearing in city hall.[286]

For an unknown reason, Voltz especially targeted the Christian Weyand Brewing Company. Weyand's, so angered by the charge, started placing large ads in the daily newspapers and put $10,000 ($286,000) on deposit with the German-American Bank if anyone could prove it produced impure beer.

In June 1899, four other Buffalo maltsters backed Weyand's assertion that it did not use corn (unlike the mega brewers) but only the best malt. The John Kam Malting Company said it had been supplying Weyand's with the best

THE MONEY IS UP FOR WEYAND.

$10,000 ON DEPOSIT

At the German-American Bank, Says That the

Christian Weyand Brewing Company

Has Always and is Now Making a . . . . Strictly Pure Beer.

Our money covers every Point made in our challenge, and MR. VOLTZ has but to name time and place to meet the president of this company and one other with himself and one other, to arrange such mode of procedure as to bring out the facts, and then the money will be turned over to the committee named by Mr. Voltz, viz.: The proprietors of the Commercial, News and Express.

Mr. Voltz Must Agree That All Proceedings Shall Be Made Public. No Closed Doors or Other Star Chamber Proceedings.

JOHN A. WEYAND, President.

CHAS. M. WEYAND, Secretary and Treasurer.

A newspaper advertisement from 1899 that the Christian Weyand Brewing Company placed to back up its pure beer claims. Maltster Christian Voltz said that Weyand used corn instead of quality malt. *Photo from the* Buffalo Courier.

malt, regardless of cost, since 1874. Joseph Kam, son of the founder said, "Yes, there are some breweries in Buffalo making bad beer, but Weyands' is not one of them." Voltz also claimed that the $10.00 ($286.00) barrel of beer the brewers sold cost them only $0.44 to make.

The Magnus Beck Brewing Company also responded, offering a total of $800 ($22,800) to charitable organizations if anyone could find it brewed beer that was not pure, but no one ever came forward. The president and primary shareholder of the Magnus Beck Brewing Company, William J. Connors, sold all his stock in the brewery and resigned as president of the company in June 1899. Edward Beck, vice-president under Connors, was elected president in his place. Adam Benzinger was made vice-president, and Albert Schelling was added to the board of directors. At the time, Connors, owner of several Buffalo newspapers, was in a battle with ten thousand striking dockworkers that threatened his profitable business enterprise. After selling his stock in Magnus Beck, he never again had an interest in any Buffalo breweries.[287]

In 1899, the Fisher Malting Company (formerly Fisher Brothers & Company) was incorporated. Up to this time, the company still used the floor process to manufacture malt, turning by hand; no drums were yet in place.[288]

Anthony Schreiber was born in Poland in January 1864. "As a young man he moved to Germany where he graduated from the University of Berlin with a degree in chemistry. He left Germany for the United States when he was 17," arriving in 1882, at which time he worked various jobs in New York City and later was a successful salesman in New England.[289] In 1899, Schreiber and an employee, F. Rawolle, settled in Buffalo. That year, they incorporated and built the A. Schreiber Brewing Company at 662–84 Fillmore Avenue in Buffalo's Polish neighborhood with $100,000 ($2,860,000) capital. Although a late entry into Buffalo's brewing industry, Schreiber built a reputation for crafting quality beer in this Polish neighborhood.

The brewery was initially capable of producing 100,000 barrels per year but would average about 70,000. One of its distinct advantages was that the company installed duplicate systems, so in case there was an accident or line failure, it could continue to brew beer.[290]

In late August 1899, representatives from the various bottler businesses formed the Western New York Beer Bottlers' Association. The main goal of the association was to wage war on persons using bottles in violation of the law.[291]

Carl Strangmann was born in Westphalia, Germany, in 1860 and came to America in 1875, living first in New York City. After a year, he went to Alexandria, Virginia, where he was employed by his uncle, brewer Robert Portner. He worked for two years, rising to shipping and office clerk. Then, in 1883, Portner organized the business into a stock company, and Strangmann was made secretary and treasurer. He also took on the role of business manager over time until 1895, when he purchased, with

The remains of the Schreiber Brewery at 662 Fillmore Avenue in 2013. The location is currently used for storage. This building was the bottling, storage and distribution space; the brewery itself was to the right (north). *Photo by Michael Rizzo.*

John M. Leicht, the George Muth Star Brewery in Cleveland, Ohio. When, in October 1897, a syndicate organized as the Cleveland-Sandusky Brewing Corporation purchased that brewery, Strangmann bought an interest in the German-American Brewing Company in Buffalo in 1899 and succeeded George Dittly as president. At the time of the purchase, the brewery was producing about fifteen thousand barrels of beer per year. Ernst Mühlhauser was vice-president, John F. Nagel was secretary and Carl J. Wideman was treasurer.[292]

In late April 1899, Strangmann agreed to purchase 698 shares of the Gambrinus Brewing Company stock from Peter Reinlander, Frederick Mersmann, Conrad Klemm, Michael Schiesel, John E. Fitzpatrick and George Kempf in return for helping to reduce the company's debt. He was then made president of Gambrinus. Under the agreement, Strangmann and Fitzpatrick were to refurbish the buildings and help improve the business. On November 6, 1899, at a board meeting of Gambrinus, Strangmann resolved that Gambrinus be sold to the German-American Brewing Company in exchange for seven hundred shares of German-American stock, followed by the voluntary dissolution of Gambrinus. He held the seven hundred shares while the other men held one hundred shares each. The stockholders said he never lived up to his end of the deal and, in 1902, sued Strangmann for $50,000.[293] The final disposition would come later.

Former state senator Simon Seibert accepted the position of general manager of Magnus Beck Brewing Company, still at Spring and North Division Streets, in 1899, succeeding Buffalo native George C. Ginther, who had been manager of the brewery since about 1879.[294] Ginther had resigned to become general manager of the Phoenix Brewery & Bottling Works, Ziegele Brewing Company, located at 851 Washington Street at Virginia Street.[295]

A war had begun at the Lion Brewery in 1899 after the death of George Rochevot. His son Oscar P.; widow, Caroline; and daughter Matilda Mesinger were left in charge of the brewery, but a battle for control of the brewery and million-dollar estate soon boiled over. Oscar and his sister Eleanora M. Beck were aligned against their mother and siblings, Albert G. and Matilda. In the end, the brewery business was left in shambles. Matilda and Oscar were, they alleged, forcefully removed from the board, and Albert was made president and recklessly ran the brewery and squandered the funds.[296]

In February 1899, city councilman Frank J. Bissing was hired as manager of the brewery, but apparently company president Albert hindered his performance and, in October 1899, bought his contract and had him removed. Additionally, Matilda's husband, Henry G. Mesinger (a local restaurant owner), was made vice-president of the firm. Subsequently, as things deteriorated, court action was started with Matilda and Oscar trying to be relieved of their duties as executors.[297] The events would worsen as time went on, and the Rochevot/Lion Brewery would slowly fade.

12

THE TWENTIETH CENTURY

CHANGE COMES TO BREWING

The dawn of a new century brought much hope for Buffalo. It was the second largest city in New York State and the eighth largest in the country, with over 350,000 residents.[298] The Pan-American Exposition was slated for May 1901, and all the world's eyes would be on this growing industrial powerhouse. Things were definitely looking up for Buffalo, and the brew and malt industries would continue to evolve.

The six-year agreement that William Simon had signed with Susan Schüssler when he purchased the Schüssler brewery had ended. Simon immediately changed the brewery's name in 1900 to the William Simon Brewery, which would go on to be Buffalo's longest-lasting brewery.

After two years in Buffalo as the Seitz Malting Company, the Queen City Malt House was leased to the Lion Brewery. This house had a capacity of 175,000 bushels of barley.[299]

After a nearly twenty-five-year run as a maltster, Jacob Weppner decided, in 1901, to retire for a second time. This time, it appears it was for good. He would die in early January 1902 at eighty-one years of age.

On March 6, 1900, representatives from sixteen of the eighteen breweries operating in Buffalo met and formed Buffalo Brewers' Exchange to "prevent the cutting of prices."[300] Any brewery deviating from a fixed price would be fined. Attorney Robert F. Schelling was elected treasurer, and Charles G. Pankow was elected president. The Christian Weyand Brewing Company and Broadway Brewing and Malting Company elected to not participate and remained independent.[301]

At the time of this picture, the John Schüssler Brewing Company was owned by William Simon. He was under agreement to keep the Schüssler name until 1900, when it would be renamed William Simon Brewery. This picture is circa 1897. *Photo from* Souvenir of Buffalo, on Occasion of the 37th Annual Convention at Buffalo, N.Y.

In September 1900, *U.S. Health Reports,* a periodical that reported on health, said of the William Simon Brewery, "A more superior brew never entered the laboratory of the United States Health Reports...This beer is absolutely devoid of the slightest trace of adulteration, but...is composed of the best malt and the choicest hops."[302] It was an official endorsement for the brewery, but whether or not it translated into actual sales is unknown.

Eugene Irr, possibly upset at the mess that Carl Strangmann had caused, left his position at Gambrinus Brewing Company in 1900 to resurrect the closed Williamsville Brewery in suburban Williamsville, New York. It would last only a year before closing.

Francis Xavier Schwab was born in Buffalo in 1874. After completing school, he went to work at a tin shop and then joined the E. and B. Holmes Company, where he made his first invention. By the time he was nineteen, he was a foreman at the Pullman Palace Car Company on Broadway near Bailey Avenue in Buffalo. Schwab was a German-language singer and traveled to Milwaukee for a saengerfest (singing festival) where Conrad Hammer of Germania Brewing Company noticed him. When Schwab returned to Buffalo, Hammer offered him a job as a brewery solicitor for Germania.[303] In this position, he visited saloons to drum up business for the brewery, at which he excelled, and was said to be the highest-paid solicitor in Buffalo. He was then a collector, salesman and saloon owner before taking a position as general manager of the International Brewing Company on Niagara Street in 1900, a position he held for five years. During that time, he also started a wholesale liquors business, the Frank X. Schwab Company.

In mid-January 1901, the partners of the Star Brewing Company at 642 Spring Street—John L. Schwartz, Joseph Phillips, Edward A. Diebolt and John S. Kellner—purchased the stock of the Clinton Cooperative Brewing Company at 18 West Bennett Street, directly across from the Clinton-Bailey Market. In

A mug compliments of Buffalo mayor and brewer Frank X. Schwab, circa 1900. The German translates roughly as "When it rains beer and snows bratwurst, we ask the heavens that the weather doesn't change" and is a verse from a well-known song. *Photo by Chris Groves, from the collection of Dave Mik.*

1882, Charles G. Pankow had purchased an interest in the Clinton Cooperative Brewing Company, and from then until 1901, he served as president of the firm.[304] Pankow, Louis Freund and Louis J. Baitz all retired from business after the brewery was purchased by the Star Brewing Company.

Led by Schwartz, the Star Brewing Company partners bought out John S. Kellner of the Star. The new officers, Schwartz as president and general manager, Moses Shire as secretary and Jacob Dilcher as vice-president, planned to shut down the Star Brewing Company, which would be converted into their ice-making and storage plant.[305] The Clinton Cooperative Brewing Company had a capacity of forty-five thousand barrels of beer per year, while the Star had only a twenty-thousand-barrel capacity. The new owners estimated the combined breweries would produce thirty thousand barrels, and the brewery would be renamed Clinton-Star Brewery. One of their signature beers would be their Pilsener Bock Beer. According to a 1902 advertisement, it was "the palest beer ever brewed in Buffalo, yet it is as strong as the darkest."[306]

The Seitz Malting Company took control of two malt houses owned by William W. Sloan on September 1, 1901. It also still owned the Queen City Malt House, which was leased to the Lion Brewery.[307]

THE HISTORY OF BREWING IN THE NICKEL CITY

In 1881, William Voetsch changed his brewery into the Clinton Cooperative Brewing Company, where only members could purchase the beer. It would later become the Clinton-Star brewery. This picture is circa 1897. *Photo from* Souvenir of Buffalo, on Occasion of the 37th Annual Convention at Buffalo, N.Y.

The John Kam Malting Company operated two malt houses until October 1901, when it just operated the plant at the foot of Hertel Avenue. The capacity of this pneumatic drum system house was 1,500,000 bushels per year, "the malt being germinated and kiln-dried on the slow process, or eight day germinating system."[308]

The Pan-American Exposition was supposed to be Buffalo's shining moment. A world's fair that would highlight Buffalo as one of the globe's leading cities. The brewers were instrumental in donating money to the effort, and President William McKinley announced he would attend. Beer was an important beverage at the expo, and Pabst Brewing Company sponsored an entire building. It had built its first storage house in Buffalo in 1875. In the end, President McKinley was assassinated at the exposition, and Buffalo gained the fame it so desired, but not in the way it expected.

One of Buffalo's prominent citizens and brewers, Jacob Scheu, died on December 7, 1901. Scheu had constructed the large brewery on Niagara Street operating as International Brewing Company, and like his brothers Solomon and William, he had been involved in Buffalo's political affairs. Scheu served as an alderman in Buffalo three times and later moved to a large mansion at 988 Main Street. He was also a Mason and an organizer and member of the German Young Men's Association. Scheu left a sizable estate valued at over $91,000 ($2,540,000), not including real estate property.[309] He is buried in Forest Lawn Cemetery.

One of the biggest brewery scandals took place in 1899, when Carl A. Strangmann convinced the stockholders of the Gambrinus Brewing Company to elect him president and transfer their shares of the business to him. He quickly took control and sold the company to the German-American Brewing Company, which he owned. Gambrinus was then legally dissolved in October 1901, but the dissolution was overturned by a judge in April 1902. The stockholders said he was supposed to improve Gambrinus, but he never lived up to his end of the deal and, in February 1902, began legal action against Strangmann. The sticking point was outstanding mortgages the original Gambrinus owners say Strangmann was responsible for and which he said were not part of the sale.[310] The trial continued.

In 1902, Henry C. Moffat realized that the Midwest malt houses were newer and bigger, and to compete, he would need to update his equipment. His facility was capable of drying 100,000 bushels, but it all had to be turned by hand, so he was at the mercy of his workers. Moffat installed a drum drying system that required no manual turning and increased his capacity to 325,000 bushels per year. The Moffat brewery was selling its beer far and wide across western New York, and in Pennsylvania, Ohio and as far away as Michigan.[311]

The C. Zwickel Malting Company at 650–56 Elk Street was formed by Christian Zwickel in 1902. It had capital stock of $100,000 ($2,790,000), and other directors were Charles Newton and F.A. Dole.[312] Zwickel was born in May 1858 in Babstadt, Baden-Wuerttemberg, Germany. He arrived in America in 1878 at age twenty. He settled in Ohio, and by 1900, he was living in Chicago before coming to Buffalo and starting his malt business. His son Albert would be secretary of the firm. By 1920, both of their families would be living in Los Angeles.[313]

On February 12, 1902, the former president of Lake View Brewing Company, George Sandrock, died at sixty-four years old. Sandrock was one of the original members of the grade crossing commission, was elected Buffalo city councilman and served as president of the German-American Bank from 1888 until his death. He was also an investor in Shaker Heights Land Company in Cleveland and owned a significant share of stock in the German-American Brewing Company. Sandrock is buried in Holy Cross Cemetery in Lackawanna, New York.[314]

The exterior of Phoenix Brewery, founded by Albert Ziegele, on Washington and Virginia Streets. This is part of the reconstructed brewery after a devastating 1887 fire destroyed the original brewery. *Photo by Michael Rizzo.*

On May 2, 1902, a tremendous fire consumed John Baker Manning's Frontier Canada Malt House at the foot of Auburn Avenue near the Erie Canal in Black Rock. It was said to be the largest fire ever seen in Black Rock.[315]

The talk of brewery consolidation came up from time to time in Buffalo as fierce competition pushed many breweries to their limits. In March 1902, a deal worth $2,000,000 ($55,100,000) was rumored to be in the works. The breweries mentioned in the consolidation were Lion, Broadway, Kaltenbach, Star, Iroquois, Beck's, Lake View, Germania, East Buffalo, International and Phoenix. Attorney Robert F. Schelling and Edwin G.S. Miller were named as those behind the consolidation. One brewer said the reason for the consolidation was "the breweries of this city have not been making the money they used to." The breweries had been "practically eating each other up" and "cutting each other's throats for years." They would also help anyone that wanted to open a saloon, even if "the applicant hadn't a dollar." The consolidation would also close between two hundred and four hundred saloons controlled by the breweries. Buffalo had more breweries "than any city in the country except possibly New York and Chicago." Beer consumption was primarily on the East Side "among the Germans and Poles" but had decreased by 1902 from a high in 1897, even though the population had grown by seventy-five thousand.[316]

By June 1903, a Cleveland group led by Henry Boehmke was rumored to be leading new takeover talks. (Boehmke was later secretary of Hoster-

A Christmas ad from Broadway Brewing & Malting Company at 815 Broadway, circa the 1900s. *Photo from* Buffalo Courier.

Columbus Associated Breweries Company in Columbus, Ohio.) The deal would make John L. Schwartz president with attorney Robert F. Schelling again engineering the deal. Together, they would have made a powerful consortium, but Schwartz and others denied the rumors.[317] In the end, neither this deal nor any other major consolidation ever took place.

A two-alarm fire in the ice machine building of the Broadway Brewing and Malting Company on Broadway and Smith Streets started the night of August 1, 1902. The employees tried to put out the blaze, but the fire department arrived and took control as flames shot out from all sides of the building. It was extinguished after two hours, and damage was about $5,000 ($138,000).[318]

Joseph L. Haberstro had embarked on a career in the brewing industry in 1859, opening J.L. Haberstro & Company on Main and High Streets. In 1886, it became the German-American Brewing Company as Haberstro went on to serve as a Buffalo city alderman, city treasurer and sheriff of Erie County. He was also a Mason and involved in Orpheus and Saengerbund societies in Buffalo. He was also elected secretary of the United States Brewers' Association at its fourth annual convention in 1864. Haberstro died on November 5, 1902, after a short illness.[319]

In late November 1902, the board of the Buffalo Cooperative Brewing Company convened in order to change the brewery bylaws to allow non-members to purchase products from the cooperative. The change was made because several majority shareholders wanted to change the business, even though manager John Honecker said he heard "no objections from the small stockholders."[320] The brewery's regular brands included Special Brew Extra 6, Phoenix Beer, as well as Stock Lager, Municher, Pilsener and Wurtzburger.[321]

Brewery fires were often devastating events. Sometimes they would cause minor damage to buildings, but often the contents of the buildings were lost. On July 18, 1903, the Moffat brewery suffered a $90,000 ($2,420,000) fire, which primarily damaged sixty-five thousand bushels of malt and ten thousand bushels of barley.[322]

Albert Ziegele Jr., secretary of Phoenix Brewing & Bottling Works, died in April 1903 after a five-week illness. He was a director in the German Institute and a member of the Orpheus and Concordia Lodge, F&AM He is buried in Forest Lawn Cemetery.[323]

In April 1901, a large block of Kaltenbach Brewing Company stock was made available for a quick sale. By 1903, the Excelsior Brewery (Kaltenbach Brewing Company), at Clinton and Pratt Streets, which had been run by

The Albert Zeigele Brewing Company on Washington Street. At the time of this image, it operated as the Phonenix Brewery.

Philip D. Stein, was now in the hands of Clemens B. Kosters. Kosters was the president of CB Kosters & Company, a manufacturer of shoe trees. Adam Boeckel continued as secretary-treasurer of the firm, and Frank X. Kaltenbach Jr. was employed as a collector by the brewery.[324] The brewery would be open only until 1908.

Complaints of an awful smell emanating from the Fisher Brothers & Company malt house on Trenton Avenue and Maryland Street prompted Buffalo's health commissioner to order the malt house to stop drying grain. The police were notified that they could enforce the ruling. At the same time, the Moffat brewery was being demolished after the June fire, and complaints were made about rotting grain there also.[325]

One of the most interesting aspects of German beer culture is beer gardens. In Buffalo, although the German population reached nearly 50 percent of the total population at one point, real beer gardens never really developed. There were locations where the German people, sometimes the elite, did gather, and some were similar to beer gardens. The Parade House on Humboldt Parkway and Teutonia Park on Fillmore Avenue were popular with the Germans in that part of the city, which was predominantly German at the time.

Weyand's restaurant, located on Main Street at the corner of Goodell Street, was open from about 1909 until Prohibition. It is now the site of the Catholic Diocese (formerly the *Buffalo Courier-Express*). The Christian Weyand Brewing Company was located next door, so the beer was cold and fresh. As was typical of German restaurants, cold dishes of Swiss cheese, ham and rye bread were popular.[326]

THE HISTORY OF BREWING IN THE NICKEL CITY

The German-American Café was located at Main and High Streets, but when Carl Strangmann took over the German-American Brewing Company, he converted it into "a beautifully decorated restaurant." He hired a New York City chef and served the "best in food and drinks for moderate prices."[327]

There were many industries that were tied to the brewing trade, and bottling was one natural outgrowth. Many of the larger breweries owned their own bottling works, but there were many companies that specialized in bottling. In 1899, the Western New York Beer Bottlers' Association was formed, but in early March 1904, the Western New York Bottlers' Association was created "for the purpose of preventing the constant theft of beer and soft drink bottles by junk dealers, who sell them in remote sections of the country." It is unknown if the original organization failed or was dissolved. The 1904 officers were George Dittly, president, German-American Brewing Company; Frederick Lochmann, vice-president, Phoenix Brewery; Edward H. Boehringer, secretary, Buffalo Cooperative Brewing Company Bottling Works; and August P. Koch, treasurer, International Brewing Company.[328]

The American Malting Company, with headquarters in New Jersey (the Buffalo branch was the former Charles G. Curtiss Company), was sued after it was found that it was illegally issuing quarterly dividends based on "paper profits." In 1904, Alexander M. Curtiss, a physician and surgeon of Buffalo, was personally held liable for $1,400,000 ($37,200,000).[329]

The Lion Brewery at 1033 Jefferson Avenue, still operated by the estranged estate of George Rochevot, had been on the market for some time. The Buffalo Brewers' Exchange attempted to purchase the brewery from Albert G. Rochevot, George's son, for $120,000 ($3,230,000) in 1905, but he declined. Then, Hugo Schoellkopf stepped in and offered the same amount, which Rochevot accepted. Schoellkopf was an active member of the management at National Aniline and Chemical Company, started by his father. He formed the Consumers' Brewing Company with Eugene L. Falk, Shire & Jellinek (attorneys Moses Shire and Edward L. Jellinek) and G.A. Wegner and purchased the brewery in late March 1905. Philip D. Stein, who had been manager of Excelsior Brewery, took over as manager of Consumers'. The sale of the former Rochevot brewery, though, was not the end of the quarreling Rochevot family. In December 1905, the estate was finally settled, but not until a large portion of the million-dollar estate had been squandered.[330]

The new owners of Consumers' planned to increase brewing capacity from 65,000 to 100,000 barrels of beer per year. To get a quick start in the marketplace, and to the ire of the other local breweries, they charged one dollar less per barrel than any other Buffalo brewery.[331]

The members of Buffalo Brewers' Exchange—Lang, Germania, German-American, Lake View, Kaltenbach, Beck, Phoenix, Iroquois and Simon—found a remedy to that problem and offered Schoellkopf and his investors $160,000 ($4,270,000) for the brewery just five weeks later, which they accepted.[332] Although initial thoughts were to close Consumers' Brewing Company, it continued in operation until Prohibition closed the doors.

In late April 1905, Charles M. Weyand, thirty-six, who was secretary and treasurer of the Christian Weyand Brewing Company, died in Buffalo. He was a prominent member of St. Louis Church, leader in the Orpheus Singing Society and other organizations.[333] A cousin, William W. Weigel (son of William J. Weigel), took over as secretary and treasurer of the brewery. He is buried in United German and French Cemetery in Cheektowaga.

One of the principal stockholders and treasurer of the German-American Brewing Company, Carl J. Wideman, was sued in New York Supreme Court by John P. Persch of New York for $100,000 ($2,730,000) in July 1905. It

A view of the remains of the Iroquois Brewery on Pratt Street. At one point the biggest by volume of Buffalo's breweries, it was the second last to close in Buffalo. *Photo by Michael Rizzo.*

was not, as you would assume, a typical lawsuit. Persch, of New York City, was in Buffalo for about six months in 1904 in order to purchase the stock of several breweries, including Wideman's stock of the German-American. In order to influence Wideman's decision, he forced his wife, Gretchen, to accompany Wideman many places to try and win his affections and make the transaction go smoothly. What Persch didn't expect was for Gretchen to fall in love with Wideman and leave him.[334] Divorce proceedings went on for several years.

Also in 1905, Frank X. Schwab, general manager of the International Brewing Company on Niagara Street, became a business adviser to Leonard Burgweger, president of Iroquois Brewing Company. Schwab would use his influence and personal connections during his twelve years with Burgweger to help Iroquois become Buffalo's biggest brewery.[335]

Michael Schamel, a brewer since 1864 and co-founder of the Union Brewery with Jacob F. Kuhn, died in 1905. He is buried in St. John's Cemetery, Cheektowaga, New York.[336]

The Moffat family continued in the brewery business when Henry's son William Leroy took over management of the brewery in 1906. His leadership would continue until the onset of Prohibition in 1919.

William Voetsch Sr., sixty-eight, a pioneer Buffalo brewer and founder of the Clinton Cooperative Brewing Company and later Clinton-Star Brewery, died suddenly on February 11, 1906. Modestia Lodge Number 340 arranged the funeral since he had been a Mason for many years. He is buried in Forest Lawn Cemetery.[337]

Lake View Brewing Company was formed in 1885, when its founder, Alois Schaefer, retired. His son Philip G. was appointed general manager upon his father's retirement and, after twenty-one years serving as acting executive, was elevated to president of the firm on April 1, 1906. It was estimated that the firm was producing about fifty thousand barrels of high grade beer, ale and porter per year by this time, with a capacity of about seventy-five thousand barrels a year. It sold its products primarily locally.[338]

Unions had long been an important aspect in the brewing industry, providing fair wages to workers. All the major breweries in Buffalo used barrels made by union coopers, but sometimes things went awry. There were two coopers' unions in Buffalo: Mixed Coopers, Local Thirty-three, and Beer, Ale and Brewery Coopers', Local Ninety-three. Local Ninety-three went on a multi-month strike against the breweries in Buffalo Brewers' Exchange around June 1906, demanding a raise from $15 to $17 ($395 to $448) per week. It had settled on $16.50 ($434) in late July or August when a committee from the Brewery Workers' Union wanted a new clause added to the contract. The coopers were upset that the Brewery Workers' Union did not side with them during the strike. It was finally approved, and the coopers returned to work.[339]

"Anthony Schreiber (of A. Schreiber Brewing Company) was a man who was deeply connected to his Polish culture. Schreiber decided to honor and promote that by naming his premium light beer after Jan Paderewski's 1901 opera, *Manru*,"[340] According to the company's trademark, it was called "the King of bottled beers."[341] Although being in business just about seven years, the demand for "Manru" lager compelled the company in 1906 to erect a large addition to its plant, which would bring brewing capacity to about 100,000 barrels per year. The company was already producing 60,000 barrels of beer per year with output steadily increasing. Their other brands included Kloster, a dark beer that debuted in 1912, and Shreiber beer.[342]

After spending twenty-nine years rising through the ranks at the malt house of Charles G. Curtiss Company (then part of American Malting Company) to become vice-president and general manager, George J. Meyer decided to start his own malt business, so with M.J. Meyer, he purchased the Niagara Malting Company plant on Niagara Street at the foot of Lafayette Avenue in September 1906. George was president and treasurer, and M.J. served as vice-president and secretary of the new firm. The renamed George J. Meyer Malting Company had a capacity of 800,000 bushels and storage for 450,000 bushels of malt.[343]

George C. Ginther had been general manager of the Phoenix Brewery & Bottling Works at 851 Washington Street since 1899. Sometime after Albert Ziegele Jr. died in 1903, it is believed that Ginther purchased a controlling interest in the brewery and was named president of the firm. His son Cyril F. joined him as treasurer of the brewery. They would operate the brewery until the onset of Prohibition.[344]

Charles Gerber, a brewing pioneer in Buffalo, died at eighty-six in December 1904 after a fall. When Gerber came to America, he worked as a butcher for some years and then turned his attention to brewing. He continued in that capacity until about 1893, when his Empire Brewing Company at 821 Main Street was no longer in existence. He was a personal friend of Grover Cleveland, a lifelong Democrat and at one time a member of Buffalo's volunteer fire department. He is buried in Forest Lawn Cemetery.[345]

In 1907, the William Simon Brewery sold a company record seventy-three thousand barrels of beer. Also in 1907, Julius Binz modernized his Broadway Brewing and Malting Company at 797 Broadway and added a two-story office.[346]

A small portion of the breweriana collection of Dave Mik. Collecting bottles and other items is a popular hobby. Included are bottles, taps and advertising items. *Photo by Chris Groves, from the collection of Dave Mik.*

An article in the *Buffalo Daily Courier* in April 1907 explained how Buffalo Cooperative Brewing Company was unlike other breweries because they did not sit on their laurels once they had a great beer, unlike other brands. They always "endeavored to furnish newer, better brands in a sufficient number." In fact, they were "a researcher in brewing, experimenting to find new brews and devising them to meet every taste." Their brands at the time included Superior Sparkling Ale (a pilsner), Superior XXX (a stock ale), Capusiner Beer (a "food beer" dark and aged), Superior Porter and Extra and Lager.[347] Most breweries would not have survived long if they had sat on their laurels.

Francis Perot's Sons Malting Company was started in Philadelphia in 1687. In 1907, it desired to capture more of the Midwest market and built a 1,000,000-bushel-capacity malt house in Buffalo, right next to the American Malting Company's house on Child's Street. The building cost $125,000 ($3,200,000) to construct. The business moved its headquarters to Buffalo but maintained its ownership through eight generations of the Perot family.[348]

On September 3, 1907, the last member of the Weyand Brewing family, John A. Weyand, died at his home after a seven-week illness. Weyand, who was forty-seven years old, began working in his father's brewery at sixteen and served as a Buffalo city park commissioner in 1893.[349] He is buried in the family plot in the United German and French Cemetery in Cheektowaga.

By 1908, the Magnus Beck Brewing Company employed one hundred people in its various operations and had a capacity of 110,000 barrels per year. The "principal products" it brewed were Salvator and Wurtzburger, while Magnus Beck Select Lager was "known throughout the eastern end of the state for its purity and general quality."[350] By 1908, the Broadway Brewing and Malting Company malting division had a capacity of 300,000 bushels.[351] The brewery's most popular beers at this time were Export Beer, Standard Beer, Sparkling Ale and Fine Porter.

Just a year after expanding his brewery, the wealthy brewer and founder of Broadway Brewing and Malting Company, Julius Binz, died in March 1908.[352] After discovering natural gas on his property in 1886, Binz co-founded the Erie County Natural Gas Fuel Company.

Said to have a temper, in July 1884, Binz assaulted a man who came to pay his bill at the brewery, slugging him and knocking him down a flight of stairs, causing him to lose teeth and be laid up for several weeks. Binz was a major in the Knights of St. John and active in other societies. He was only sixty-one at his death and left an estate valued at $500,000 ($13,100,000).[353] He is buried in the United German and French Cemetery in Cheektowaga.

His son, Frank X. Binz, took over as president of the brewery; another son, Joseph O., was vice-president; son-in-law Charles W. Belzer was general manager and treasurer; and Frank W. Adolph was secretary of the firm.[354]

Wealthy Buffalo maltster John Baker Manning died in late April 1908. Manning was named president of the National Association of Maltsters when it held its first annual convention in Niagara Falls in 1881. That same year, he was nominated for mayor of Buffalo, but when Grover Cleveland's name was brought up, he dropped out, and Cleveland won the election. When Cleveland resigned (because he had been elected governor of New York), Manning was encouraged to run for mayor, which he did, winning the special election. He lost reelection after his one-year term and did not seek public office again.[355] He is buried in Forest Lawn Cemetery.

In 1908, Buffalo breweries produced 31 million gallons of beer, most of which was consumed locally, making the per capita consumption approximately 77.5 gallons for every man, woman and child in the city of Buffalo.[356]

John F. Nagel, secretary of the German-American Brewing Company, partnered with inventor Edward Zahm in 1908 to form the Zahm Manufacturing Company at 430 Niagara Street. The primary products sold were sterilizing systems and brewers' supplies. Zahm was born in Ohio in about 1876; his father was from Germany and his mother from England. Nagel most likely provided the needed capital to start production, and Zahm provided the

The remains of the William Simon Brewery at Emslie and Clinton Streets. Though much of the old plant is gone, what remains is in sound shape and owned by William Simon III, who has an interest in bringing his family's legacy back again one day. *Photo by Michael Rizzo.*

skills to develop new products. The company is still in business today as Zahm & Nagel Company, Incorporated. It manufactures testing instruments and carbonating equipment for the food and beverage industry.[357]

In November 1908, William Simon incorporated his brewery as the William Simon Brewery with $500,000 ($13,100,000) capital stock. Simon's son William J. was born in Buffalo in October 1880. After graduating from Canisius College and Bryant & Stratton Business College, he went to work for his father at the brewery in 1902 and spent four years learning every aspect of the brewery. He then went to Milwaukee, where he worked for Valentine Blatz Brewing Company and attended the Hautkes Brewing School. Afterward, he returned to Buffalo, where he went back to work at the brewery.

When the company was incorporated, William J. was made vice-president. William J.'s brother Gerhard J. joined the brewery in 1908 and was made secretary while son-in-law Joseph G. Schaff was made treasurer. William held the majority shares and was the brewery's first president. On November 30, 1908, just eleven days after incorporating, Gerhard resigned as secretary, not returning until 1910. William Simon took a salary of $25,000 ($653,000) per year.[358]

Henry Diehl, one of Buffalo's pioneer maltsters, died in February 1909. Starting in 1871, Diehl had built a malting business that would include his sons at 406 Niagara Street. He was eighty-four years old and is buried in the United German and French Cemetery in Cheektowaga.[359]

Oftentimes, business owners or managers took the daily receipts home and would deposit them the following morning. August P. Koch was manager of the International Brewing Company at 1076 Niagara Street and lived at 457 Normal Avenue. On May 9, 1908, Koch was walking home when he was attacked by two men, hit over the head and knocked down, but he quickly jumped up and fought back. A second blow struck him, but he continued fighting, and the would-be robbers were frightened off by his resiliency. He survived the attack, but the assailants were not caught. Koch, it turned out, wasn't carrying any money that night.[360]

The Clinton-Star Brewery at 10 West Bennett Street had been in business since 1901 after the merging of the Clinton and Star Breweries. After a successful run, the firm was dissolved, and in mid-September 1909, John L. Schwartz, former president and general manager of the Clinton-Star, formed the John L. Schwartz Brewing Company in its place.[361] Schwartz was president and treasurer; his son Karl A. was secretary of the new business.

One of America's pioneer brewers, Albert Ziegele Sr., died on June 21, 1909, at the home of his daughter in Sacramento, California. He was the first brewer in Buffalo to erect an ice machine and the first to install an engine in his plant. Ziegele was a founder of both the German Insurance Company and the German Bank and was a director of both. He contributed to the construction of the music hall, was possibly the oldest Mason in Buffalo and

John L. Schwartz, founder of multiple breweries, including the Clinton-Star Brewing Company and John L. Schwartz Brewing Company at 10 West Bennett Street. *Photo from* Men of New York.

was involved in many German organizations, as well as many other cultural and arts organizations in Buffalo.[362] Ziegele's legacy and the early life of Buffalo's brewing industry were recorded in a handwritten memoir that is at the Buffalo Historical Museum. His estate executors were George C. Ginther and Robert F. Schelling, and he is buried in Forest Lawn Cemetery.

In 1909, George F. Stein, one of the founders of Germania Brewing Company, moved to Medina, New York, and purchased the Medina Brewery, which he would operate as Stein's Ale Brewery until 1918. His son George

Why Liberty Brew Is So Popular

The reason Liberty Brew, the new soda fountain beverage, is meeting with such decided favor is because it is a really pure, wholesome soft drink that quenches the thirst and helps the health. It contains in the most palatable form the food and tonic properties of barley-malt and hops.

LIBERTY

BREW

A Malt Extract

is manufactured solely of household ingredients and could be made in any home. Men, women and children find its nourishing qualities of pronounced benefit to their health. It is strictly non-intoxicating and practically non-alcoholic, containing much less alcohol than the government permits in soft drink beverages.

Sold Only in Bottles, and Every Bottle Pasteurized. Order *From Your Dealer For Home Use, or Phone Us*

Gerhard Lang Brewery
Bell, Oxford 643   Frontier 3643

An ad from the Gerhard Lang Brewery for its Liberty Brew malt extract, which was sold before and during Prohibition, undated. *Photo from* Buffalo Courier.

C. would join him after receiving his brewmaster's diploma from Schwartz Brewing Academy in New York City.[363]

The Gerhard Lang Brewery developed a new soda fountain drink made from malt extract in 1909 called Liberty Brew. The company called it a "really pure, wholesome soft drink that quenches the thirst and helps the health." A 1909 advertisement said that it contained "much less alcohol than the government permits in soft drink beverages."[364] It was something the company would need to help survive Prohibition. By this time, the brewery had a capacity of 300,000 barrels of beer per year.[365]

Surprisingly, in late 1909, a new brewery sprang up in the Queen City. Buffalo Brewing Company (today it is Battenfeld-American) purchased one and a half acres of land for the brewery at 1561–75 Clinton Street at the corner of Bailey Avenue. The new brewery was organized in mid-November 1909 with $350,000 ($9,240,000) capital from Syracuse, New York investors. Ground was broken on the $150,000, 150,000-barrel-per-year brewery on November 29, 1909.[366]

John J. Hagan (or Hagen) was born in Leitrim, Ireland, in 1854. He came to America and settled in Buffalo in 1871, working in an iron-rolling mill for eight years before opening a hotel and saloon at 477 Elk Street. Hagan dealt in real estate, owned a farm and was a director and treasurer of International Brewing Company on Niagara Street starting in the 1880s. He was named president of the new brewery; his son James J. was vice-president; and John J. Cummings, treasurer of Dunfee Construction Company of Syracuse, was general manager. They expected to have their building erected and production started by May 1, 1910. One of their products was Bellweiser Bock Beer.[367]

13
THE 1910s

THE ROAD TO PROHIBITION

The years leading to Prohibition brought the death of many of Buffalo's leading brewers and maltsters, as well as changes in the industry, and the brewers saw the writing on the wall as the temperance movement gained steam across the country.

Charles R. Rauch, treasurer for the Buffalo Cooperative Brewing Company, died in 1910 at seventy-four years old. Rauch was born in 1835 in Germany, coming to America in 1848 and finally arriving in Buffalo in 1852. From 1868 to 1887, he ran the Captain and Sailors Boarding House and saloon by the Erie Canal on Commercial Street. When his wife died, he inherited fourteen shares of stock from the brewing company, worth $700 ($16,200), which he may have used to secure a seat on the board of directors. Possibly after closing or selling the saloon, he joined the brewing company. He is buried in the United German and French Cemetery in Cheektowaga.

On July 24, 1910, the corporation known as the German-American Brewing Company ended. It is not known what happened or why. On April 11, 1913, a law was passed reviving the corporation with the same rights it had in 1910.[368]

Christian G. Voltz, maltster with his brother John S., died in November 1910 at sixty-five years old. Voltz made headlines starting in 1899, when he accused Buffalo brewers of brewing impure beer. In 1900, he became a vocal opponent of city hall corruption and was assaulted by the city clerk after a meeting. He became more vocal, and in April 1901, Voltz announced his candidacy for mayor of Buffalo, but he did not win. It appears he and his brother retired around 1908. He is buried in the United German and French Cemetery in Cheektowaga.[369]

Henry L. Schaefer, seventy-four, who spent most of his life in the Schaefer Malt House at Seventh and Jersey Streets, died on May 21, 1911, after a long illness. His sons, Walter E. and Henry G., were still involved in the business. Henry L. was a Mason and member of the Harmonia lodge and Germania chapter RAM.[370] He is buried in Forest Lawn Cemetery.

Augustus F. Scheu, former maltster, died in early March 1912. Scheu had a colorful life, including as a city park commissioner, public works commissioner, as chairman of the grade crossing commission and a member of the terminal commission. He had also been a member of the board of police commissioners. His funeral was attended by hundreds, and several city offices were closed for the day. Pallbearers included Philip G. Schaefer, John F. Nagel, George J. Meyer and Joseph Phillips.[371] He is buried in Forest Lawn Cemetery.

Conrad Hammer Jr. was born in St. Louis, Missouri, in October 1877. While an infant, his parents moved to Buffalo, where his father, Conrad Sr., found employment after traveling the United States. He attended local schools, including Canisius College, before joining his father at the Germania Brewing Company, which he founded, where he rose to general manager.[372]

In August 1912, the Christian Weyand Brewing Company and the Germania Brewing Company were consolidated under the Weyand name. The Weyand brewery was updated, and Germania closed.[373] Hammer Jr. became president of the merged firm and stayed in that position until the onset of Prohibition in 1919.

William W. Weigel, who had been secretary and treasurer of the pre-merger Christian Weyand brewery, was made vice-president at the same time. Weigel, who was the grandson of Christian Weyand, was born in Buffalo in 1883. After attending St. Joseph's Collegiate Institute, he graduated from the United States Brewery Academy. His first business venture was Weyand's Restaurant at Main and Goodell Streets.[374]

In December 1912, John Kreitner, a former director and vice-president of the Iroquois Brewing Company, sued the company president, Leonard Burgweger, and Philip Bartholomay after he contended they took $50,000 ($1,240,000) from the business. Kreitner said Burgweger and Bartholomay illegally awarded themselves raises and misappropriated company funds for their own use, including thousands of dollars "for entertaining patrons." A Buffalo judge, in February 1915, said that Bartholomay owed the company for part of his salary increase and

The Iroquois Brewing plant, circa 1897. In 1893, the Roos brewery was purchased by a group that demolished it and built this brewery, which would go on to be the second-longest-running brewery in Buffalo. *Photo from* Souvenir of Buffalo, on Occasion of the 37th Annual Convention at Buffalo, N.Y.

Burgweger owed the company for a telephone installed in his home that he had charged to the brewery, but they were not responsible for any entertaining expenses, including wedding gifts to the children of patrons, Christmas presents to customers and presents for bartenders, up to that point in time.[375]

Just six years after the forming of the George J. Meyer Malting Company, the business turned out 2,500,000 bushels of malt in a single year, four times the original output. The construction of a new malting plant at 1314 Niagara Street must have had some impact on those numbers, but the growth was directly attributed to Meyer himself.[376]

The German-American Brewing Company perfected a process to bottle its beer without pasteurization in 1912, thereby preserving the taste of the beer. It claimed to be the "first brewery in the world" to succeed at the process and advertised the same to Buffalonians. "Filtered through germ proof filters," its Maltosia beer won a gold medal at the Antwerp Exposition. Its signature brews at the time were Maltosia Pale and Maltosia Dark. Its advertisements touted, "Order a case of Maltosia today and apply the final test. You'll easily recognize its superiority."[377]

In June 1911, the Fleischmann Malting Company of Cincinnati (related to Gustav Fleischmann of Buffalo Distilling Company and Fleischmann's Yeast) purchased the Charles G. Curtiss Company on Niagara and Albany Streets and Riverside Malting Company at 2212 Niagara Street (previously

Bullymore Malt House, sold in 1907). Fleischmann amassed five malt houses in several cities, with a total capacity of 4,000,000 bushels of malt.[378]

When George F. Stein purchased the Medina Brewery in Medina, New York, in 1909, it was a small brewery with a modest capacity. After spending at least $22,000 ($526,000) upgrading the brewery, the production capacity was eight thousand barrels per year (or seventy-five per day) of its Sparkling Ale. It had two icehouses and was powered by electric, a rare occurrence for the time. The ale that it produced was a "product that is refreshing,

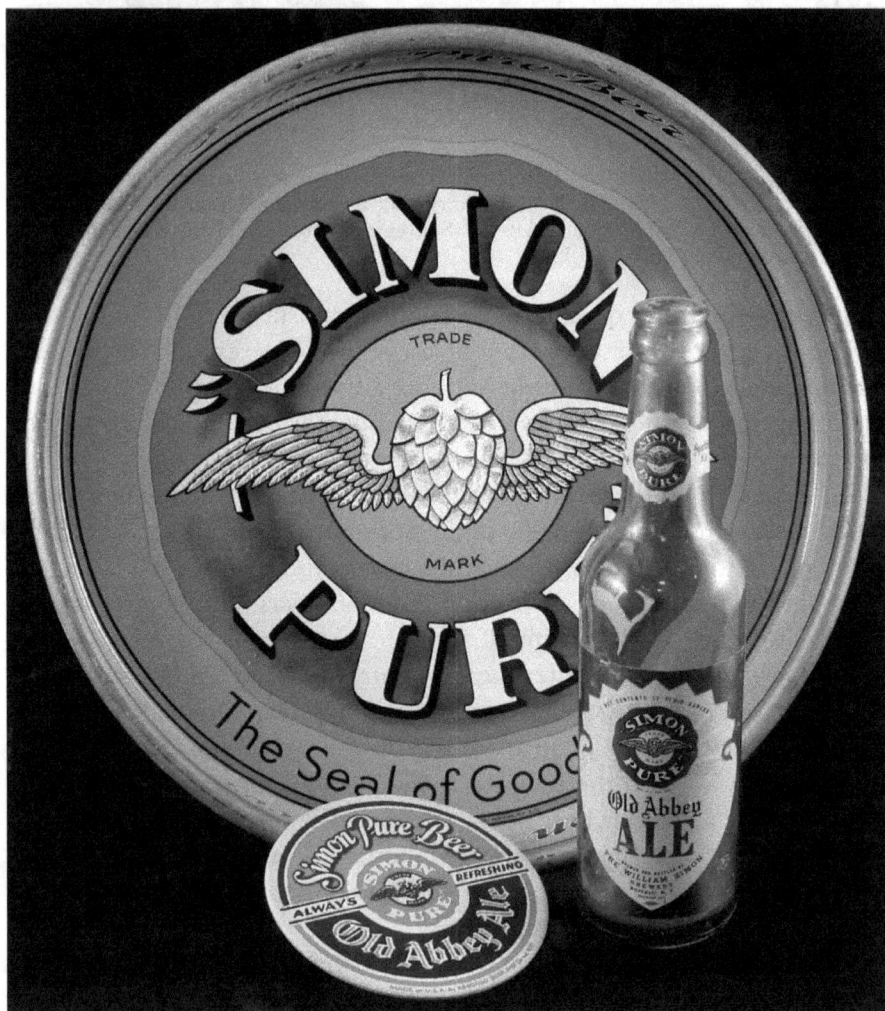

A Simon Pure Old Abbey Ale tray, bottle and coaster, circa the 1950s. *Photo by Chris Groves, from the collection of Dave Mik.*

stimulating and healthful."[379] Stein also secured the distribution rights for Iroquois Beer in Medina and handled about fourteen thousand barrels per year of that beer. Stein would have a Buffalo connection again in a few years.

The year 1913 was good to the William Simon Brewery, as it produced the most beer in its history to that point.

The New Jersey government rejected the bid for the merger of the American Malting Company and American Malt Corporation for monopoly reasons. The companies appealed the decision to the Supreme Court, which ruled against them.[380] American Malting Company owned the former Charles G. Curtiss Company plant in Buffalo.

The year 1915 would prove fatal to many in Buffalo's brewing industry. In late January, Edward G. Becker, sixty-two, one of the founders of Buffalo Cooperative Brewing Company, died. Becker was born in Buffalo in October 1852. In 1871, he joined the German Bank and advanced to cashier in 1878. After two years, he joined Buffalo Savings Bank and advanced to secretary and trustee, positions he held until his death. Becker was also a Mason and member of other fraternal, social and business organizations.[381] He is buried in Forest Lawn Cemetery.

One of Buffalo's finest citizens passed away in 1915 as well. Jacob F. Kuhn established J.F. Kuhn & Company, which was later known as Union Brewery and sold to Gambrinus Brewing Company in 1891. Kuhn, eighty-five, was heavily involved in affairs of the city. He was a master of the Modestia Masonic Lodge, treasurer of the Western New York Masonic Hall Association, Germania chapter member and a founder of Buffalo Brewers' Association. Kuhn was said to be a strict father and had his buggy pick him up from work at the exact same time every day.[382] He is buried in Forest Lawn Cemetery.

In late February 1915, Gustav Fleischmann, sixty, who had been in Florida for his health, died.[383] Fleischmann was the former owner of Buffalo Distilling Company and president of both the Baynes Crematory Company and Frontier Elevator Company, among other business interests. The funeral took place in Baltimore, Maryland.

Carl Strangmann came to Buffalo in 1899, when he purchased a controlling interest in the German-American Brewing Company. On October 2, 1915, Strangmann died suddenly. Under his "guiding spirit," the brewery had grown from fifteen thousand barrels to about forty thousand barrels per year. As a lover of books, Strangmann had one of the largest private libraries in Buffalo. He served "as an officer of the United States Brewers' Association and a trustee of the New York State Brewers'

Association."[384] His widow, Mary, was left a fortune, including brewery stock and gems. He is buried in Alexandria, Virginia.

Gerhard Lang Brewery filed plans with the city building department in 1915 for a brick, concrete and steel constructed brewhouse to be seven stories high that cost $20,000 ($471,000), exclusive of equipment.[385]

Colman Curtiss—son of Alexander M. Curtiss and formerly connected with the Charles G. Curtiss Company—and associates purchased the C. Zwickel Malting Company, 650–56 Elk Street, from Christian Zwickel in late 1915. Curtiss assumed the president and general manager positions of the malting concern, and the business continued under the old name. Curtiss was with the Fleischmann Malting Company as assistant general manager the previous four years. In September 1916, the firm was officially renamed the Curtiss Malting Corporation.[386]

Ziegele Brewing Company at Washington and Virginia Streets was granted a permit to make alterations to its storage cellars, which cost about $7,000 ($165,000), in November 1915. In 1916, the Ziegele Brewing Company remodeled its cold storage plant at 843 Washington Street at a cost of $7,000 ($151,000).[387]

The president of Gerhard Lang Brewery, Edwin G.S. Miller, died after a short illness on November 3, 1915, at seventy years old. Miller had became manager of Gerhard Lang Brewery, owned by his father-in-law, in 1884. He was president of the German-American Bank and the first president of Buffalo Traction Company. In December 1895, he became part owner of the *Enquirer* and was once owner of the *Volksfreund*, both Buffalo newspapers.[388]

After Miller's death, his wife, Anna Maria Emma Lang Miller, began construction on a twelve-thousand-square-foot mansion on Nottingham Terrace in Buffalo, the former grounds of the Pan-American Exposition. She died before the house was completed in 1933. The house would later become Nichols Middle School.

The Millers are interred in the family mausoleum at the United German and French Cemetery in Cheektowaga, and the family continues to own property in Canada.

Conrad Hammer Sr., the founder of Germania Brewing Company, died in March 1915, leaving his wife, two sons and attorney Robert F. Schelling as executors.[389] The story of his estate would continue to play out for several years. He is buried in the United German and French Cemetery in Cheektowaga.

Another family's troubles continued when Caroline Rochevot, family matriarch and widow of Lion Brewery founder George Rochevot, died in early March 1916. The family struggled to run the brewery and settle George's estate after his death, with Caroline in the middle of the fray. Her youngest son, Oscar P., had been treasurer of the brewery, but after Caroline took over as president, her eldest son, Albert G., who had been foreman of the brewery, succeeded her as president.

After Caroline's death, Albert and his sister Eleanor (Rochevot) Beck had the body exhumed to determine if she had died of natural causes, which she had. When her will was finally probated, she left $50 ($1,090) to each of her children and left the bulk of the estate to another daughter, Matilda (Rochevot) Mesinger, with whom she had lived since her husband's death. Albert and Eleanor were then sued for $50,000 ($1,090,000) by Matilda's husband, Henry G. Mesinger, for libel related to exhuming his mother-in-law's body.[390] The family would continue to make headlines for several more years, though.

The Zahm Manufacturing Company at 430 Niagara Street, manufacturer of the Zahm beer sterilizer and brewers' supplies, erected a new brick building to accommodate its growth. This company's sterilizing system was installed in a number of breweries across the country (and in Buffalo) to bottle a stable beer.[391]

Many Buffalo breweries updated their plants in 1916. Breweries spent thousands of dollars as national sentiment toward Prohibition grew. It's possible that the brewers were blinded to the fact that Prohibition could actually happen.

The International Brewing Company installed a new bottling plant, which included a Zahm sterilizing system. The Broadway Brewing and Malting Company made extensive improvements by updating its bottling department also using the Zahm system.[392]

Also in 1916, the William Simon Brewery erected a $6,000 ($129,000) addition to its bottling plant; the Gerhard Lang Brewery added to its bottling house equipment. The Lang brewery was enlarged to handle an expected increase of business the following summer; and the German-American Brewing Company installed four additional bottling tanks and an additional two-hundred-barrel Zahm sterilizer. The Phoenix Brewery added to its bottling equipment. The Broadway Brewing and Malting Company installed a one-hundred-barrel Zahm system and a bottle sterilizer. To accommodate its continuous growth, the Gerhard Lang Brewery ordered a new conveyor and bottling line.[393]

The days of the horse and wagon were ending in Buffalo, and the Ziegele Brewing Company began fading out horses in their hauling service in 1916

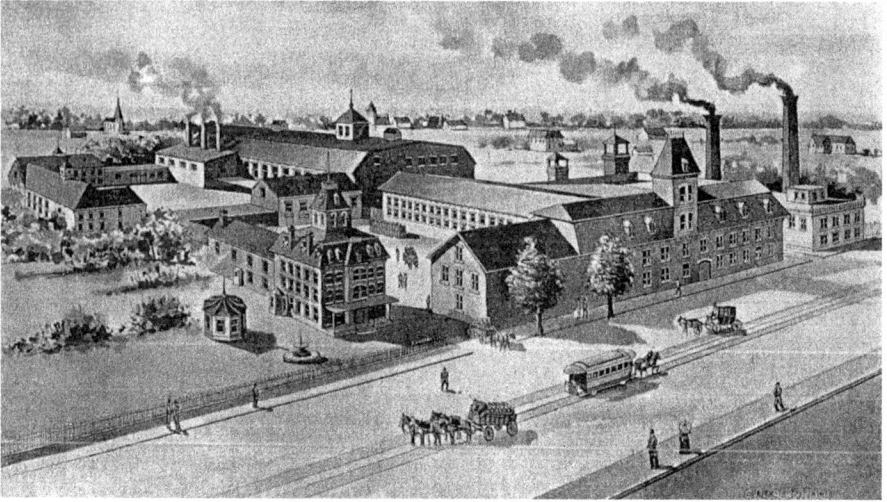

George Rochevot began brewing in Buffalo in 1857. This 1890 scene of Rochevot's Lion Brewery, at 1013–39 Jefferson Avenue, shows the hard work these men put into building their businesses. *Photo from* Buffalo Illustrated: Commerce, Trade and Industries of Buffalo.

and replacing them with new trucks. A large garage was erected to protect its growing fleet of vehicles. Change was afoot.[394]

In August 1916, the A. Schreiber Brewing Company was made defendant in a suit brought by Johann Stumpf on the charge of infringement of a patent on a steam engine.[395] That same month, John F. Nagel, president of German-American Brewing Company, purchased the plant and equipment of the defunct Canandaigua Brewing Company for $30,500 ($658,000).[396]

From October 1 to 3, 1916, the convention of the Master Brewers' Association was held in Buffalo. At the close of the convention, Gustav Braun, president of the Master Brewers' Association of the district of Buffalo, was elected first vice-president of the Master Brewers' Association of the United States.[397]

The Central and Western New York Brewers' and Maltsters' Mutual Insurance Company of New York was formed on July 1, 1914, to jointly represent the brewing and malt industries. In 1917, the directors included a who's who of Buffalo malt and brewing: John L. Schwartz, John F. Nagel, Joseph Phillips, Simon Seibert, George J. Meyer, George C. Ginther and several others. In August 1919, the name was changed to Central Mutual Insurance Company of New York.[398]

Respected Buffalo attorney Robert F. Schelling died on December 17, 1916, after a long illness. Schelling was a critical part of the brewing scene in Buffalo for many years. Born in Buffalo in 1850, he was admitted to the bar in 1873 and, after working for several law firms, began business for himself in the German Insurance building. His specialty was corporate law, and he was involved in the formation of many breweries in Buffalo.

Schelling was a director and attorney for the German Bank that failed, and he and other directors were scrutinized for allowing it to happen. Schelling was also vice-president of the German-American Bank when it nearly failed in 1894. He was a director and executive of the 1901 Pan-American Exposition and was a member of the Buffalo Club and Buffalo Orpheus. His younger brother Albert was also a Buffalo attorney who worked with the breweries.[399]

Simon Seibert, manager of Magnus Beck Brewing Company and a prominent Buffalo politician, died on October 18, 1917. Seibert became manager of the brewery in 1883 and had been general manager since George C. Ginther retired in 1899. His business acumen made him reputedly one of the highest-paid brewers in the state.

Seibert was also a well-known politician, serving as a New York State assemblyman and state senator, both for two terms, losing reelection to the senate when the Raines Excise Bill was passed and there was a revolt against Republicans. He was also an Elk and Mason and involved in other fraternal and business organizations.[400] Seibert is buried in Forest Lawn Cemetery.

As part of the war effort for World War I, the use of grains in brewing was severally restricted in order to save the grain for food. At this time, many states began statewide Prohibition during the war. In April 1918, the United States government ordered all the Buffalo malt plants to close because they were "non-essential" to the war effort. Before it went into effect, some strong lobbying must have been persuasive because most of the malt required by Buffalo brewers was made locally and the government changed the order to allow the malt houses that supplied Buffalo breweries to stay open.[401]

In 1917, Frank X. Schwab, assistant to Iroquois brewery president Leonard Burgweger and in charge of the bottling department since about 1905, became vice-president and general manager of Buffalo Brewing Company at Clinton and Bailey Avenues. Simultaneously, the brewery was enlarged and modernized its bottling department.[402] John W. Gates was president of the firm, William Merrill treasurer and Lorenz Schwab manager of the bottling department.

On October 1, 1917, the Buffalo Brewers' Exchange members agreed to reduce the number of saloons they controlled by 25 percent, from 1,650 to 1,200. John F. Nagel, president of the German-American Brewing Company, possibly in a move to appease the temperance movement, said

The former plant of Buffalo Brewing Company at Clinton Street and Bailey Avenue. It was one of the last breweries to open in Buffalo in 1909. It's the current home of Battenfeld-American. *Photo by Michael Rizzo.*

they were "going to clean house," and "all disorderly places, fake hotels and questionable cabaret houses" would be shut down.[403]

The Rochevot family reared its ugly head in the news once again in mid-December 1917. After family trouble over property litigation in which Albert G. Rochevot blamed his son-in-law, Dr. John M. Schaefer, Rochevot went to his daughter's house and shot Schaefer twice, killing him. He then shot his daughter once but did not kill her and escaped in his son-in-law's car. Police tracked Rochevot to his office on Jefferson Avenue, where they found him dead from self-inflicted gunshot wounds.[404] This was the final, tragic end to the once prosperous Rochevot brewing family.

The John L. Schwartz Brewing Company had several popular drinks, including its Alma beer. With World War I and the curtailing of grains used in beer, the Schwartz brewery came out with a non-alcoholic drink it named Cleo that could be "freely partaken as pure water."[405] It also announced a plant enlargement due to the demand for Cleo.[406]

By March 1918, the monopoly known as American Malting Company (the former Charles G. Curtiss Company plant) had sold all its malt and barley and began liquidating its plants.[407] By 1922, the company was dissolved.

In 1918, George F. Stein moved back to Buffalo from Medina, New York, where he had been living since 1909 and running Stein's Ale Brewery. He immediately found work as brewmaster at Broadway Brewing and Malting Company, which lasted until the onset of Prohibition.[408] His son George C. followed him back to Buffalo after the closing of the Medina Brewery.

George C. Ginther, president of the Phoenix Brewery for about eighteen years, retired in 1917. He thought he would relax, but in 1918, he was asked to direct the receivership of the bankrupt German-American Brewing Company. After he discharged all the brewery's liabilities, he once again retired.[409] The brewery building at 23 High Street was then converted into an apartment building.

In late 1918, the Oswego Milling Company purchased the John Kam Malting Company plant on Hertel Avenue for $750,000 ($11,600,000).[410]

The customer-friendly, bearded founder of the William Simon Brewery, William Simon, died on October 22, 1918, at sixty-six years old. His death and

The William Simon family plot, located in the United German and French Cemetery, Cheektowaga, New York. *Photo by Michael Rizzo.*

the impending start of Prohibition would affect the brewery tremendously. Simon was on the board of directors of many financial institutions in Buffalo, was a member of numerous clubs and fraternal organizations and, according to Michalak, "took an active part in public affairs of the city."[411] He is buried in the family plot in the United German and French Cemetery in Cheektowaga. His sons, already in management positions in the brewery, would continue operations, but in later years, a battle for control of the concern would nearly destroy the family.

The former manager of the Magnus Beck and Gerhard Lang breweries, Peter Drexelius, died in 1919. He had been chairman of the Erie County Democratic Party, was dairy commissioner under New York governor David Bennett, chief clerk of the Internal Revenue Service under President Grover Cleveland and water commissioner of Buffalo.[412] He is buried in the United German and French Cemetery in Cheektowaga.

The Moffat brewery did not want to let the factory or its workers down due to Prohibition, so in January 1919, it converted the factory—said to be the oldest manufacturing plant in Buffalo at the time—to a flour mill and was able to keep some people employed.

In May 1919, the executives of the Iroquois Brewing Company, preparing for the inevitable, filed incorporation papers as the Iroquois Beverage Corporation to manufacture ice cream and soft drinks. Only one year had passed since it had registered Indian Head Beer. Starting in 1917, it would manufacture Iro, a cereal beverage.[413]

John F. Nagel was president of the German-American Brewing Company when a secret indictment by a grand jury in Buffalo charged him with taking $60,000 ($808,000) from Rocky River Development Company (of which he was treasurer) and funneling it into the brewery. The court ruled in May 1919 that the brewery owed Rocky River Development Company $38,790 ($522,000).[414]

George J. Meyer, president of the large malting firm bearing his name, died on July 14, 1919. Meyer was known as an "unselfish advocate of a Greater Buffalo movement" and active in many projects.[415] A Democrat, he was one of the leaders of the Democratic Party's formation in Erie County and served as county chairman for two years. Meyer was made Buffalo postmaster in 1916 and donated his entire postmaster salary to the Red Cross and other war efforts. He left an estate valued at $500,000 ($6,730,000), as well as an enormous obelisk and family burial plot in the United German and French Cemetery in Cheektowaga. He served as Buffalo park commissioner, was a member of various organizations and held an honorary degree from Canisius College.[416]

Gorgeous color ad printed in 1901 from Christian Weyand Brewing Company, located at 793 Main Street. The photo also shows Weyand's buffet from Main and Goodell Streets. *Photo by Chris Groves, from the collection of Dave Mik.*

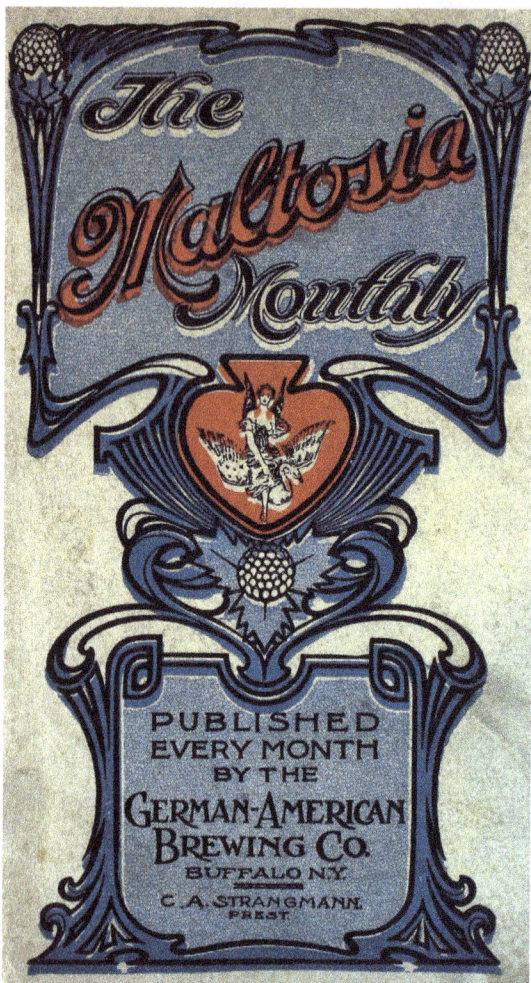

Left: *Maltosia Monthly*, the publication of German-American Brewing Company, started by Joseph Haberstro. This June 1911 copy is the only month collectors have found. *Photo by Chris Groves, from the collection of Dave Mik.*

Below: A display of bottles from Iroquois prior to the company being sold to International Breweries, Incorporated, in 1955. Bottles shown include beer, ale, bock and other labels. *Photo by Chris Groves, from the collection of Dave Mik.*

Opposite, bottom: A collection of rare, pre-Prohibition labels from some of the lesser-known breweries. *Left to right*: Moffat & Service, German-American Brewing Company, Clinton-Star Brewing Company, J. Schüssler. The later dates from the 1890s while the first three are all circa early 1900s. *Photo by Chris Groves, from the collection of Dave Mik.*

Left: Several items from the William Simon Brewery on Clinton Street. Simon was the last of Buffalo's breweries to close in late 1971. Shown are a bottle, a tray and a coaster, all relating to the company's Abby Ale and circa 1930s. *Photo by Chris Groves, from the collection of Dave Mik.*

Right: A swing-top bottle circa 1900 from the Buffalo Cooperative Brewing Company, which was located at Main and High Streets. *Photo by Chris Groves, from the collection of Dave Mik.*

Above: One of the Webster-Citizens Ice Company's storehouses. This was located on Essex Street on Buffalo's West Side. *Photo by Michael Rizzo.*

Left: A collection of post-Prohibition Simon Pure bottles, including a rare prototype bottle of the never-released Cavern Spring Water. *Photo by Chris Groves, from the collection of Dave Mik.*

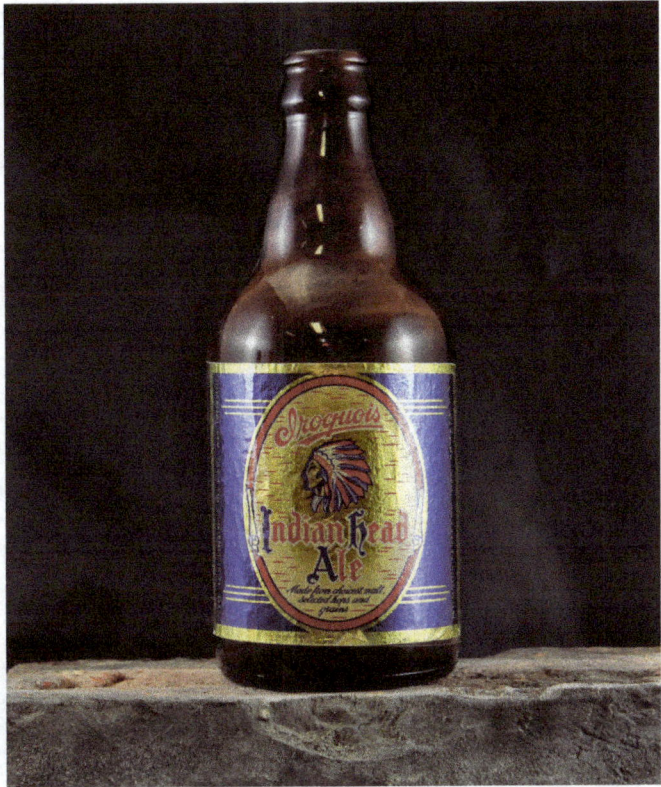

Right: An Indian
Head Ale bottle
from the Iroquois
Brewery, circa 1940.
The metallic label
denotes it being an
anniversary edition.
*Photo by Chris Groves,
from the collection of
Dave Mik.*

Below: A collection
of post-Prohibition
tap handles
spanning the 1940s
to '60s. *Top, left
to right*: Lang's,
Phoenix, Steins.
Bottom, left to right:
Iroquois, Simon
Pure, Iroquois.
*Photo by Chris Groves,
from the collection of
Dave Mik.*

Opposite, top: A remarkable collection of a circa 1900 Iroquois tray with three bottles depicted, as well as the three bottles themselves. Salvator was likely a dopplebock because of the history of the -ator suffix in German brewing. *Photo by Chris Groves, from the collection of Dave Mik.*

Opposite, bottom: A selection of Iroquois bottles and a tray. While the tray dates from the 1940s, the bottles themselves are mostly from the 1930s. *Photo by Chris Groves, from the collection of Dave Mik.*

Right: An Iroquois bock beer bottle, circa 1930. *Photo by Chris Groves, from the collection of Dave Mik.*

Below: Sunny Kid was a Prohibition-era product from the brothers Schwab. F.X. would also serve as a mayor of Buffalo, running on an overtly anti-Prohibition platform. He had a long history in the brewing industry. *Photo by Chris Groves, from the collection of Dave Mik.*

STEP UP! . . . AND ASK FOR

Sunny Kid
BEVERAGES
Made Famous - "FOR QUALITY"

SPECIAL BREW
A. Schwab
ALE

A. Schwab

SPECIAL BREW
A. Schwab
BEER

BROAD-SMITH CO., Inc.
575 Jefferson Buffalo, N.Y.

Pre-Prohibition breweriana, circa 1900, from the Buffalo Cooperative Brewing Company, including a tray, the bottles depicted thereon and a period corkscrew bottle opener. *Photo by Chris Groves, from the collection of Dave Mik.*

An assortment of pre-Prohibition beer glasses, dating from around 1900. *Left to right*: Lion (Rochevot), Iroquois, Broadway Brewing & Malting Company. *Photo by Chris Groves, from the collection of Dave Mik.*

A tray from the Broadway Brewing Company, circa 1910. *Photo by Chris Groves, from the collection of Dave Mik.*

A collection of brewer badges. *Top left*: Phoenix-sponsored Old Home Week in the late 1890s. *Top right*: Lang's welcomed the Grand Army of the Republic to Buffalo in 1897. *Bottom left*: An Iroquois pin circa 1900. *Bottom right*: The Lion Brewery welcomed exposition-goers to Buffalo in 1901. *Photo by Chris Groves, from the collection of Dave Mik.*

A collection of promotional mugs from the Weyand Brewing Company, circa 1900.
Photo by Chris Groves, from the collection of Dave Mik.

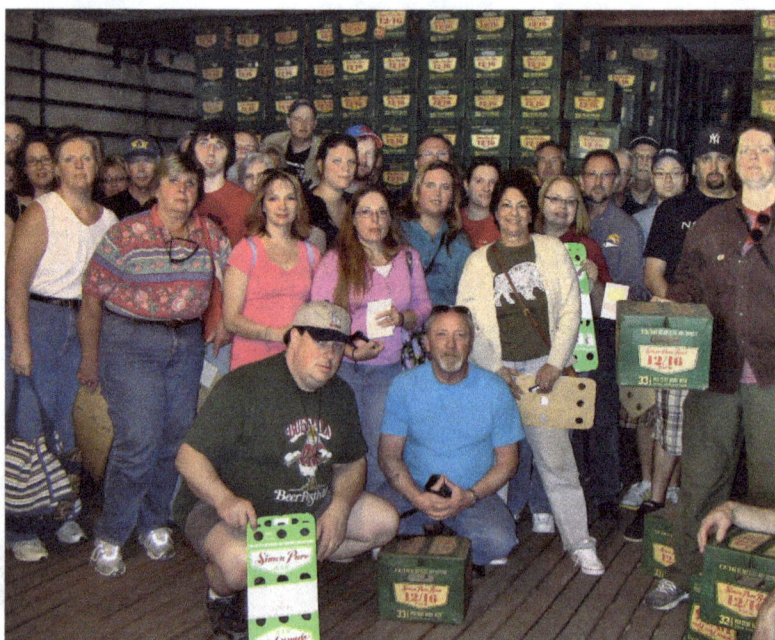

A tour group in the old cold storage room of the William Simon Brewery, 2012.
Photo by Michael Rizzo.

Above: An assortment of bottles from the collection of Dave Mik. Many Buffalo beers are shown, including Downs, Phoenix, Manru, Simon and Lang. *Photo by Chris Groves, from the collection of Dave Mik.*

Right: An ad from the Iroquois Brewing Company in the 1950s reminds us that brewery tours, and the enjoyment of a brewery-fresh beer in a brewer's own taproom, is hardly a new idea. *Photo by Michael Rizzo.*

The founders of Community Beer Works. *Left to right*: Christopher Smith, Rudy Watkins, Dan Conley, Ethan Cox, Matthew Daumen and Gregory Tanski, circa April 2013. *Photo by Ethan Cox.*

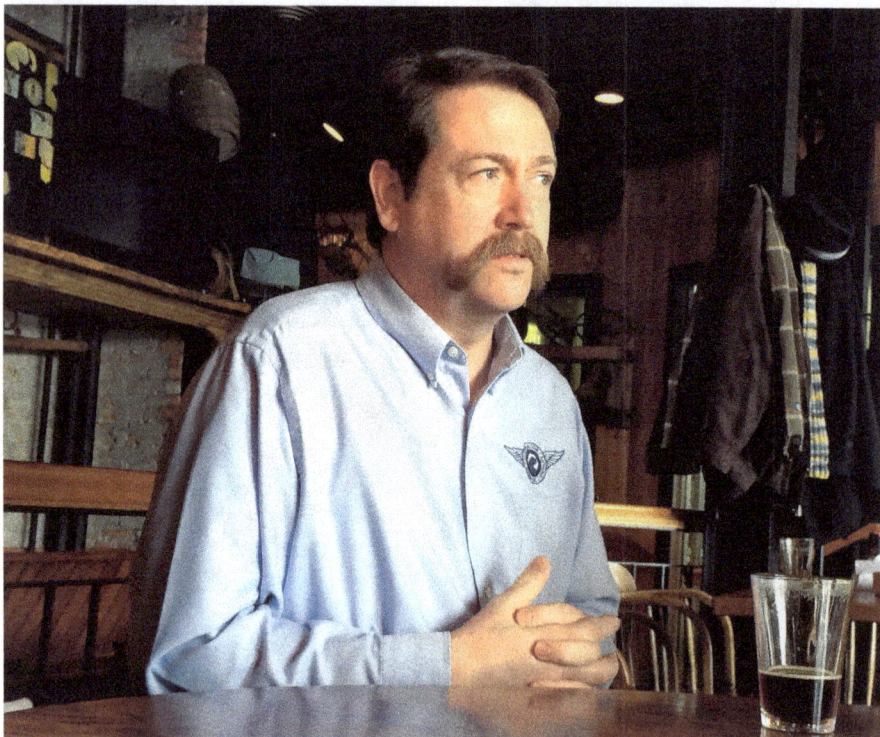

Flying Bison Brewing Company founder Tim Herzog speaking at the Pearl Street Grill in 2013. *Photo by Ethan Cox.*

Opposite, bottom: A nice view of the bar at Gene McCarthy's, featuring Old First Ward beers and tap handles. *Photo Jennifer Reed.*

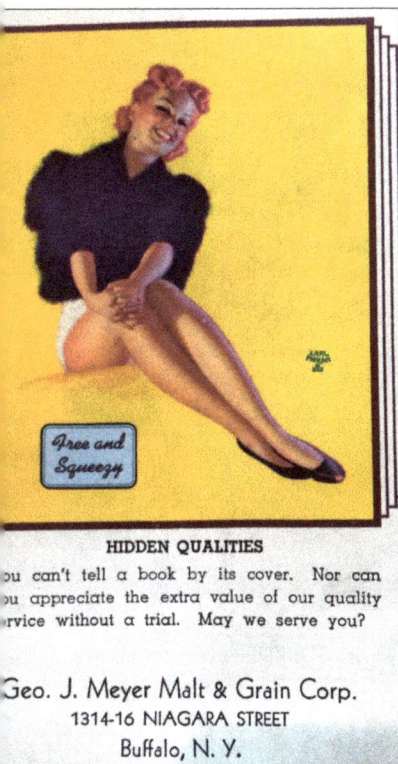

Left: An advertising card circa 1930s for the George J. Meyer malting company at 1314–16 Niagara Street. Meyer was one of the last to remain in business in Buffalo. *Photo by Chris Groves, from the collection of Dave Mik.*

Right: Big Ditch Brewing founders Matt Kahn and Corey Catalano in their brewery in late August 2014. The brewery is located at 55 East Huron Street. *Photo by Ethan Cox.*

Resurgence Brewing Company is another of the new breweries in Buffalo. Here are tasting glasses and paddles. *Photo Buffaloeats.org.*

John Kam opened two large malt plants in Buffalo, one along the Erie Canal and one on the East Side. This fine letterhead shows drawings of both plants as they appeared in the early 1910s. *Photo by Ethan Cox from the collection of Dave Mik.*

The taps at Gene McCarthy's for Old First Ward Brewing Company, 2014. *Photo by Jennifer Reed.*

The bar at Resurgence Brewing Company, located at 1250 Niagara Street, 2014. *Photo by Matthew McCormick.*

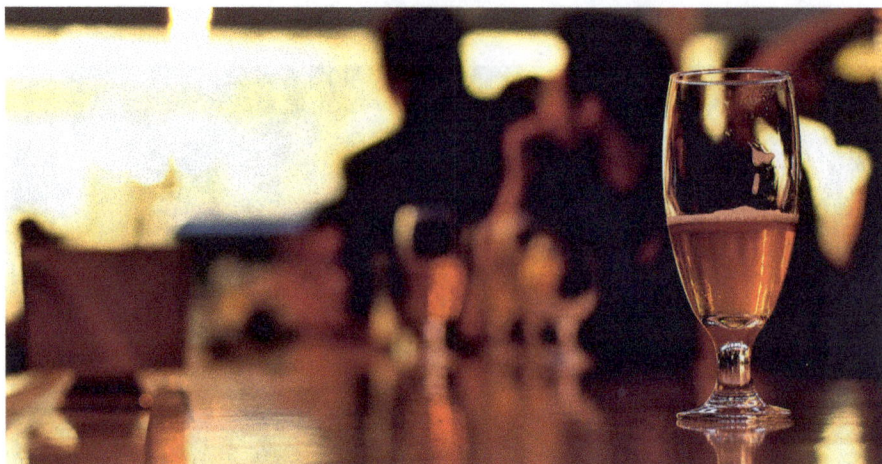

A glass of beer at Resurgence Brewing Company, 2014. *Photo by Matthew McCormick.*

A glass of Community Beer Works' Frank Pale Ale sits at the brewery's retail counter. Community Beer Works was founded in 2010 and began serving beer in April 2012. *Photo by Ethan Cox.*

Henry J. Kam, president of the John Kam Malting Company, died in late June 1919 after a long illness. He had been with the company started by his father for forty years. He was fifty-six years old and is buried in the United German and French Cemetery in Cheektowaga.[417]

Prohibition had a profound impact on the alcohol industry and beer producers in Buffalo, which is why it is interesting to note that "eminent ecclesiastical authorities...recognized beer as an important factor"[418] against temperance. Those same authorities apparently also claimed "beer does not create an appetite for whisky or other strong liquors."[419]

That didn't stop Congress, which, in 1917, voted to make the Eighteenth Amendment to the Constitution law. Three-quarters of the states needed to ratify the amendment in seven years in order for it to become law. It took just thirteen months, enabling the Volstead Act, which enforced the national Prohibition of alcohol.[420] The Volstead Act defined an alcoholic beverage as one containing half of 1 percent of alcohol, which eliminated even light beers and wines.

President Woodrow Wilson, though, would have none of it and vetoed the Volstead Act, but his veto was overridden by Congress on October 28, 1919.[421] Frank X. Schwab, a likable brewery man, would base his platform against Prohibition to run for mayor of Buffalo in 1921 and appeal to the large German population with which he was friendly because they were generally against the new law.

The International Brewery Company, Incorporated, looking to find new work during Prohibition, filed incorporation papers in early September 1919, stating that it would become a realty construction and warehouse business. With $250,000 ($3,370,000) in capital stock, Joseph Phillips, former vice-president of International Brewing Company, headed the concern, with Otto H. Krotz, bottling department manager, and John J. Hagan, treasurer, as the other investors.[422]

In October 1919, the United States Patent Office ruled in favor of Iroquois Brewing Company, which had sued American Brewing Company of Rochester, New York, for infringing on its patents from 1894 and 1906 of its logo with the head of an Indian woman.[423]

Another son of the founder of the John Kam Malting Company, John Kam Jr., died in early November 1919, just weeks after his brother Henry died. Kam was forty-eight years old.[424] He is buried in the United German and French Cemetery in Cheektowaga.

The thought of a long, drawn-out Prohibition forced the hands of many brewery executives. On December 3, 1919, the Iroquois Brewing Company announced it was selling all the property it owned in western New York, including in Woodlawn Beach, Batavia, Sloan and its entire brewery on Pratt Street, including all the machinery.[425]

14
THE 1920s

PROHIBITION AND THE END

T he 1920s could not have begun on a more sour note for the brewing
industry across America. At midnight on January 17, 1920, Prohibition
went into law, and hundreds of workers lost their jobs in Buffalo. Political
leaders were reminded of this over and over, but the will of the temperance
movement, which had been pushing for Prohibition for many years, won out.

No one knew how long it would last or if it would ever end. That didn't end
the availability of alcohol, though, as beer and hard alcohol were available
through various illegal means. This in itself fueled a new business model,
which gave rise to mafias. Some taverns in Buffalo never stopped selling beer
but continued to purchase it on the black market.

With Prohibition in effect, the German-American Brewing Company at
11 High Street shut down. In mid-February 1920, it sold the brewery to the
Buffalo Commercial newspaper for $300,000 ($3,490,000).[426] The building was
later converted to apartments and was finally demolished in 2006.

What happened to the other breweries? Well, the Magnus Beck Brewing
Company on North Division Street, which had a capacity of 150,000 barrels
of beer per year, was dismantled during Prohibition, and some of the land
was sold. The Christian Weyand Brewing Company on Washington Street
was sold to Trico, the windshield wiper company, for construction of a new
manufacturing plant. Weyand's Restaurant on Main and Goodell Streets was
sold to the *Buffalo Courier-Express* newspaper, where it erected a new building.
The former International Brewing Company brewery at 1088 Niagara
Street was sold to American Gelatine Corporation. It was later owned by

William W. Weigel and William J. Connors holding the cornerstone from the former Weyand Brewery after it was demolished to make room for Connor's new *Buffalo Courier-Express* newspaper building. Today, it is home to the Catholic Diocese. *Photo from* Buffalo Courier-Express.

Gulf Oil Corporation and Hygrade Petroleum Company and today is a brownfield site.[427]

The Lake View Brewing Company at Porter and Seventh Streets was converted to a laundry during Prohibition. The Buffalo, Schwartz and Consumers' breweries were all dismantled, and their property was sold. Most of the rest, if not idle, would manufacture other products during Prohibition.[428]

All breweries across the United States were closed due to Prohibition, or at least they were supposed to. It didn't take long before Buffalo Brewing Company at Broadway and Bailey Avenue was raided and seized by the Internal Revenue Service department for brewing beer with an alcohol content higher than half of 1 percent and then not paying taxes on said beer.[429]

The manager of Buffalo Brewing Company was Frank X. Schwab, and John W. Gates of Syracuse was president at this time. Schwab, who would go on to be elected mayor of Buffalo in 1921, said it was a conspiracy from those who were angry he was making money from near beer because he wasn't a member of the Buffalo Brewers' Exchange. While the plant was detained by federal agents, someone broke in and stole 250 cases and 40 half-barrels of beer. A lawyer for the brewery said the higher alcohol content beer had been made before Prohibition.[430]

In late April 1920, the Buffalo Brewing Company, now under the leadership of William W. Weigel (previously with Christian Weyand Brewing Company), purchased the trade and output of the Buffalo Cooperative Brewing Company, including about five thousand barrels of beer. The company was renamed Mohawk Brewing Company and manufactured under the Mohawk name.[431]

Prior to Prohibition, almost every brewery owned saloons or held the mortgages on them. They often leased them to the saloon proprietor and would deduct expenses from the monthly beer sales. This control allowed the breweries to dictate which beer was sold in the saloon, generally only theirs. For example, William Simon Brewery owned 165 pieces of property in Buffalo and Erie County before Prohibition.[432] Breweries used this tactic to keep competition out and would buy properties that other breweries had taverns on.

After the onset of Prohibition, a big sell-off of saloon properties occurred. But because the brewery owners had bought and sold so much real estate, they had become experts at property evaluation. So when Prohibition shut down the breweries, several of them ventured into real estate, including the International Brewery Company, Incorporated, owners.

Henry C. Moffat, owner of Moffat's Brewery, died on December 30, 1920. Moffat Flour Mills, Incorporated, at West Mohawk and Eagle Streets, was sold and demolished in 1922 in order to make way for a new parking garage,

The A. Schreiber Brewery at 662 Fillmore Avenue. Anthony Schreiber's most famous beer was Manru, named after Jan Paderewski's opera of the same name. This is a view of the remains of the brewery in 2013. *Photo by Michael Rizzo.*

which, coincidentally, was never built. Henry C. Moffat is buried in Forest Lawn Cemetery.

During Prohibition, one of the breweries that stayed open was the A. Schreiber Brewing Company plant on Fillmore Avenue. It started roasting coffee and named it Manru, after its popular beer. It also manufactured other food products, including Solido, a cereal beverage.[433]

Polarizing, outgoing, loyal and anti-Prohibition brewer Frank X. Schwab ran for mayor of Buffalo in 1921 on the Democratic ticket against incumbent mayor George S. Buck. Schwab, a native East Sider, lost the primary but won the general election in November 1921, with the majority of his support coming from the Polish- and German-dominated East Side neighborhoods of Buffalo.[434]

Newly elected Mayor Schwab aimed to make a stand early in his term. Within his first week, he said he wanted the vice and dry squads of the police department "out catching crooks, not snooping around." The Anti-Saloon League and Federation of Churches, which were pro-temperance movement and Prohibition, declared that with Schwab as mayor, the streets would "run red with booze."[435] They weren't far off.

Prohibition provided an unintended boost to a criminal organization that would come to be known as the mafia. Based in Niagara Falls, a powerful Sicilian man named Stefano Magaddino had arrived from Brooklyn and, for the next fifty years, ran a subversive organization that defied the laws; ran gambling and vice rings, unions and politics; sold illegal booze; and is believed to be responsible for numerous murders. Magaddino stated that at one point in the 1920s, he was making $10,000 ($133,000) a week.

Not everyone was happy with Prohibition, especially those East Side immigrants who enjoyed their beer. Illegal booze also fueled another gang, this one Polish. It ran its own brewery, supplying saloons across the area, from the East Side to Cheektowaga to Lancaster. John "Korney" Kwiatkowski was a dapper, well-dressed killer. His Korney Gang would pull off multiple daring daylight payroll robberies and eventually end up in prison. The Great Experiment was flawed from the start, and those who knew how to take advantage of it certainly did.

Most breweries had closed completely, unable to secure any other type of work to keep their employees occupied. Some did surreptitiously continue to manufacture beer because there was a desire for it. And why not? Illegal "wildcat" breweries, as they were called, sprang up all over the city. Enforcement was lax; police were often on the take. When Korney Kwiatkowski was acquitted of murder in 1929, parties sprung up across the East Side, the liquor flowed freely and the Buffalo police turned a blind eye.

Frank J. Illig—who, with Conrad Hammer, had helped found Germania Brewing Company—died in 1922. In the 1890s, he was Buffalo police commissioner, later was an excise commissioner and a sales agent for the New York state prison system and, in 1911, was keeper of Erie County Penitentiary.[436] He is buried in the United German and French Cemetery in Cheektowaga.

In early 1922, Broadway Brewing and Malting Company and 797 Broadway and East Buffalo Brewing Company at 300 Emslie Street were both charged with violating the national Prohibition act, as were officials from both concerns. Although already illegal, the government placed temporary injunctions against the companies prohibiting them from "manufacturing, transporting or selling high-powered beer."[437]

On March 1, 1923, Broadway Brewing and Malting Company and East Buffalo Brewing Company were both fined $2,000 ($26,900), the temporary injunctions that had stopped them from manufacturing "high-powered" beer were made permanent and officials from both breweries were fined. Frank W. Adolph, secretary, and George F. Stein, brewmaster, both of Broadway, as well as Henry W. Brendel, president; John C. Schenk, secretary-treasurer; and Frank Feltes, assistant treasurer and brewmaster, all of East Buffalo, were fined $750 each ($10,100). Additionally, taxes and penalties for Broadway were estimated to be over $285,000 ($3,830,000) and $17,831 ($240,000) for East Buffalo.[438]

In mid-February 1922, Frank M. Beck was elected president of the Iroquois Brewing Company at 230 Pratt Street and replaced Joseph Phillips as general manager of the firm. Just two months later, the Magnus Beck Brewing Company, with offices listed at 12 Buffalo Insurance Building, purchased the assets of Iroquois Brewing Company for $350,000 ($4,860,000). The Iroquois Beverage Corporation was then incorporated with $50,000 ($695,000) capitalization, and Frank M. Beck, Edward Beck, Albert Schelling and William W. Weigel were made directors of the new company. Weigel was "confident that Prohibition would not last [and] he acquired most of the plants of various Buffalo breweries."[439]

Frank X. Binz of Broadway Brewing and Malting Company died in July 1922. After his father, Julius, died in 1908, he had taken over as president of the brewery and ran it until Prohibition. He is buried in the United German and French Cemetery in Cheektowaga.

During Prohibition, the breweries that stayed afloat often did so by manufacturing other products. George F. Stein partnered with Frank

X. Schwab to start Broadway Products Corporation in 1931 at 797–807
Broadway (in the former Broadway Brewing and Malting Company building)
to make liquid malt and malt syrup products. Stein served as president, with
Theodore J. Stein as vice-president and Joseph C. Stein as treasurer.[440]

One of the businesses that the Lang brewery formed to keep active during
Prohibition was Lang's Creamery, Incorporated. Founded by Jacob Gerhard
Lang in 1923, the dairy, one of many in the city at the time, was a very
successful business.[441] Lang experienced a few hiccups during the growth
of the business, including a problem with colored bottles. In the late 1920s,
researchers determined that green bottles would prevent the milk from
turning rancid. The Owens-Illinois Glass Company manufactured green
bottles for Lang's in 1932 for eggnog. Consumers, though, did not like the
colored bottle since they could not see if the product was rancid.[442]

Eugene Irr, one of the founders of Gambrinus Brewing Company and a
well-known "cultured" man of Buffalo, died in late November 1925. After
Gambrinus closed in 1904, Irr found employment with the Iroquois Brewing
Company. He had been a member of several organizations, like many of
Buffalo's brewers. He is buried in the United German and French Cemetery
in Cheektowaga.

In September 1924, the former William Simon Brewery was leased
to the Nomis Beverage Company, Incorporated, for $3,000 ($40,900)
per month. Nomis (which is Simon spelled backward) was developed to
produce near beer by the Simon family.[443]

On April 24, 1926, federal agents seized the Nomis Beverage Company,
Incorporated, located in the former William Simon Brewery on Clinton and
Emslie Streets, after two truckloads of "high-power" beer were found inside.

The plan backfired, and in June 1926, a federal grand jury indicted seven
men in connection with the manufacture of illegal beer at the Nomis cereal
plant. William J. Simon; his brother Gerhard J. Simon; their brother-in-law
Joseph G. Schaff, former state senator and president of the company; Samuel
J. Ramsperger, treasurer and secretary; Frank J. Frankenberger, vice-president;
Frank A. Haag; and Carl Lehmann, brewmaster for Nomis and the former
Simon brewery, were all indicted. Nomis was leasing the brewery under the
auspices of producing near beer, a cereal beverage, when they were indicted.

Near beer was made by brewing beer at full alcohol content and then
de-alcoholizing it, possibly using equipment manufactured by Zahm
Manufacturing Company of Buffalo. Blame was placed squarely on the
brewmaster, Carl Lehmann, who had apparently allowed a truck to leave
that April morning when it was seized by federal agents.[444]

During that time, William J. Simon got back into the beer business when he purchased the Copeland Brewing Company of Toronto, Ontario, in May 1926. The president of the firm was Eugene J. Meyer, and Daniel Sutter of Pennsylvania was vice-president. William's brother Gerhard J. Simon was also believed to be an investor. The firm kept the original Copeland Brewing Company name and began making deliveries on June 1, 1926.[445]

The former president of the Buffalo Brewers' Exchange and the International Brewing Company, Joseph Phillips, died on June 10, 1926, after a long illness.[446] Phillips was one of the partners in the Star Brewing Company and other brewery interests. He is buried in the United German and French Cemetery in Cheektowaga.

The buildings of the Moffat Flour Mills, Incorporated, at 1035 Seneca Street were engulfed in flames in a three-alarm fire on September 30, 1926, that caused $50,000 ($658,000) in damages. Henry J. Rengel, treasurer of the company, said fifty thousand bushels of grain were stored in the building. Fire officials believed the fire was caused by spontaneous combustion of the grain. This was the end of Moffat Flour Mills, Incorporated.[447]

In 1926, William E. Kreiner and his son, William Jr., incorporated their malt business as Wm. E. Kreiner & Sons, Incorporated, with $200,000 ($2,630,000) in capital, the vast majority of which was held by William Sr. and William Jr. and a second son, Howard.[448]

As Prohibition lingered on, former brewery men in Buffalo were itching to get back into the business. While Prohibition in the United States prohibited the sale and manufacture of alcohol, in Ontario, Canada, their prohibition law allowed companies to manufacture as long as the product was exported to countries such as the Caribbean.

Frank M. Beck, president of Iroquois Beverage Corporation, along with other investors, purchased the Welland Brewery in Welland, Ontario, in June 1926, hoping to capture some of the lost business. In May 1927, Beck was able to bring together a group of men to reopen the Cronmiller and White Brewing and Malting Company Limited of Welland, Ontario. The group had plans to brew Iroquois' Indian Head Beer, "as popular in Canada as it was in Buffalo."[449] While Beck would serve as chairman, William M. German, ex-member of the Canadian Parliament for Welland, was president of the concern. The brewery was ready to start shipping on June 1, 1927.[450]

When Conrad Hammer Sr. died in 1915, his widow, two sons and attorney Robert F. Schelling were named as executors of the estate. Schelling died shortly after, and Hammer Jr.'s brother left him in charge of the estate. In 1922, the executors decided to change banks and had a check for $20,000 ($269,000) drawn up, along with new signature cards. But Hammer Jr. alone deposited the funds and made new signature cards bearing just his name. From October 7, 1924, to November 21, 1925, he proceeded to withdraw $20,500 ($275,000) for personal use. After his mother died in April 1927, the remaining executors demanded an accounting of the estate, and the fraud was discovered. Anticipating the outcome, Hammer Jr. died mysteriously of asphyxiation in his garage in March 1927 before the accounting was undertaken.[451]

Hammer had been named manager of Cronmiller and White Brewing and Malting Company Limited shortly before his death and was associated with his brothers in soft drink bottler Hammer Bottling Company, as well as multiple fraternal and social organizations.[452] He is buried in the United German and French Cemetery in Cheektowaga.

After five years of litigation, Marine Trust Company was found responsible for the fraud and forced to repay $27,346 ($466,000) to Conrad Hammer Sr.'s estate.[453]

Not seeing an end to Prohibition in sight and unable to do anything with its brewery, in August 1927, Lake View Brewing Company at 128 Lake View Avenue put its plant up for sale.[454]

Near beer could contain half of 1 percent alcohol, making it nothing more than a beer-flavored drink. Several Buffalo companies had tried to stay afloat during Prohibition by brewing near beer, including the East Buffalo Brewing Company.

When Ontario, Canada, started producing beer, including some Buffalo brands, it pretty much killed any chance the local breweries had of making money with near beer due to smuggling or consumers just traveling to Canada. In early February 1928, dry agents discovered five thousand barrels of pre-Prohibition beer worth $160,000 ($2,180,000) at the Ebbco Beverage Company, operators of East Buffalo Brewing Company at 300 Emslie Street. The company agreed to surrender its cereal beverage permit and retire from the brewing business, and the beer, all five thousand barrels of it, was destroyed.[455]

Peter Mergenhagen, one of the founders of Buffalo Cooperative Brewing Company, died on February 22, 1929. Mergenhagen, ninety-five, was a friend of Grover Cleveland before his political star rose. He owned a hotel and restaurant on Exchange Street and Michigan Avenue with his brother, operating for fifty years and purchasing much of the property in the area. He served as president, vice-president and director of the brewery over the years.

Mergenehagen was asked in 1923 what the "recipe" for old age was, and he said, "Plenty of hard work—and don't forget a little good beer also helps—that is if you can get it."[456] He deplored Prohibition and later said he

THE HISTORY OF BREWING IN THE NICKEL CITY

Buffalo Cooperative Brewing Company, circa 1897. This brewery formed after purchasing the former Hoefner Brothers brewery. In 1897, it suffered a major fire, which necessitated the building of a new brewery. *Photo from* Souvenir of Buffalo, on Occasion of the 37th Annual Convention at Buffalo, N.Y.

threw away better beer than was being sold during Prohibition. He is buried in the United German and French Cemetery in Cheektowaga and left an estate valued at $218,133 ($2,970,000).[457]

The Lang family had started several businesses to combat the loss of brewing during Prohibition and, in early April 1929, added two more. Gerhard Lang Meats and Provisions, Incorporated, and Gerhard Lang Properties, Incorporated, were both started with Jacob Gerhard Lang, Raymond E. Lang and Carlton J. Clement as the directors.[458]

Colonel John L. Schwartz—the founder of the Star, the Clinton-Star and the John L. Schwartz Brewing Companies—died in late June 1929. His last brewery was open until the start of Prohibition. Schwartz served as vice-president of the Buffalo Brewers' Exchange and was a trustee, vice-president and president of the New York State Brewers' Association. He was active in the Catholic Church and a leader in the Knights of St. John, the title colonel often added to his name. He was also a member of the Elks, Royal Arcanum and Buffalo Orpheus and was president of the Alumni of Canisius College organization. He is buried in Mount Calvary Cemetery in Cheektowaga.

In January 1924, the East Buffalo Brewing Company at 300 Emslie Street deeded its property to Albert Holding Corporation, and in June 1929, the

139

A view of the east wall of the Christian Weyand Brewing Company's cold storage facility, showing context of the surrounding building, corner of Goddell and Ellicott Streets. *Photo by Michael Rizzo.*

two companies merged to form one corporation.[459] This would become the Phoenix Brewery Corporation in 1934.

Another founder of Buffalo Cooperative Brewing Company, John Honecker, died in 1929. Honecker, who died in October, was a partner with Peter Mergenhagen in real estate transactions in Gardenville and Ebenezer, New York, and left an estate valued at over $20,000 ($268,000), primarily to his family. His son, John Jr., died just four days after his father.[460]

Like most of Buffalo's breweries, the Christian Weyand Brewing Company had closed in 1919 due to Prohibition. In 1929, the building, located at the former Trico windshield wiper plant on Washington and Ellicott Streets, was torn down. There is still a portion of the plant standing, the former icehouse, as it was incorporated into the Trico plant on Ellicott Street.

For companies that wanted to stay in business during Prohibition, there was a fine line that some of them operated on. Anecdotal stories tell of several breweries brewing low alcohol content near beer and real beer in separate vats, hoping that if an inspector showed up, he would check only the near beer.

15

THE 1930s

REBIRTH

Although the 1930s brought about the Great Depression, Prohibition ended and Buffalo breweries were angling to get permits, update their factories and prepare for the coming onslaught of demand.

Some breweries had produced other products, including liquid malt and cereal beverages, during Prohibition. In early January 1930, the federal government indicted Iroquois Beverage Corporation at 230 Pratt Street and Mohawk Products Company at Michigan and High Streets and the men said to be involved in the businesses for manufacturing liquid malt, which could be used to make real beer.[461]

Iroquois president Frank M. Beck, vice-president Edward Beck, secretary William W. Weigel and attorney and treasurer Albert Schelling, as well as Mohawk's president Albert A. Weigel and secretary and treasurer Frank G. Kager, were all charged with conspiracy to violate the national Prohibition law. The companies, in their defense, said they were within their legal right to manufacture liquid malt.[462]

In early November 1930, the judge overseeing the conspiracy to violate Prohibition case against Mohawk Products Company and Iroquois Beverage Corporation instructed the jury to declare a verdict of not guilty, saying the government never proved its case.[463]

Prohibition was destined to fail from the start, especially in cities like Buffalo, where the European population was so large. A writer from the *London Daily Mail* said that the "Peace Bridge across the Niagara River serves the national thirst better than a pipe line," and hush-hush trains

(trains crossing the river loaded with liquor) averaged more than $50,000 ($697,000) a day.[464] Moreover, while Ontario and other Canadian provinces had their own forms of prohibition, they never excluded manufacturing and effectively ended prohibition by 1927.

A large three-alarm fire swept through a seventy-foot tower at the Kreiner & Lehr malt house, 467 Spring Street, at one o'clock in the morning on November 6, 1930. William E. Kreiner estimated the damage at $100,000 ($1,390,000), mainly to the tower and barley stored in it.[465]

Frank M. Beck was born in Buffalo in 1865, the son of Magnus Beck. After his education, he joined his father and brother Edward in the brewery that bore his father's name. By the time Prohibition had become law, Beck was secretary of the brewery. With his brother Edward, he formed the Iroquois Beverage Corporation in 1922, and he was president of that concern. Beck was taken ill and died in early February 1931. He had been close friends with former mayor Frank X. Schwab and sat on several boards, including the city hospital commission and Frontier Bridge Commission. Schwab said that Beck had given more to the poor than anyone would ever know.[466] The Beck residence had been burglarized several times over the years with the same jewelry stolen both times. Beck left an estate of over $300,000 ($4,590,000) and is buried in Forest Lawn Cemetery.

George C. Ginther, retired president of the Phoenix Brewery at Washington and Virginia Streets, died on June 15, 1931. Ginther was vice-president of Erie County Savings Bank, a member of the Buffalo club and the Elks. He was seventy-five and was buried in the United German and French Cemetery in Cheektowaga.[467]

Former mayor of Buffalo and perennial mayoral candidate Frank X. Schwab began legal action in September 1931 against his former business partner in the Broadway Products Corporation, George F. Stein, for $50,000 ($754,000) and one-half interest in the Cataract Products Corporation. Prior to that, Stein had begun foreclosure proceedings against Schwab and Broadway Products Corporation. Schwab alleged that Stein started the Cataract business without him and issued additional shares of Broadway stock (including to Schwab's own son), reducing his voting rights.[468]

None of this stopped Schwab or Stein from business, though. The Frank X. Schwab Brewing Corporation, under his direction, purchased the Tonawanda Brewery in Tonawanda, New York, in December 1931 and planned to spend $20,000 ($306,000) to update the plant to manufacture liquid malt products. The brewery had been purchased in 1924 by men from Albany, New York, who had made near beer, and one story said

SCHWAB'S LIQUID MALT
Delivered in Sanitary Glass Containers

Schwab's Liquid Malt is being used in thousands of homes in Buffalo, the Tonawandas, Rochester, Niagara Falls and surrounding territory. It is manufactured in a mammoth plant at 300 Emslie Street, Buffalo, under the supervision of Frank X. Schwab, who has spent the greater portion of his life as a manufacturer of beverages. He is thoroughly conversant with the nutritious value of Malt and has approval of those who recognize the worth of its health building properties.

In the accompanying illustration, the magnitude of the plant can be gleaned, and the scrupulous methods used to furnish liquid malt that can be relied upon for its sanitation and the healthfulness of the product.

As Soon as Alterations are Completed in Our Local Plant, Schwab's Liquid Malt Will be Manufactured in The Tonawandas.

Where the sanitary containers are cleaned.

Not a germ remains after the sterilizing process.

Your Local Dealer Is

WM. E. KILLEWALD

209 Delaware St.
Tonawanda

Phone Tonawanda 1499

Sanitary method used in filling 5-gallon glass containers with Schwab's Liquid Malt.

Storage House and Office
former

Tonawanda Brewery

Niagara Street,
Tonawanda

Phone Tonawanda 685

The final spraying of the filled container before packing.

Schwab's Liquid Malt packed in cartons ready for shipment.

Buffalo mayor Frank X. Schwab ran the Tonawanda Brewery on Niagara Street in Tonawanda. During Prohibition, it sold liquid malt to consumers. They just had to add yeast and they could brew beer at home, undated. *Photo from* Tonawanda News.

that trucks from the brewery rumbled through the streets at night to the railroad yards.[469]

The Schwab company then purchased the former East Buffalo Brewing Company plant at 300 Emslie Street. "Considerable sums" were spent to update the plants, anticipating the end of Prohibition. The liquid malt that Schwab sold was nearly beer, all it needed was yeast, so when the deliveryman dropped the malt off, he also added liquid yeast, and individuals could have homemade beer, almost legally.[470]

George F. Stein must have seen the writing on the wall when it came to Prohibition ending. The tide was turning across the country, and Stein wanted to be ready, so in 1931, with his son George C., he purchased the former Broadway Brewing and Malting Company at 797–807 (formerly 815) Broadway; formed the George F. Stein Brewery, Incorporated; and waited for the Great Experiment to end.[471]

Philip G. Schaefer, former president of the Lake View Brewing Company started by his father, died on May 15, 1932, at seventy years old. Born in Buffalo on May 29, 1862, he attended Canisius College and Bryant & Stratton Business College before joining his father, Alois, in the brewery. Schaefer had been involved in numerous civic, political, charitable and fraternal organizations, including the Buffalo Launch Club (of which he was commodore) and the board of visitors at Buffalo State Hospital.[472] He is buried in the United German and French Cemetery in Cheektowaga.

Another Buffalo brewer died in 1932, Philip Bartholomay, son of a Rochester, New York brewer. He came to Buffalo in 1902 to join the Iroquois Brewing Company as treasurer, the same position he had held at the Bartholomay Brewing Company in Rochester, and continued in that position until Prohibition, at which time he retired. Bartholomay, who was seventy-six years old, left an estate based on a patent claim for long-distance telephone service of $300,000 ($5,120,000).[473] He is buried in Mount Hope Cemetery in Rochester, New York.

In early December 1932, former mayor Frank X. Schwab, president of Frank X. Schwab Brewing Corporation, confident that Prohibition would be repealed, prepared his two breweries by offering stock in his corporation. The combined Tonawanda, New York and 300 Emslie Street breweries could produce 125,000 barrels of beer per year. The initial stock offering suggested the numbers were conservative, and Schwab anticipated a swell of business.[474]

Simon Mergenhagen, who, with his father and others, started the Buffalo Cooperative Brewing Company in 1880, died in late January 1933.

Mergenhagen, who had been secretary of the brewery until Prohibition, was seventy-six years old and is buried in the United German and French Cemetery in Cheektowaga.[475]

Prohibition, the failed temperance experiment, was repealed by nineteen states. By mid-March 1933, in New York, with the state legislature working on legislation in case it was repealed, the Buffalo Brewers' Exchange was re-formed, with William W. Weigel chosen as its first president. The organization was vastly different than before Prohibition, with only Lang's, Schreiber's, Mohawk, Iroquois, Broadway, Magnus Beck and Simon left from Buffalo. Now included were Fred Koch Brewery of Dunkirk, Frank X. Schwab Brewing Corporation of Tonawanda, Cataract of Niagara Falls, Tonawanda Brewery and two Olean firms.[476]

One of the Olean firms was Empire State Brewery, in which John Montana, William F. Schwartz and other Buffalo men were involved.[477] Montana, it would come out in 1958, attended the infamous mafia gathering in Apalachin, New York, in 1957 and is believed to have been the secret underboss to Stefano Magaddino while he was also serving as a Buffalo city councilman.

One of Lockport's well-known breweries, the Downs Brewing Company on Van Buren Street, was purchased in April 1933 by Buffalonian Frederick J. Munn. The brewery had been known for its fine beer until Prohibition shut it down, during which time ice cream was manufactured in the former brewery. With Prohibition ending, Munn installed new equipment and prepared the brewery to begin brewing once more. The new company would be named Van Buren Products Company, Incorporated, with beer produced under the Downs name.[478]

The German-American Brewing Company (which had gone bankrupt prior to Prohibition and sold its facility) was revived and purchased the former John L. Schwartz Brewing Company at 10–20 West Bennett Street in November 1933. Under the guidance of brewmaster and vice-president Conrad Haberstrumph, the company planned to spend $700,000 ($12,600,000) to update the facility to be "the most modern brewery between New York and Chicago." Arthur W. Kistner was president and treasurer, and Alfred W. Sudrow was secretary of the company. It was a reorganization of the Maltosia Products Company, which had produced "Eagle Liquid Malt" during Prohibition.[479]

The father-and-son Stein brewery team was ready when Prohibition ended in 1933. They had purchased the former Broadway Brewing and Malting Company in 1931, renamed it the George F. Stein Brewery, Incorporated, and immediately updated the machinery and began beer production.[480]

Stein's would produce Pilsener Beer, Dry Hop Ale and Canadian Brand Cream Ale, among others.

The tide against Prohibition was growing, and on March 22, 1933, the Cullen-Harrison Act was signed by President Franklin D. Roosevelt, authorizing the sale of 3.2 percent beer (thought to be too low an alcohol concentration to be intoxicating) and wine. Meanwhile, states considered the Twenty-first Amendment, which would repeal the Eighteenth Amendment, thereby ending Prohibition.[481] Iroquois Beverage Corporation, the only Buffalo brewery that held on to its cereal beverage permit, was able to begin bottling the night before. Company president William W. Weigel and general manager William Schramm were in charge of the operation. The first case of beer came off the Iroquois conveyor at 12:01 a.m. and was personally delivered to Buffalo mayor Charles Roesch. Unfortunately, his home was dark, so the delivery had to wait until the following day.

Weigel would not allow one case of beer to leave the plant until after midnight, when the law went into effect, but the trucks were quickly filled. Lang's and Iroquois had already taken hundreds of orders for beer, but the demand was so great that, on April 10, 1933, Iroquois placed an ad in the *Buffalo Courier-Express* thanking Buffalonians for demanding its beer, but it could not make beer fast enough to supply everyone who wanted to buy it. Iroquois knew it would need a better delivery system and purchased a large fleet of Buffalo-built Stewart Motor Corporation delivery trucks, keeping the money local.[482]

The 3.2 percent alcohol content irked some brewers, who vowed to brew pre-Prohibition alcohol of 6 or 7 percent. But Anthony Schreiber, president of A. Schreiber Brewing Company, debunked that, saying, "Analysis of 30 well known brands of beer of pre-war days showed none to exceed 4 percent."[483] That is why brews such as lager were considered "non-intoxicating."

Schreiber, anticipating the amendment being repealed, began updating the equipment at his brewery around the beginning of 1933. He was granted a permit to manufacture beer in June and assured customers that by July 1, 1933, Manru and Kloster beers would be available for purchase.[484] Some customers later complained that their beer tasted like coffee.

The William Simon Brewery was ready to begin production and reorganized its board in May 1933. The board had been in continuous operation during Prohibition, to the point of providing $12,000 ($216,000) annual salaries for Gerhard, William J. Simon and Joseph G. Schaff. Schaff had been employed by the company since 1891, and when the business was incorporated in 1908, he was made treasurer. When the company

1842   1933

APPRECIATION
and APOLOGY to BUFFALO
from IROQUOIS

A Message from W. W. Weigel

"WE want Iroquois!" By phone, telegraph, letters and personal call literally tens of thousands have expressed that desire within the past few days. And how we wish we could have made all of you happy!

But if each of us at the Iroquois had a dozen hands—if our brewing capacity had been multiplied ten-fold—if it were possible to answer the thousands of calls that jammed our telephone lines — even then we could not have answered the overwhelming demand for Iroquois Beer...

Our single regret is our inability to supply everyone quickly. But, if you have not been able to reach us, if your order is unfilled, if we have seemed impatient or hurried, we know you'll understand...

Appreciative Buffalo, for the moment, has simply swamped us. But soon we expect to be in a position to take care of our many good friends who are bearing with us so patiently.

Naturally, we're proud of the tribute Buffalo has paid us... in remembering so well the pre-prohibition superiority of Iroquois Indian Head Beer. Equally gratifying is the proof that we were right in deciding that some day beer would be restored to the nation, and that we should keep our brewery active, clean, intact, and modern, so that we could be ready for Buffalo's call.

We are conscious, too, of our good fortune in being able to participate in a program which will give employment to hundreds of our fellow citizens and put millions of dollars to work in Buffalo.

"Is Iroquois Beer as good as it used to be?" Doubtless you've wondered; so let us free your mind of all question. Made under the same formula, by exclusive processes that have been handed down from generation to generation... with the advantage of the newest and most modern equipment, Iroquois of today is even better than ever before. You'll find it even more delicious in every respect, and just as satisfying as when it was the choice of the connoisseur in Buffalo's finest hotels, restaurants, clubs and homes.

You who drink Iroquois, may depend upon it being of the highest possible quality always... brewed and lagered in the most scientific and sanitary manner known to the art. We intend to keep Iroquois, not only Buffalo's finest brew; but as fine as there is in the nation!

President

IROQUOIS BEVERAGE CORPORATION
212-256 Pratt Street, Buffalo, N. Y.

Iroquois
INDIAN HEAD BEER
UNCHANGED WITH THE PASSING OF YEARS

Demand for beer after Prohibition was so great that Iroquois Brewing could not make it fast enough. The company placed an ad in the *Buffalo Courier-Express* on April 10, 1933, apologizing to its customers. *Photo from* Buffalo Courier-Express.

To Our Friends and Neighbors in Buffalo and Western New York State

GREETINGS

IN answer to thousands of inquiries by mail, telephone and personal meetings, we make the public announcement that SIMON PURE BEER will again be on the market and ready for our many friends and customers when certain important situations are worked out.

SIMON PURE BEER was not available on April seventh for two reasons which we frankly present, realizing that our many former patrons are entitled to know our position.

(1) Our brewery, located at 143 Emslie Street, Buffalo, New York, has been under lease for an extended period, and under the terms of this lease we have been unable to take possession for a period of sixty days after the President of the United States signed by the President of the United States. We are happy to state that the machinery and equipment is in good condition and with some modernizing repairs and improvements we will be ready to distribute a brew which will be the equal of the finely flavored quality SIMON PURE beer which we first offered our customers 41 years ago (1892) under the William Simon name. The same master brew which William Simon offered as brewmaster under the predecessor name of John Schueler which brewery was established in 1859. Seventy-four years ago the brew known to Buffalo in 1919 as SIMON PURE BEER was first offered to cheer. The friendly glass of fellowship is not to be only a recollection of the past but will shortly return to bring back the memories and sentiments of yesterday.

(2) The repairs and improvements and necessary distributing equipment and essential free working capital mean cash which is not currently available. For 41 years this business has been entirely owned in the Simon family but following the modern corporate procedure we propose to shortly offer our friends and the public, an invitation to join with us in the ownership of this business, on a basis which will be consistent with the fair trade policy which has always governed our practices. This business has always been profitable as recorded in credit establishments. We have consistently made substantial profits, without exception, through the many long years of our brewing activity.

Partial customer ownership and public participation in part of these profits seems the sensible thing to do, and after much consideration of this matter we propose to follow the policy of modern business and divide the ownership of our business with a new and larger group of people, thus keeping our plant and equipment unchattled and our profit expectations unhampered by fixed charges of any character. We have made the simple determination to "cooperatively" divide profits among stockholders rather than to inaugurate a policy of paying interest and carrying charges on mortgages or bonds. By such a plan all fixed assets will be, as now, free and clear of any encumbrances.

This announcement is obviously the forerunner of an offering of participation in this old established business in the new day of our opportunity.

THE WILLIAM SIMON BREWERY

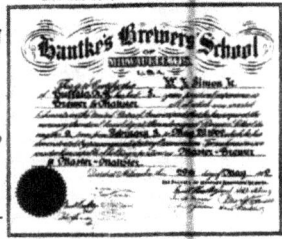

The William Simon Brewery, after surviving Prohibition, needed money to update and repair its brewery, so it sold stock to the public. The family owned 500,000 shares, and 250,000 were sold. This was the general offering notice the company had printed. *Photo from* Buffalo Courier-Express.

met to prepare to ramp up production, Schaff was appointed treasurer and chairman of the board.[485]

But the Simon building and brewing equipment were not ready for production and were in need of repair and updating. To raise the needed capital, the company issued 750,000 shares of stock. The Simon family held

500,000 shares, and 250,000 shares were sold to the public. In May 1933, a new board of directors was elected with William J. Simon as president, Gilbert W. Klink as vice-president and general manager, Joseph G. Schaff as treasurer and Gerhard J. Simon as secretary.[486]

In early 1933, William L. Moffat passed away, and the end of the Moffat brewery empire was thought to be over. But after the repeal of Prohibition, one of the beers that reappeared was Moffat's Ale. This was curious, since none of the Moffat family was involved. A charter was issued in September 1933 to attorney Henry J. Rengel, who had been the manager of the brewery from 1882 until the onset of Prohibition (and treasurer of the flour mills), and attorney James T. Driscoll. Rengel had also been the executor of Henry C. Moffat's estate after his death in 1922. The duo purchased the former East Buffalo Brewing Company at 300 Emslie Street from the Frank X. Schwab Brewing Corporation and renamed it Phoenix Brewery Corporation (not to be confused with the former Phoenix Brewery, started by Albert Ziegele Sr., but maybe to confuse consumers of the day) with the goal of producing the exact same Moffat's Ale, pale ale, cream and stock beers from pre-Prohibition days. Thus, it was one of few breweries producing ales at the time.

To further confuse matters, Cyril F. Ginther was elected president of the newly formed brewery. Ginther had been treasurer at the Phoenix Brewery on Washington Street, which had been run by his father, George C. Ginther, until Prohibition closed its doors. John H. Schenk was vice-president, Raymond G. Danahy was secretary and Charles A. Buerk was treasurer.[487]

Former Buffalo mayor and brewery executive Frank X. Schwab had applied for a permit to manufacture beer at the former East Buffalo Brewing Company at 300 Emslie Street, which was granted in early June 1933. The problem was he had since sold the property to the Phoenix Brewery Corporation after financial woes hobbled his start-up. Schwab originally did not sell enough stock to finance the business, but by late July 1933, he had found New York City investors to back the project and expected beer to be flowing from his other brewery in Tonawanda, New York, by September 1933.[488] Prohibition may have been over, but some of the players were still struggling to find their way.

December 5, 1933, was a glorious day in the United States as the Twenty-first Amendment to the United States Constitution was ratified when Utah became the thirty-sixth state to approve it. New York was the ninth state to ratify it on June 27, 1933. Prohibition and the Great Experiment were officially over. Beer was free to flow once again, and more Buffalo breweries wanted in on the action.

Also in December 1933, Depew, New York businessman John B. Konsek Sr. was granted a license to operate a new brewery, Great Lakes Brewing Company (at the former Lake View Brewing Company on Lake View Avenue). The Phoenix Brewery Corporation at 300 Emslie Street was also granted a license to start beer production once again.

The German-American Brewing Company, which had had high hopes of reliving pre-Prohibition glory, closed in 1934, less than a year after reopening. The property was sold in March 1935.[489]

With Prohibition over, Americans were ready for legal beer. The William Simon Brewery was ready to supply the thirsty Buffalonians and produced record output in 1934. But that was overshadowed by the fact that there was a bitter internal battle for control of the brewery. Although the Simon family controlled 500,000 of the 750,000 shares of stock outstanding, nothing was guaranteed. In 1934, William J. Simon was ousted as president of the board and replaced by Gilbert W. Klink. Arthur T. Danahy became chairman; Joseph G. Schaff was replaced as treasurer by James F. Austin and Gerhard J. Simon rose from secretary to vice-president.

The complaints were that profits weren't high enough, even though they had high start-up costs associated with reopening. William J. Simon, former president, said that his brother Gerhard, vice-president, had used his own stock as collateral on a loan, and William believed Gerhard had forfeited the stock. Early in 1934, Gerhard lined up enough votes (including his sister, whose husband was Sylvester B. Eagan) to take over the board from William. When the annual meeting took place in May 1935, William was able to regain his position as president of the company.[490]

One of the reasons Gilbert W. Klink was ousted was because he had used company funds to support his reelection, which was seen as a no-no by many shareholders.[491] Another stock battle occurred in 1940, but William J. Simon prevailed, and a Simon heir never lost the seat again.

George J. Weckerle, best known as a local dairyman, was hired by Cyril F. Ginther, president of the Phoenix Brewery Corporation, in February 1934 and promoted to general manager in April 1934.[492]

After Prohibition ended, the government wanted better controls to monitor and tax the breweries. U-permits were one aspect added but were dropped after a year; another control was government-installed meters in the breweries so accurate taxing could be done. The A. Schreiber Brewing Company at 662 Fillmore Avenue was the first in Buffalo to get the meters.[493]

The George F. Stein Brewery, Incorporated, in an effort to attract more business from Niagara County, decided to open "Lockport's only electrically refrigerated beer warehouse" in late June 1935. Its goal was to manufacture, transport and store its beer and ale refrigerated at all times, so no loss of quality would occur. That same year, George F. Stein Sr. announced that he was retiring after many years in the brewing business.[494]

Joseph G. Schaff, sixty-six, manager of the William Simon Brewery, died in early 1935. Schaff was born in April 1868 in Buffalo and, after school, became a salesman. For many years, he was employed by the Barnes, Hengerer Company, but in 1893, he married William Simon's daughter Julie and not long after was hired by his father-in-law. He worked at the brewery as treasurer and manager.[495]

William J. Simon sued his brother Gerhard J., president of the firm, in order to collect on promissory notes. Gerhard said he was fraudulently induced to invest in the Copeland Brewing Company, Limited, in Toronto during Prohibition. William was able to get a default judgment for $20,975 ($356,000) and wanted Gerhard's equity in the Simon brewery sold to satisfy the judgment.[496] That never happened, but the brothers would feud on and off, including a stock battle for control of the brewery in 1940.

In 1935, the Tonawanda Brewery that Frank X. Schwab had owned and where he made liquid malt at the end of Prohibition, was sold to a group that renamed it Frontier Brewing Company.[497] The company would brew Premium Beer, Malz-Brau Ale and Gold Label Ale. That was the end of Schwab's interest in breweries.

In March 1933, Henry J. Rengel, the manager of Moffat's Brewery prior to Prohibition, had attempted to get written authority to reproduce Moffat beer and use the Moffat name from Alice Moffat Bentley. Although that did not succeed, he co-founded the Phoenix Brewery Corporation and Moffat's Ale Brewery, Incorporated, at 300 Emslie Street and began producing Moffat beers with recipes from before Prohibition. In 1936, the heirs of Henry L. Moffat sued the corporation to prevent them from profiting off the Moffat name.[498]

In late January 1935, Rengel, who was thought to be the only person to know the beer recipes, sold his stock in Moffat's Ale Brewery Incorporated to attorney James T. Driscoll, another founder, and was no longer employed by the company. This was only about six months after his employment began. Driscoll then sold the stock to the Phoenix Brewery Corporation and continued selling the beer under the Phoenix name.[499] The suit would play out in the courts for several years.

The William Simon Brewery profit jumped 80 percent in 1935, with sales of $1,846,538 ($31,300,000), gross profit was up and William J. Simon said the plant was being updated to handle more product.[500]

A full-page ad for the William Simon Brewery touting three generations of brewing experience. *Photo from* Buffalo Courier-Express.

Buffalo breweries were always trying to outdo one another, whether it was with a garden restaurant (German-American), an ornate building (Lang) or original artwork (Schreiber). The A. Schreiber Brewing Company commissioned Danish artist Johannes Nielsen in 1936 to decorate its second-story mural room. What it received was a series of murals depicting the history of beer. These six murals depicted Egypt, Louis Pasteur, Emil Christian Hansen and others. The artwork has since been moved off site and is being restored.

The son of the founder of the Voetsch and Clinton-Star Breweries, William E. Voetsch Jr., died in late May 1936. Voetsch, seventy-three, worked in his father's breweries for several years before he ventured into real estate in 1886, purchased land and founded Edgewater Park in Grand Island, New York. There he built a picnic ground and hotel. In 1892, the hotel burned but was rebuilt. Voetsch Jr. continued to manage the hotel until his death.[501]

Philip L. Haberstro, son of Joseph L. Haberstro, died in late June 1936. Haberstro had studied at a brewing college in Bavaria before joining his father in J.L. Haberstro & Company. He served as a superintendent in the New York State Forestry Department and was instrumental in founding Adirondack State Park. He was also a founder of the original Buffalo Athletic Club and had invented some brewing equipment. He was eighty years old.[502]

The Iroquois Beverage Corporation, headed by William W. Weigel, had purchased the former Buffalo Cooperative Brewing Company on Michigan and High Streets in 1920 at the start of Prohibition. It was closed in 1936, after brewing Iroquois Ale for three years but would reopen as a brewery again.[503]

The Phoenix Brewery Corporation registered a trademark in September 1937 for "Phoenix Old German" for a type of beer it produced. It was subsequently sued by the Gerhard Lang Brewery, Incorporated, for $100,000 ($1,620,000), claiming it had been using "Old German" since 1900. Ultimately, in April 1939, Lang won the case but no monetary damages, and Phoenix was forced to stop using the name, the judge stating that Phoenix was competing unfairly.[504]

In April 1937, more than six hundred brewery workers—members of the drivers', bottlers' and brewers' unions—received $3.00-per-week ($48.70) raises after negotiations with the breweries.[505]

The founder of George F. Stein Brewery, Incorporated, died on October 9, 1938, just three years after retiring from active business. George F. Stein Sr. ran several breweries over the years and was a master brewer himself. He was a member of the Elks, the Boreal Club and the Old German Society. Stein was seventy-three years old at the time of his death.[506] He is buried in Mount Calvary Cemetery in Cheektowaga.

One of Stein's contemporaries also died in 1938, Anthony Schreiber. The founder of A. Schreiber Brewing Company at 652 Fillmore Avenue passed away on November 9, 1938, at his home in East Aurora, New York. The seventy-four-year-old president of the brewery was responsible for establishing Polish libraries and preserving Polish culture and was a censor of the Polish National Alliance. His home, known as the Lilacs, was featured in periodicals. Schreiber did substantial work to the property during his ownership.[507]

Schreiber "never ceased to take a living interest in the welfare and history of his native land, and he is a representative figure in the movement to bring about unity among Polish-Americans."[508] He was a member of various social organizations and Supreme Master of the Polish National Alliance.

During the late 1920s, several mega brewers experimented with canning near beer for the first time. When Prohibition ended, Pabst Brewing Company was the first mega brewer to begin canning its beer. In Buffalo, bottling beer was still the norm, but with the advent of this new, cheaper and lighter form of storage, Iroquois Beverage Corporation became the first Buffalo brewery to can its beer in the late 1930s. It canned its Indian Head Beer and Ale.[509]

The Downs Brewing Company of Lockport took over the former John L. Schwartz Brewing Company (and later German-American Brewing Company) at 10–20 West Bennett Street in Buffalo in 1939, where it would begin production of beer for distribution in Buffalo.

The Frontier Brewing Company in Tonawanda, owned since 1935 by Klocke & Deckop, was sold to Julius C. Belzer in 1939. Belzer, both president and secretary of the firm, was son of Buffalo brewer Charles W. Belzer and grandson of Julius Binz (both of Broadway Brewing and Malting Company). They had four different brewmasters at the brewery during his ownership, and the company's most popular beer was Malzbrau.[510]

16
THE 1940s

Usher in New Growth

T he 1940s brought about more challenges for the brewing industry. With World War II, rationing, strikes and increased competition from mega brewers, Buffalo breweries had to continue to evolve or die.

In 1940, the New York State Liquor Authority charged the Beck, Phoenix and Lang breweries with using practices that influenced retailers. All three breweries would lose their licenses if they could not explain the practices of helping saloon owners get into business and subsidizing their rent, among other things. This allowed the breweries to control saloons and what products they served in the saloons. Often, the proprietor would be in debt to the brewery, but as kegs were sold, a portion went toward the rent. The Beck and Phoenix breweries pleaded guilty to making gifts and providing illegal services to retailers, but the charges against Lang were dropped.[511]

Gerhard J. "Garry" Simon was reelected treasurer of the William Simon Brewery in 1941 after a five-year absence to pursue other goals.[512]

Three brewery-related unions and one thousand workers were ready to walk off the job in early June 1941, but a strike was averted. A six-dollar-per-week wage increase was agreed to by the nine breweries of the Buffalo Brewers' Exchange to avoid the strike, which would have affected 1,500 taverns and 1,000 stores, as well as thousands of consumers. The breweries affected were Iroquois, William Simon, Downs, Schreiber, Lang, Phoenix, George F. Stein, Magnus Beck and Frontier of Tonawanda.[513]

Four Buffalo breweries lost their licenses in June 1941 after violating the New York ABC liquor control laws. A. Schreiber Brewing Company, William

Simon Brewery, Van Buren Products Company, Incorporated, and George F. Stein Brewery, Incorporated, had to pay fines for their illegal dealing with retailers in order to renew their licenses.[514]

It is believed that Iroquois Beverage Corporation was about to release its Half & Half porter/ale in cans when, in May 1942, the canning of beer for civilian use was ended in order to save metal for the war effort. The company scrapped the unused cans.

With a scrap metal campaign begun in September 1942 to aid in the war effort, the George F. Stein Brewery, Incorporated, contributed to the effort by sending large metal gates from its plant at 797 Broadway.[515]

The former Buffalo Cooperative Brewing Company at Michigan Avenue and High Street, owned by the Iroquois Beverage Corporation and closed in 1936, was razed to save taxes in June 1942. Not all was lost, though. A six-thousand-pound copper brewing vat was used for the defense effort, and "several hundred thousand bricks" were used in the defense housing project adjacent to Kenfield. It covered an acre and a half.[516]

Most breweries saw the importance of advertising and sponsorships—from bowling, softball and baseball teams to television and radio shows. The George F. Stein Brewery, Incorporated, sponsored Stein's Korn Kobblers, a "daffy musical unit" that was known for its twice-weekly radio shows.[517]

"Without warning in the summer of 1943,"[518] Frontier Brewing Company in Tonawanda announced it was stopping all deliveries to local businesses to concentrate on the contract it had received to supply the United States armed forces during World War II. Frontier's beer had been widely enjoyed in Tonawanda. For the war effort, "substitute ingredients"—including yam syrup—were used, the aging time was shortened and the quality had deteriorated to the point that it was not popular with the servicemen.[519] Consequently, its local reputation probably also suffered.

In 1944, the canning of beer in olive drab cans (made so they would not reflect on the battlefield) for military use began. Thirty-five larger breweries spread around the country were chosen to can beer for the military. Iroquois canned Iroquois Beer and Ale with an olive drab J-spout during World War II.[520]

"Buffalo's oldest brewmaster, in age and years of service, Gustav Braun,"[521] died on July 14, 1944. Braun was born in Germany and came to Buffalo in 1890. He was a master brewer for fifty-four years, including at Broadway Brewing and Malting Company, Buffalo Cooperative Brewing Company and the final fifteen years with Iroquois Beverage Corporation. Braun had served as president of the Western New York Brewmasters'

A Case of Beer FREE

when you BUY A BOND at the

BUFFALO BREWERS WAR BOND RALLY

LAFAYETTE SQUARE

Tuesday, June 19, 1945
12:00 to 1:00 P. M.

You Can't Lose--Here's Why

1. A case of beer will be given FREE to every purchaser.

2. By buying a Bond, you may WIN A BOND to be given away to the holders of lucky numbers.

PEPPY MUSIC   **GOOD ENTERTAINMENT**
DON'T MISS THE FUN!

BUFFALO BREWERS' ASSOCIATION

Magnus Beck Brewing Co., Inc.	Phoenix Brewery Corp.
Downs Brewery	Schreiber Brewing Co., Inc.
Iroquois Beverage Corp.	Wm. Simon Brewery
Gerhard Lang Brewery	Geo. F. Stein Brewery

BUY, BUY WAR BONDS-BYE, BYE JAPAN

During World War II, the sale of war bonds was instrumental in raising funds for the war effort. In June 1945, the Buffalo Brewers' Association held a rally at Lafayette Square to sell war bonds and gave a free case of beer with each sale. *Photo from* Buffalo Courier-Express.

Association and was vice-president of the national association. He was a member of various organizations and, at his death, was seventy-three years old.[522]

When the United States was thrust into World War II, everyone became patriotic. The war caused rationing on all kinds of goods, from meat and gasoline to metals. There were often war bond drives to help raise funds for the effort. Buffalo brewers (George F. Stein, Magnus Beck, Schreiber, Iroquois, Lang and Downs) did their part in late June 1945 when they sponsored a rally at Lafayette Square. To entice sales, the companies offered a free case of beer to every purchaser, held a drawing for a bond and had music and other entertainment. Five hundred Buffalonians turned out to get their free cases of beer and war bonds. The breweries and their employees raised $218,670 ($2,790,000), with the William Simon Brewery and employees raising the most at $64,000 ($816,000).[523]

In 1933, the Downs Brewing Company on Van Buren Street in Lockport, New York, became Van Buren Products Company, Incorporated, when Frederick Munn purchased the closed brewery. In 1939, the company had purchased the former John L. Schwartz Brewing Company at 10 West Bennett Street in Buffalo. The principal stockholder was Leo Potter, who, in July 1946, became chairman of the board. Beer produced under the Downs brand included Arf and Arf (a triple-aged blend of beer and ale), Special India Pale Ale, a lager beer, Bock Beer and a cream ale.[524]

Potter had come to Buffalo from New York City in 1942 to run the brewery. The well-known businessman and financier died in January 1947 at fifty-three years old, months after assuming chairmanship of the company. The growth of the Downs brand was credited to "his ability as a merchandiser and financier."[525]

William Schramm, assistant secretary and general manager of Iroquois Beverage Corporation, died in early July 1946 at seventy-two years old. Schramm was born in Buffalo and began as a bottle washer at the Christian Weyand Brewery, eventually rising to office manager until Prohibition. In 1932, Schramm joined Iroquois Beverage Corporation as general manager and was later appointed assistant secretary.[526] He is buried in Forest Lawn Cemetery.

When the war ended in 1946, breweries were once again allowed to begin packaging their beer in cans.

The Frontier Brewing Company at 533 South Niagara Street in Tonawanda had ceased local sales to concentrate on sales to the military during the war. After the war, it tried to regain what it had lost during the war but never could gain traction. A small sales peak during an artificial shortage in 1946 was its only spotlight. Various factors, including labor costs, mismanagement and most likely the sub-par beer it was brewing, led to the company's closing in 1947, ending decades of brewing at the facility.[527]

William J. Simon, president of the Simon brewery, announced in 1947 that the brewery would expand over a five-year period.[528] Some of the popular

The William Simon Brewery on Clinton and Emslie Streets was the last brewery to close in Buffalo. This is a rare, circa 1910s Simon Pure tray. *Photo by Chris Groves, from the collection of Dave Mik.*

brands the brewery produced were Maltina Vitaminada, Pure Export Beer, Pure Bock Beer, Old Abbey Ale, Pure Ale and Pure Ale Extra Pale.

In June 1947, William W. Weigel, president of Iroquois Beverage Corporation, announced the company was purchasing the Downs Brewing Company at 10 West Bennett Street from Van Buren Products Company, Incorporated. Under the purchase agreement, the Downs brand name would be discontinued and the plant would be leased to become Iroquois Plant Number Two, which increased its output by 100,000 barrels per year. Shortly after, Iroquois announced a modernization program, with plans to increase production to 300,000 barrels per year. It planned to spend $1,000,000 ($10,400,000) to enlarge its brewery at 230 Pratt Street and add a new brewhouse and two new bottling lines.[529]

In 1947, president and founder of the Wm. E. Kreiner & Sons, Incorporated malting company, William E. Kreiner Sr., died at age ninety. He was a lifelong Republican and served on the common council in 1900.

After his death, his sons William Jr. and Howard ran the business. William was "prominent in the promotion of the malting industry nationally" and was a fifty-year member of the Master Brewers' Association.[530] He is buried in Forest Lawn Cemetery.

In April 1948, the Brewery Workers' Union went out on strike, closing the eight Buffalo breweries of the Buffalo Brewers' Exchange while negotiations over higher wages were discussed.[531]

The A. Schreiber Brewing Company installed a new $300,000 ($2,900,000) addition to the plant at 662 Fillmore Avenue with a state-of-the-art bottling line in March 1948. Company president Joseph R. Schwindler said a total of 255 bottles per minute had been added to the output of the shop.[532]

The Copeland Brewing Company in Toronto, Ontario, which William J. Simon and partners had reopened during Prohibition, was sold to Labatt Breweries, Limited, in 1946 because "it was a good business move."[533]

The Gerhard Lang Brewery at 400 Best Street was, without a doubt, one of Buffalo's most successful breweries prior to the start of Prohibition. On January 15, 1949, company president Jacob Gerhard Lang announced that the brewery was shutting down for good, without providing a reason for the closing. The brewery became the second of the post-Prohibition breweries to shutter its doors. The other businesses Lang started during Prohibition, Lang's Bakery, Incorporated, Hyan Dry Soft Drinks and Lang's Creamery, Incorporated, were not immediately affected.[534] Lang's produced multiple brands of beer over the years, including Liberty Brew, Lang's Beer, Old German Brand Beer, Percolated Beer, Tru-Keg Beer, Tru-Keg Ale, Bohemian Type Beer, Crown Ale, Genuine Pale Ale, Premium Beer, Horse Head Pale Ale, Horse Head Dry Hopped Ale, Horse Head Pale Beer, Old Bounty Beer and Buffalo Beer.

Just a few months into 1949, another Buffalo brewery would begin its demise. The Schreiber family sold the A. Schreiber Brewing Company at 662 Fillmore Avenue to a group headed by Guy H. Lovelace for an undisclosed amount. All the associates were brewery experts and Lovelace was the president of the new company. Cornelia Schreiber Haley, Anthony's daughter, was also on the board. Lovelace had the Schreiber beer and ale lab tested for quality and said it would stand up against any in the country.[535]

To celebrate its fiftieth anniversary, Schreiber produced a special beer to mark the occasion, Manru Golden Anniversary. The company produced special patches with the new logo for the employees to wear and for the bowling team it sponsored that year.[536]

A period ad for the Schreiber Brewing Company on Fillmore Avenue for its Manru Golden Anniversary Beer and Ale. It would close shortly after. *Photo from* Buffalo Courier-Express.

A strike by United Brewery Workers in April 1949 left taverns and delis struggling for supply. The walkout included truck drivers, bottlers, brewers and garage maintenance workers. The George F. Stein Brewery, Incorporated, was not affiliated with the unions and was thus unaffected but probably stressed.[537]

The former president of the Phoenix Brewery Corporation at 300 Emslie Street and treasurer of the Phoenix Brewery at 851 Washington Street, Cyril F. Ginther, died on June 6, 1949, at sixty-six years of age. At the time of his death, Ginther was trustee and, like his father, senior vice-president of Erie County Savings Bank. He had also been a director of Third National Bank of Buffalo. He left an estate valued at $159,970 ($1,540,000) and is buried in the United German and French Cemetery in Cheektowaga.[538]

THE 1950s

THE DECLINE OF REGIONAL BREWERIES

The 1950s brought new challenges for local manufacturing. With the world war over, the Cold War began and manufacturing costs for local businesses started increasing. It was a time when mega corporations were shipping beer (and many other products) to Buffalo for less than it cost the local companies to produce theirs. Sometimes, people think nostalgically about the old breweries, but oftentimes they complain that the local companies did not produce good beer. So why buy OK local beer when you can buy OK cheaper beer from a mega brewer?

After the end of World War II, Buffalo breweries hoped to see a resurgence in sales, but for the A. Schreiber Brewing Company, even the installation of a $300,000 ($2,930,000) bottling line, new owners and celebration of the company's fiftieth anniversary were not enough. On August 7, 1950, the company became the third of the post-Prohibition class to file for voluntary bankruptcy protection. In early October 1950, the plant was sold for a paltry $90,200 ($873,000), which included a $218,000 ($2,110,000) mortgage.[539] The brewery would not reopen.

The stealth purchaser of the Schreiber brewery was a man named Nathan Benderson. He had a portion of the brewery dismantled and sold the metal for scrap. This would be one of his first purchases and would lead to one of the largest portfolios of real estate holdings in several states.[540]

The Iroquois Beverage Corporation was the market leader in Buffalo for years. Sometime after 1950, it began producing five different cans for its beers. In 1952, it produced 500,000 barrels of beer, employed 550 men and,

The remains of the Iroquois Brewery on Pratt Street. The buildings remaining were largely office space or for packaging, as buildings purposed for brewing and malting operations were generally harder to repurpose. *Photo by Michael Rizzo.*

through the 1950s, 40 percent of all beer drank in Buffalo was said to be from Iroquois. In addition, the company produced more than its four biggest competitors in Buffalo combined.[541]

In April 1952, Canadian grocery chain Loblaws opened the largest store in its chain on property the Gerhard Lang Brewery once occupied after it had acquired the former Lang's Bakery, Incorporated, and used that for bakery production for its local supermarkets.[542]

The George F. Stein Brewery, Incorporated, had been in production since 1933, when Prohibition was repealed, but one thing it had not done was can its beer. In 1952, it began canning its Stein's Ale, Stein's Beer, two Canandaigua beers and a Canadian cream ale. Beer can collecting is a rather large hobby, and there are several known variations of the Stein's cans.[543]

A group of Detroit-based businessmen formed International Breweries, Incorporated (IBI), in 1955 and purchased breweries in Frankenmuth, Michigan; Findaly, Ohio; Tampa, Florida; and Covington, Kentucky. Termed a "combine" by then IBI president Bruce Berckmans, he said that each brewery would keep its local identity. In mid-1955, William W. Weigel, president of Iroquois Beverage Corporation at 230 Pratt Street, announced the company was being sold to IBI for $6,000,000 ($52,200,000).[544] Weigel had been ill for nearly a decade, which might have been a deciding factor in his decision. The Iroquois plants would produce beer from all the breweries, but they were the only plant to produce Iroquois Beer. Frankenmuth was one of their biggest production lines, shipping the beer to the Midwest.

William K. Simon, grandson of the founder of the brewery emblazoned with his name, was named president of the William Simon Brewery in 1956. Simon, born in Buffalo, had a formal brewery education before working under his father in nearly every department, honing his skills.[545]

William Weyand Weigel, president of Iroquois Beverage Corporation until he sold the company to International Breweries, Incorporated, in 1955, died in April 1956. Involved in the brewery business since birth, he was instrumental in consolidating Buffalo's breweries after Prohibition. He built Iroquois Beverage to be the largest brewery in Buffalo. Weigel had been ill for the last decade of his life and was often bed-ridden, but he still managed the minute details of the brewery from his bed until finally selling it in 1955.[546]

Weigel was a member of the U.S. Olympic Committee in the 1930s, and two of his daughters competed in figure skating at the Germany Winter Olympics. He even built an indoor skating rink in one of the breweries where his daughters could practice. (His daughter Louise married Edward A. Atwill, a longtime Iroquois vice-president.) He was a member of many clubs and organizations, was an avid outdoorsman and owned extensive property in Canada. Weigel left an estate valued at $2,041,789 ($17,500,000), half left to his wife and the rest in trust for her until her death.[547] He is buried in the United German and French Cemetery in Cheektowaga.

Local ownership of Buffalo breweries continued to end in 1957, when International Breweries, Incorporated, of Detroit announced it was purchasing the Phoenix Brewery Corporation at 300 Emslie Street for $318,000 ($2,590,000). The brewery, which was running under capacity, would produce its own Phoenix brands, as well as International's Frankenmuth brands. Majority shareholder and board chairman George T. Driscoll said his family approved the sale to IBI.[548] Under the International label, Phoenix produced Phoenix Light Lager Beer, Phoenix Premium Beer, Governor's Club Ale, Phoenix Cream Ale, Phoenix Bock Beer, Moffat's Pale Ale and Phoenix Three Star Special Beer.

Phoenix wasn't the only brewery struggling, though, as the George F. Stein Brewery, Incorporated, at 797 Broadway decided to take on contract work around 1957 to keep its lines running and employees busy. Some brands

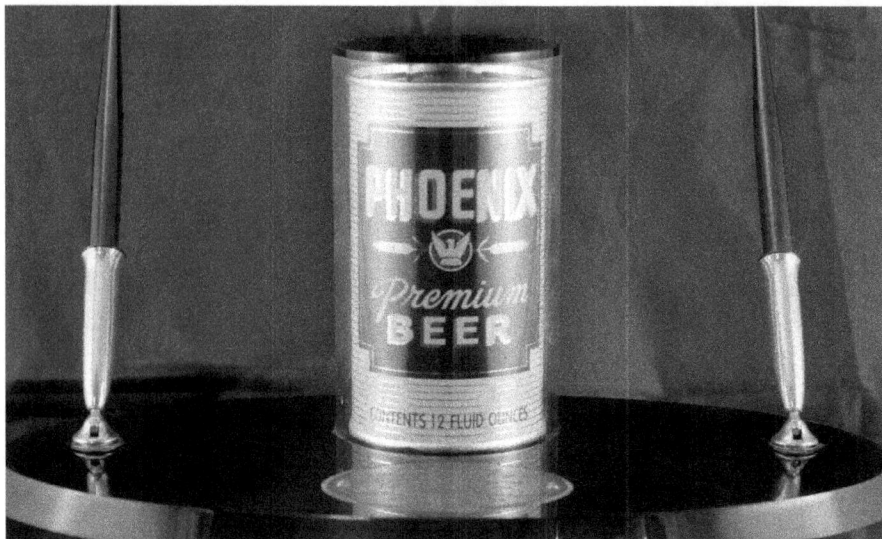

A Phoenix beer can in lucite and a pen set, dated March 12, 1958. The set was created to commemorate the first canning run, using cans produced in nearby Fairport, New York. *Photo by Chris Groves, from the collection of Dave Mik.*

the company brewed included Tudor Ale and Beer and Kol. Tudor was the store brand for the A&P grocery store chain. Stein was one of at least nine different breweries across the country that brewed it.[549]

William J. Simon, seventy-seven, chairman of the board of directors of the William Simon Brewery, died in mid-January 1958. His father started the brewery bearing their name, and he succeeded him as president in 1918. He was a member of the Master Brewers' Association, the Rotary, the Elks and other organizations.[550]

The George F. Stein Brewery, Incorporated, at 797 Broadway was one of the last breweries still locally owned. The pressure to modernize and compete with the mega brewers was tough on the local breweries, which relied on the local population to stay in business. In late January 1958, Stein's finally succumbed to the pressure to sell. The Leisy Brewing Company of Cleveland announced it was purchasing the company, but only for Stein's recipes and current business. The actual brewery was not included in the deal. Company president Joseph C. Stein refused to offer any details at the time but did say Stein's Beer would continue to be brewed, in Cleveland, and then shipped to Buffalo for sale.[551] If the company could not sell enough beer while in business in Buffalo, one can question how much it thought it would sell when the beer was produced in Cleveland.

Phoenix Brewery Corporation began canning its Phoenix Beer about 1958, but the end of the line was near. In 1959, International Breweries, Incorporated, which also owned the Iroquois Beverage Corporation plant on Pratt Street, purchased the Phoenix brewery, but the Phoenix plant was closed by May 1960, and an auction of all the contents and the real estate was held on May 10, 1960.[552]

International's other Buffalo property, Iroquois, did pick up some additional contract work from other breweries in the late 1950s, including Blackhawk Beer, Stolz and Cleveland-Sandusky Brewing Corporation (formerly owned by Carl Strangmann). The company was also producing Iroquois Tomahawk Ale and Indian Head Beer, and in 1967, it introduced Draft Beer in a can.

One of Buffalo's prominent businessmen and founder of multiple companies, Jacob Gerhard Lang, died on May 31, 1959. Lang was born in Buffalo in 1871, the son of Gerhard Lang. After attending the Brewers' Academy in New York City, he joined his father's brewery. When Prohibition took away the beer business, he organized several businesses: Lang's Products, Incorporated, to manufacture Hyan Dry soda; Lang's Bakery, Incorporated; and Lang's Creamery, Incorporated. After Prohibition was repealed, Lang modernized the brewery and reopened it with himself as president. In 1949, the brewery was closed, and the other businesses closed several years later.

Jacob Gerhard Lang was instrumental in developing real

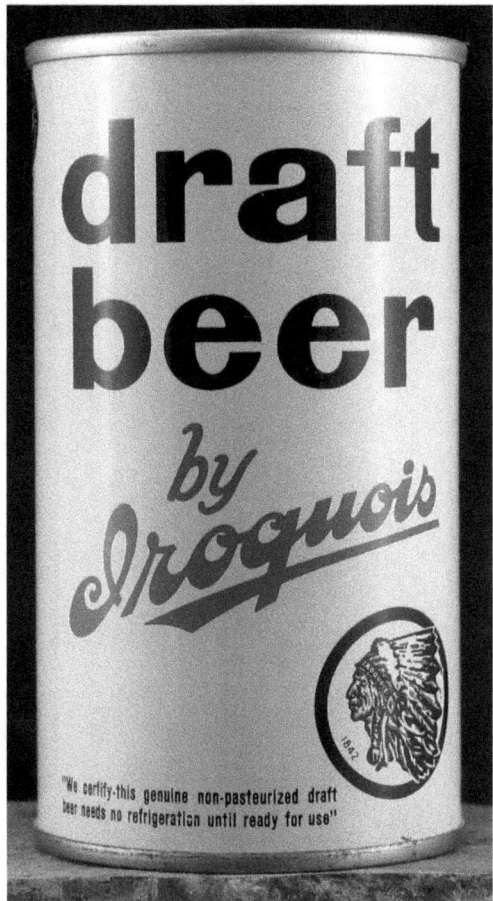

Classic design in a circa 1960s Iroquois beer can that, paradoxically, claims to contain draft beer. *Photo by Chris Groves, from the collection of Dave Mik.*

estate known as Langfield at the former Lang Farm. He owned numerous horses and was a member of several clubs in the city. His estate was valued at $339,976 ($2,720,000), and he is buried in the United German and French Cemetery in Cheektowaga.[553]

In September 1959, Lang's sister, Mrs. Sylvester B. Eagan, was elected president of Lang's Creamery, Incorporated. Her deceased husband had operated Hotel Broezel on Seneca Street and had real estate holdings, and the former Eagan building at 529 Main Street was named for him.[554]

18

THE 1960s

MORE SHRINKAGE

The 1950s saw the merger and closing of several of Buffalo's beloved breweries. The 1960s would continue the trend as the march to the end of local ownership and manufacturing continued.

William E. Kreiner Jr. and his brother Howard dissolved their business, Wm. E. Kreiner & Sons, Incorporated, in 1960 and reorganized as Kreiner Malt Company. William died in 1968, and Howard carried on until 1971, when he died. The malt house at 50 Elk Street was sold to a company called Buffalo Malting Corporation, who operated it for about twelve years. It is currently abandoned.[555]

In June 1961, one of the last vestiges of the Gerhard Lang Brewery empire, Lang's Creamery, Incorporated, was sold to the Jones-Rich Milk Corporation of Buffalo, the largest independent milk company in the country. Founded by Jacob Gerhard Lang, Lang's Creamery was one of several operating in the city at the time and operated as a wholesale business after Prohibition was repealed until the final sale.[556]

George C. Stein, the co-founder of George F. Stein Brewery, Incorporated, with his father George F., died in August 1962 at sixty-nine years old. He received a diploma from the Schwartz Brewing Academy in New York City and then joined his father at his brewery in Medina, New York. After Prohibition ended, they opened the George F. Stein Brewery, Incorporated, at 815 Broadway, the former home of Broadway Brewing and Malting Company. In 1962, he took over the brewery and, with his brothers, ran it until it was sold in 1958. He was former president of the Western New York District, Masterbrewers of America.[557]

Francis Perot's Sons Malting Company had a history dating back to the seventeenth century and the early twentieth century in Buffalo. After the closing of American Malting Company in 1918, the Perot malt house became the largest in Buffalo, surviving Prohibition, an expansion and an eventual decline in business in Buffalo. The company was dissolved in late November 1963, ending nearly three hundred years in business.[558]

Karl A. Schwartz, son of John L. Schwartz, died in early January 1968. Karl was secretary of the John L. Schwartz Brewing Company until Prohibition. He was then involved in real estate and spent twenty-eight years as secretary of Buffalo Elks Lodge Twenty-three. Schwartz was seventy-four years old.[559]

According to William K. Simon, president of William Simon Brewery, by 1964, "one bottle out of every six sold in Erie County is Simon Pure Beer or Ale."[560] The brewery built a strong local following for its products, particularly Simon Pure Beer and Old Abbey Ale. By the early 1960s, the William Simon Brewery played off the fact that it was the only locally owned brewery in Buffalo by advertising as "Buffalo's Only Independent Brewers."

The Iroquois Beverage Corporation plant on Pratt Street had been part of International Breweries, Incorporated, of Detroit since 1955. International had since been selling off or closing some of its unproductive

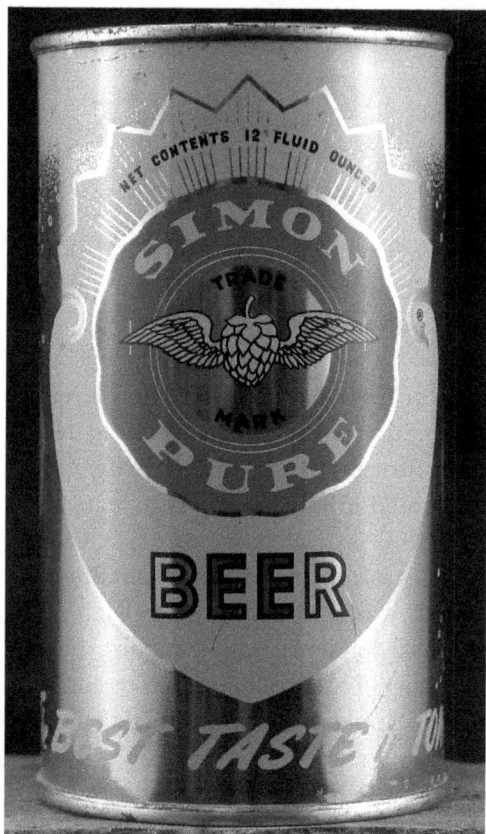

A Simon Pure beer can. Simon canned beer from around 1955 until 1968. While only one can design ever was produced, there are a number of subtle variations on the can itself, especially the tops. Most common are the coin-slot can tops, which were a bank-based promotional tie-in. *Photo by Chris Groves, from the collection of Dave Mik.*

plants, including the Phoenix Brewery Corporation in 1960 and, eventually, was left with just the Iroquois plant, which became the company's headquarters.[561]

Terry J. Fox was made International president in August 1965 and decided to concentrate on business in Buffalo, where Iroquois was a strong seller. Apparently it worked, as Fox reported a profit of $86,321 ($620,000) for the first six months of 1966 compared to a loss of $707,936 ($5,230,000) the previous year. Fox said sales of Iroquois in the local area reached an all-time high in November 1965. That coincided with the opening of the Rathskeller, a bar and restaurant inside the Iroquois brewery and "the climax of tours of the brewery by local groups and organizations."[562]

In June 1966, Peter Wheeler Reiss, a wealthy young lawyer and stockholder from Wisconsin, attempted to purchase control of William Simon Brewery by offering to purchase 300,000 shares of outstanding stock at twice what the stock was selling for. Reiss said since the company was losing money (it had in 1965 and 1966), he wanted to take control.[563] Through a very public battle and eventual litigation, Reiss was not able to tender enough offers and rejected them all.[564] At the August 1966 shareholder meeting, company president William K. Simon announced that Terry J. Fox (of International Breweries, Incorporated) had also bid on the brewery.

In late November 1966, John B. Konsek Sr. died. Konsek had started the Great Lakes Brewing Company in 1933 and had run it for a short time before shutting it down. Afterward, he ran J.B. Lounge on Memorial Drive in Buffalo. He was seventy-five years old.[565]

In March 1967, International Breweries, Incorporated, purchased the Aberdeen Management Corporation of New York City in what was the beginning of company diversification. Shortly after, the business was renamed Iroquois Industries, Incorporated, and Iroquois Beverage Corporation became a subsidiary of Iroquois Industries.[566]

After Peter Wheeler Reiss's unsuccessful bid for the William Simon Brewery in 1966, he sold his shares of Simon stock to Iroquois Industries, Incorporated, and by August 1967, Iroquois had amassed almost 10 percent of the shares.[567]

In February 1968, two years after Reiss had tried to take over the company, Buffalo attorney Edward C. Hall, who owned 61,851 shares, over 5 percent of the outstanding shares, and whose family owned the Crystal Beach amusement park, began looking to make a bid for the company. Simon had lost $140,583 ($928,000) in fiscal year 1967 but had slowed the money drain to $98,187 ($648,000) in fiscal year 1968.[568]

With only two breweries left in Buffalo by the late 1960s, consolidation was considered but never happened. This is a stock certificate issued to Iroquois Industries in 1967 for one thousand shares of William Simon Brewery stock. *Photo by Ethan Cox.*

At the 1968 shareholder meeting, the company changed its incorporation papers to diversify the business, which would allow it to invest in businesses other than brewing.[569] In the end, Hall abandoned his plan to purchase the Simon brewery.

The William Simon Brewery started using a new water source in 1967, after having used Lake Erie water for many years. With the declining quality of the lake water, the company began using water from Onondaga Limestone Caverns "because it is the closest thing to ideal brewing water we can find anywhere." The company touted its Cavern Spring Water and would later attempt to sell the water.[570]

Iroquois Industries, Incorporated, invested in numerous business sectors over the next couple of years, including pharmaceuticals, bitters, electronics and specialty foods.[571]

Kearny J. Suto was an Iroquois Beverage Corporation and International Breweries, Incorporated executive who was sent to Kentucky to oversee its Bavarian Brewery from September 1965 until it was sold in April 1966. Suto returned to Buffalo and served as vice-president of sales for Iroquois until December 1966. He then was named vice-president and general manager. In April 1969, he was named president of the Iroquois Beverage Corporation division of Iroquois Industries, Incorporated, a position he held until the brewery closed.[572] Outgoing company president Terry J. Fox had relinquished his position to concentrate on other Iroquois Industries companies.

William K. Simon, president of the William Simon Brewery, told shareholders in August 1969 that he was determined to make the company profitable, despite five straight years of losses. One way was by bottling the Cavern Spring Water the company used in its beer. The company had lost $178,401 ($1,190,000) in fiscal year 1968, claiming most of it was due to new union wages. The board of directors at the time comprised some familiar names in Buffalo brewing, including Kam and Hiemenz.[573]

19

THE 1970s

THE END OF BREWING IN THE NICKEL CITY

By the 1970s, the brewing industry in Buffalo was almost nonexistent. Two major breweries were battling with each other and the mega brewers as the population of the area declined and unemployment rose. The combination did not bode well for Buffalo.

Gerhard J. Simon, former vice-president, secretary and treasurer of the William Simon Brewery, died on July 21, 1970, at eighty-five years old. Simon was also president of the Buffalo Bisons baseball team in 1915 and 1916, when the team won consecutive International League pennants.[574] He is buried in Mount Calvary Cemetery in Cheektowaga.

There were still two Buffalo-owned breweries, William Simon Brewery and Iroquois Beverage Corporation, which was a subsidiary of Iroquois Industries, Incorporated. In August 1970, William K. Simon, president of William Simon Brewery, announced that the company had discussed merging with Iroquois Beverage Corporation.[575] Several talks were held, but the two could not come to an agreement.

Unfortunately, mega beer, changing tastes and aging equipment finally rang the death knell for Iroquois on May 5, 1971, when the company shut its doors for the very last time and beer-making operations were shifted to Meister Brau Brewery in Toledo, Ohio.[576]

Although it was no longer producing beer, the brand was well known, and it was kept alive for several years by a succession of breweries—Meister Brau (closed in 1972), August Wagner Brewery (closed 1974), Erie Brewing (closed 1976) and Fred Koch Brewery, which produced it until about 1985. On October

Detail of the remains of Buffalo's largest brewery, the Iroquois Brewing Company on Pratt Street. *Photo by Michael Rizzo.*

1, 1971, Iroquois Industries, Incorporated, moved the company headquarters from Buffalo to Greenwich, Connecticut, to put it closer to four of its subsidiaries, thus ending the local tie that had existed since the 1840s.[577]

For the William Simon Brewery, the lone survivor of the Buffalo beer wars that lasted for over one hundred years, it should have been time to celebrate. Instead, it, too, was counting the days until it would shutter its doors forever. Sales had peaked in 1966 at $4,094,427 ($29,400,000) but were steadily declining as the decade wore on. Things got worse, though. By late 1971, losses had mounted, totaling over $660,000 ($3,800,000), and the brewery suspended its brewery operations.[578]

On December 1, 1971, the William Simon Brewery announced it was going out of "the business of brewing beer."[579] The Fred Koch Brewery of Dunkirk, New York, was granted a temporary non-exclusive franchise to brew and market Simon Pure beer and ale. The temporary agreement was voided in June 1972 when the William Simon Brewery filed for bankruptcy.[580]

On August 11, 1972, the Fred Koch Brewery subsidiary Dominion Distributors, Incorporated, agreed to purchase Iroquois Brewing Distribution, a division of Iroquois Industries, Incorporated.[581]

A second temporary agreement was entered between the stockholders of the William Simon Brewery and the Fred Koch Brewery in November 1974 that allowed Koch's to brew and sell Simon Pure and Old Abbey Ale and use of its trademarks, copyrights and name.[582] The Fred Koch Brewery would continue to sell and market the Iroquois and Simon Pure brands until it, too, closed in 1985. Buffalo's brewing industry, which dated back to the War of 1812, had finally ended.

THE 1980s AND BEYOND

BREWING RESURRECTED

S outh Buffalo's Irish four-term mayor James "Jimmy" D. Griffin loved his beer. A former grain scooper, when the city was buried by a devastating blizzard in 1985, Mayor Griffin encouraged citizens to "stay inside, grab a six-pack, and watch a good football game." Unfortunately, there was not a good Buffalo beer to drink.

Joseph C. Stein was born in Buffalo in 1898. With his father and four brothers, he ran the George F. Stein Brewery at 815 Broadway. Joseph was the last president and owner of the brewery when it was sold to Leisy Brewing Company of Cleveland in 1958. He went into real estate until the mid-1970s, when he retired. Stein died on September 6, 1988, at ninety years old.[583]

For a city that could once count nearly half of its residents as German or German-American, there is no discernible German neighborhood anywhere in the city, or within Erie County for that matter.

William Simon III purchased his grandfather's brewery and one day would like to restore part of it as a small craft brewery utilizing some of the family's old recipes. Until that time, a large portion of what's left of the brewery is leased out.

In 1986, Buffalo Brew Pub opened at 6861 Main Street in suburban Williamsville. It was the first microbrewery in the Buffalo area and today is the oldest brewpub in the state. In 1990, it opened a production location on Abbott Road in Lackawanna, which was closed in 1996 when it shifted the brewing to Pennsylvania.

William Simon III (center) at a private tour of the former Simon brewery (which he owns) explains how the brewery ran when he was young. *Photo Michael Rizzo.*

Brewing returned to Buffalo when Breckenridge Brewing Company of Colorado opened a new brewpub in the restored Market Arcade building at 617 Main Street in 1995. It is best known for skipping town in the middle of the night, taking everything, even things it didn't own, and leaving the city of Buffalo with a $1 million tab in 1998, just three years after opening. The city dumped twelve thousand gallons of beer down the drain.

The location was then taken over by Empire Brewing Company, which was based in Syracuse, New York. The location was open a short time before closing in the early 2000s. Lastly, restaurateur Steve Calvaneso opened Ya-Ya Bayou Brewhouse in the location, hoping he could make it work.

Calvaneso, who at the time ran multiple restaurants, was in the midst of a race to be mayor of Buffalo when it was revealed that he was losing money at the brewpub. He admitted to wanting the brewpub to succeed and eventually dropped out of the mayoral race. He closed the pub in the fall of 2005, and that was the end of brewing in that building. After three unsuccessful tries, it was time to end it.

Pearl Street Grill & Brewery opened at 72–76 Pearl Street in 1996, in an 1870 building that was initially a dressmaking factory and warehouse and subsequently both a hardware store and a restaurant. Immediately prior to

A view of the cellar at Flying Bison's new location at 840 Seneca Street.
Pictured are several primary fermentation vessels of different sizes and makes.
Photo by Ethan Cox.

Pearl Street's inception, it was the home of Garcia's Irish Pub. The original partnership included John Hickenlooper, famous for opening the Wynkoop Brewery in downtown Denver, which had sparked the revival of the LoDo district and a wave of new urban gentrification, which the owners sought to emulate in Buffalo. In 1997, Earl Ketry and Drew Gedra became sole owners of the restaurant, brewery and banquet space.

Their fifteen-barrel Specific Mechanical system was helmed originally by a Wynkoop brewer; he was succeeded by Alec Campbell. From 2000 to 2005, the head brewer was Paul Kohler, currently the director of cellar operations for Flying Bison Brewing Company. Following Kohler, brewer Phil Dobler held the position, quickly replaced by Jay Malone until 2005. Originally hired as Malone's assistant brewer, Phil Internicola (formerly of Flying Bison Brewing Company) took the position from 2007 to 2012, assisted by Kathryn Takats and, toward the end, by Noah McIntee and Chris Herr. In 2013, McIntee and Herr started as co-brewers at both Pearl Street and the sister brewery at the Lafayette Hotel, the Pan-American Grill & Brewery, which began operation in 2013.

In 2014, McIntee left, and Herr was joined by assistant brewer Brian Vaughn. Pearl Street produces about two thousand barrels per year and packs some twelve lines to eight bars on four floors. It brews many styles of beers from IPAs to Octoberfest beers to light, sessionable golden ales. The beers are available on-premise only, though Pearl Street can sometimes be found at Sportsman's Tavern. In 2013, owner Ketry and partner David Swift announced the RiverWorks Project, a brewery to occupy land on the Buffalo River in an area historically bustling with grain elevators and processing, including malting. This project, which will include hockey, curling and roller rinks, in addition to a brewery in an old grain silo, is expected to be completed in 2015.

After five years of navigating state and federal requirements, in 2000, homebrewers Tim Herzog and Phil Internicola opened Flying Bison Brewing Company at 491 Ontario Street in the Riverside section of Buffalo. They had a twenty-barrel Criveller system. In 2007, Internicola went to Pearl Street Grill & Brewery, where he was made brewmaster. In 2010, facing closure, Flying Bison was bought out by Utica-based F.X. Matt Brewing Company, makers of Saranac beer. Herzog was kept on as brewmaster.

In 2013, with business growing, Flying Bison Brewing Company purchased a parcel of land at 840 Seneca Street in Buffalo's Larkin District to construct a new brewery. The brewery moved and opened in October 2014.

Community Beer Works was founded in April 2012 by a group of friends, with the brewery located at 15 Lafayette Avenue. Ethan Cox is president, Rudy Watkins is head brewer, Dan Conley is webmaster and Gregory Patterson-Tanski is building expert. The nanobrewery's goal is to produce high-quality craft beer for Buffalo and the surrounding region. The brewery produces a variety of brews, including Frank, the Whale, the IPA, Rutherford B. Haze, De Maas and the Double IPA. It is also open for retail sales of its beers.

Right: Flying Bison Brewing Rusty Chain beer and bottle. The Rusty Chain brand was started as a special for a biking organization in Buffalo, but it was so well received that it became a standard. *Photo Beerclubguide.com.*

Below: The exterior of the new building of Flying Bison Brewing at 840 Seneca Street. As of this writing, brewing operations are underway, and the taproom opened on November 8, 2014. *Photo by Ethan Cox.*

The brite tanks at Community Beer Works. These three-barrel brite tanks were manufactured by SMT. They are the final stage of beer making before packaging, where the beer clarifies, chills and gets carbonated. From these tanks, the beer is packaged into kegs for delivery. *Photo by Ethan Cox.*

In 2012, partners Bill Metzger, Kirsten Rose and Matt Conron purchased a classic neighborhood tavern, Gene McCarthy's, and began its initial transformation into a craft beer destination. While the tavern interior remained very much as it had been in the years since its 1963 opening, the coolers began to be stocked with less mainstream beers, and soon enough, the taps all turned over to craft beer. Many of the loyal clientele continued to put back their Buds and Blues, but the craft-curious were starting to trickle in, lured by the selection and, increasingly, by events. Famously, Bill Metzger, in his Beer Messiah persona, held monthly Beer School nights where styles and breweries were explored. Informed by his long run as publisher of the regional *Brewing News* newspapers, Metzger had been bringing interesting kegs and bottles into the area's craft-conscious bars and restaurants for many years. Now operating his own place, his plans grew in scope.

Gene McCarthy's tavern at 78 Hamburg Street in Buffalo's storied First Ward began another change in 2013, when the lot next door saw the groundbreaking for the structure that was to become Old First Ward Brewing

An interior view of the brewery at Old First Ward Brewing, 78 Hamburg Street, 2014. Founded by Bill Metzger, Kirsten Rose and Matt Conron of Gene McCarthy's. *Photo Jennifer Reed.*

Company. Completed in the spring of 2014, the three-barrel brewhouse is overseen by Matt Conron, who was formerly a brewer at the Breckenridge Brewing Company during its run in the 1990s. Several guest brewers and interns also contribute, giving OFW's beer variety and personality. The draft lines run under the ground from the separate structure over to the original bar, and the area in front of the brewery itself serves as a cozy beer garden.

Resurgence Brewing Company at 1250 Niagara Street was founded by Jeff Ware in 2013 after he saw a need for more locally crafted, high-quality beer in Western New York. Head brewer Dave Collins joined Resurgence in the fall of 2013. Dave had previously worked as the head brewer for Gordon Biersch in Syracuse, New York, after attending the Niagara College of Canada Brewing School.

The brewery offers high-quality, small-batch beer for local enjoyment. It also has a beer garden and community gathering space. Its beer varieties include IPA, Session IPA, Sponge Candy Stout (a collaboration with Watson's Chocolate), Loganberry Wit and Summer Saison.[584]

Big Ditch Brewing Company opened a production brewery in downtown Buffalo in 2014. The management team consists of Matt Kahn, president; Corey Catalano, vice-president and head brewer; and Wes Froebel, chief of

Resurgence Brewing Company head brewer David Collins working on the pilot system, 2014. Photo by Matthew McCormick

Opposite, bottom: The brewhouse at Community Beer Works. This recirculating, infusion-mash system was designed by Psychobrew and employs kettles from Stout Tanks and Kettles. It is a 1.5-barrel system, handled by head brewer Rudy Watkins. *Photo by Ethan Cox.*

sales and marketing. The brewery consists of a twenty-barrel brewhouse with five forty-barrel fermenters. Big Ditch occupies about fourteen thousand square feet at 55 East Huron Street on the corner of Ellicott Street. The space includes the brewery, warehouse space, office space and space for a taproom, which is expected to open in the fall of 2014. Big Ditch expects to brew approximately 1,200 barrels its first year.[585]

Buffalo is no longer the grain king it once was, but that is changing. Prior to the opening of the Erie Canal, there was no grain handled in Buffalo. In 1830, workers handled 146,000 bushels of grain, and ten years later, it was ten times that amount. In 1842, Joseph Dart developed what would be known as the steam-powered elevator. This allowed grain to be unloaded at one thousand bushels per hour.

Within a short time, ten additional elevators were built on Buffalo's waterfront, and it was the world's largest grain port. By the 1930s, Buffalo was also the largest flour milling city in the world. When the Welland Canal in Welland, Ontario, opened in 1932, it allowed larger boats to bypass Buffalo.

In 1959, the St. Lawrence Seaway opened, and Buffalo was essentially cut out of the shipping chain.[586]

As of this writing, malting is returning to Buffalo. Queen City Malting will be opening in the Barrel Factory, at Hamburg and Republic Streets in the city's Old First Ward. Queen City's "focus will be on using top quality, sustainable grains from local New York State farms."[587]

New York State–grown hops, which at one time were considered some of the best, have started to rebound. They emerged as a major crop in 1830 in New York State. By 1849, New York led the nation

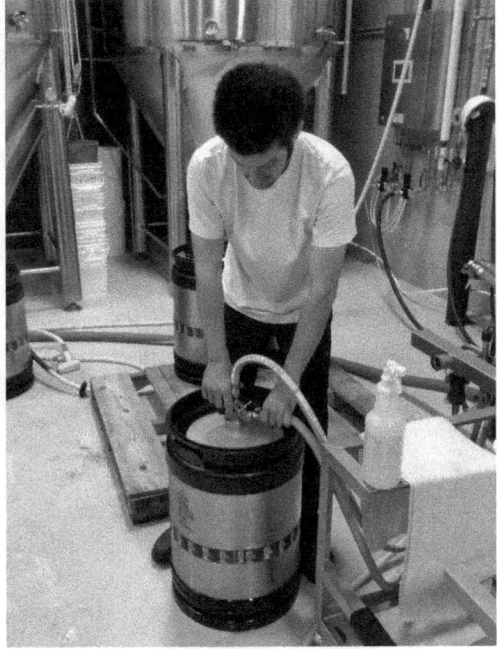

Corey Catalano from Big Ditch Brewing, one of the newest breweries in Buffalo, filling a keg. *Photo by Big Ditch Brewing.*

Tim Herzog, on the left, founder and brewmaster, explains the process of brewing to a tour group in the original Flying Bison brewery on Ontario Street in 2012. *Photo by Michael Rizzo.*

in hop production, and by 1855, over three million bushels were being grown annually. By the Civil War, almost 90 percent of hop production was in New York.

The problem started when many New York farmers plowed their land and planted hops, while at the same time, farmers on the West Coast began planting hops, and their yield per acre was far higher. After prices became volatile, New York farmers began cutting their crop size, and then, in 1909, a mildew (erroneously called a blight) destroyed smaller crops. According to Vang, in 1914, an attack by hop aphids reduced the yield again, and finally Prohibition eliminated "virtually all needs for hops."[588] By the time Prohibition ended, most farmers had already changed crops, and production was left to the Pacific Northwest.

In 2011, there were about a dozen hops growers in New York. As of this writing, there are more than 140, with at least a dozen in Erie and Niagara counties.[589] So, hop growing is starting to return in New York as the craft beer movement continues to grow, and Buffalo is poised to continue a new century of growth in the brewing and malting industries.

NOTES

CHAPTER 1
1. *Buffalo Daily Courier*, September 3, 1874, 1.
2. *Buffalo Courier*, October 26, 1910, 14.
3. Warton, *Poetical Works*, 181–82.

CHAPTER 2
4. Smith, *History of the City of Buffalo*, 51.
5. *Schenectady Cabinet*, August 30, 1820.

CHAPTER 3
6. Powell, *Rushing the Growler*, 21.
7. *Buffalo Courier*, January 29, 1911, 48.
8. Smith, *History of the City of Buffalo*, 152.

CHAPTER 4
9. *Buffalo Courier-Express*, November 4, 1943, 6. An ad for Iroquois Beer said Roos started in 1835.
10. *Buffalo Courier*, March 30, 1890, 3.
11. Smith, *History of the City of Buffalo*, 247.

CHAPTER 5
12. Kiefer, "Brewing."
13. Kriegbaum-Hanks, *History of the Germans*.
14. Buffalo History Works, "Grain Elevators."

15. City of Buffalo, *Directory for the City of Buffalo*, 1839.

16. *Buffalo Courier,* October 26, 1910, 14.

17. *Buffalo Daily Courier,* January 13, 1879.

18. *One Hundred Years of Brewing*, 158.

19. *Buffalo Courier-Express,* July 22, 1934, 5; *Buffalo Courier,* January 12, 1913, 44.

20. Smith, *History of the City of Buffalo*, 153.

21. Ibid., 247.

22. Ibid.

23. Findagrave.com, "Valentine Blatz."

24. *Memorial and Family History*, 178.

25. Powell, *Rushing the Growler*, 153.

CHAPTER 6

26. White, *Our County and Its People*.

27. *One Hundred Years of Brewing*, 251.

28. Hubbell, Dolan and Jordan, *Our Police, Our City*, 611–13.

29. *Buffalo Evening News,* January 29, 1897, 5.

30. Powell, *Rushing the Growler*, 153.

31. *Buffalo Daily Courier,* January 13, 1879.

32. Marthens, *Commerce, Manufactures and Resources*, 138.

33. Kiefer, "Brewing."

34. City of Buffalo, *Directory for the City of Buffalo*, 1851–1861.

35. U.S. Census Bureau, "Federal Census."

36. Buffalo Brewers' Association, *Souvenir of Buffalo*.

37. City of Buffalo, *Directory for the City of Buffalo*, 1852, 1854.

38. Powell, *Rushing the Growler*, 154.

39. Ibid.; *Memorial and Family History*, 178; Powell, *Rushing the Growler*, 155.

40. City of Buffalo, *Directory for the City of Buffalo*, 1854.

41. Per interview with beer historian Dave Mik, July 2014.

42. U.S. Internal Revenue Service, "Products of Industry."

43. *One Hundred Years of Brewing*, 581.

44. *Buffalo Express*, December 19, 1871, 1.

CHAPTER 7

45. Buffalo Brewers' Association, *Souvenir of Buffalo*.

46. Powell, *Rushing the Growler*, 155.

47. William W. Sloan, B.L. Cary Family Tree, http://trees.ancestry.com/tree/57840760/person/30030687084 (accessed September 10, 2014); *One Hundred Years of Brewing*, 581.

48. *Buffalo Illustrated*, 112.

49. Ibid.

50. Smith, *History of the City of Buffalo*, 247.

51. *One Hundred Years of Brewing*, 582.

52. *Buffalo Courier*, December 12, 1904, 7

53. City of Buffalo, *Directory for the City of Buffalo*, 1860.

54. Ibid.

55. Barbara Scheu, Charvat/Scudder Family tree, http://trees.ancestry.com/tree/9183971/person/7034790440 (accessed September 7, 2014); *Buffalo Courier*, November 6, 1902, 7.

56. City of Buffalo, *Directory for the City of Buffalo*, 1861.

57. Smith, *History of the City of Buffalo*, 151; "New York State Census, 1855." Ancestry.com (accessed June 5, 2014).

58. U.S. Census Bureau, "Federal Census"; City of Buffalo, *Directory for the City of Buffalo*, 1859.

59. Onlinebiographies.info, "Biography of Anselm Hoefner."

CHAPTER 8

60. Bailey, *Illustrated Buffalo*, 206; White, *Our County and Its People*, 62.

61. *One Hundred Years of Brewing*, 251.

62. Powell, *Rushing the Growler*, 109; Smith, *History of the City of Buffalo*, 249.

63. Rizzo, *Through the Mayors' Eyes*, 133.

64. Ibid., 134.

65. "New York State Census, 1855," Ancestry.com; U.S. Internal Revenue Service, "Products of Industry," 1863.

66. City of Buffalo, *Directory for the City of Buffalo*, 1860–1870.

67. *One Hundred Years of Brewing*, 581.

68. Albright-Knox Art Gallery, "Buffalo Cotton Factory"; *One Hundred Years of Brewing*, 251.

69. Rizzo, *Through the Mayors' Eyes*, 153.

70. Ibid., 153; City of Buffalo, *Directory for the City of Buffalo*, 1862; Smith, *History of the City of Buffalo*, 250.

71. "United States, Passport Applications, 1795-1925," Ancestry.com (accessed September 23, 2014); *One Hundred Years of Brewing*, 251.

72. *Memorial and Family History*, 412.

73. Charles F. Schuh, MacMurray/Schuh Family Tree, http://trees.ancestry.com/tree/26195360/person/12560470507 (accessed September 8, 2014).

74. Smith, *History of the City of Buffalo*, 247.

75. U.S. Census Bureau, "Federal Census," 1860.

76. City of Buffalo, *Directory for the City of Buffalo*, 1864.

77. Jacob Baumgartner, Carr Family Tree, http://trees.ancestry.com/tree/37299430/person/19124539791 (accessed September 8, 2014).

78. Hubbell, Dolan and Jordan, *Our Police, Our City*, 611–13; Smith, *History of the City of Buffalo*, 249.

79. *Men of New York*, vol. 1, 420–21.

80. *Utica Morning Herald*, December 20, 1880, 1; City of Buffalo, *Directory for the City of Buffalo*, 1866.

81. City of Buffalo, *Directory for the City of Buffalo*, 1866.

82. Ibid., 1867.

83. *Buffalo Daily Courier*, January 13, 1879.

84. Ibid., November 30, 1867.
85. Marthens, *Commerce, Manufactures and Resources*, 128.
86. Rizzo, *Through the Mayors' Eyes*, 153.
87. *One Hundred Years of Brewing*, 582; City of Buffalo, *Directory for the City of Buffalo*, 1870.
88. *One Hundred Years of Brewing*, 231.
89. Ibid., 232.
90. *Buffalo Daily Courier*, November 26, 1868.
91. City of Buffalo, *Directory for the City of Buffalo*, 1868.
92. Ibid., 1868, 1869.
93. History of Buffalo, 245; Marthens, *Commerce, Manufactures and Resources*, 127.
94. *Buffalo Courier & Republic*, July 7, 1869.
95. Craemer, *Royal Bavarian Castles*, 134–35; Kriegbaum-Hanks, *History of the Germans*.
96. Kriegbaum-Hanks, *History of the Germans*.
97. *One Hundred Years of Brewing*, 582.
98. *Buffalo Courier*, November 5, 1922, 93.

CHAPTER 9
99. Powell, *Rushing the Growler*, 83.
100. City of Buffalo, *Directory for the City of Buffalo*, 1870, 1873.
101. Smith, *History of the City of Buffalo*, 249; *Buffalo Courier*, February 12, 1906, 3.
102. Smith, *History of the City of Buffalo*, 250
103. *Buffalo Daily Courier*, February 17, 1871, 1.
104. Smith, *History of the City of Buffalo*, 249
105. Onlinebiographies.info, "Biography of William Simon."
106. Smith, *History of the City of Buffalo*, 250
107. *Buffalo Express*, December 19, 1871, 1.
108. Ibid.
109. Sloan, B.L. Cary Family Tree.
110. *History of the City of Buffalo: Its Men*, 128.
111. *Buffalo Courier*, January 12, 1913, 44.
112. Ibid., February 17, 1909.
113. Bailey, *Illustrated Buffalo*, 87.
114. Genealogy.com; Marthens, *Commerce, Manufactures and Resources*, 80; Bailey, *Illustrated Buffalo*, 87.
115. City of Buffalo, *Directory for the City of Buffalo*, 1886.
116. *One Hundred Years of Brewing*, 582; *Buffalo Express*, April 29, 1873, 1.
117. U.S. Internal Revenue Service, "Products of Industry," 1871.
118. City of Buffalo, *Directory for the City of Buffalo*, 1873.
119. *Western Brewer*, July 1915.
120. *Buffalo Courier*, November 10, 1912, 41.
121. Smith, *History of the City of Buffalo*, 128.
122. Marthens, *Commerce, Manufactures and Resources*, 51.
123. Smith, *History of the City of Buffalo*, 249.
124. *Buffalo Illustrated*, 110.

125. *Men of New York*, vol. 1, 420–21.

126. Smith, *History of the City of Buffalo*, 249–50.

127. *Buffalo Daily Courier*, March 25, 1871.

128. Albright-Know Art Gallery, "Buffalo Cotton Factory."

129. *Buffalo Courier*, April 14, 1894, 5.

130. *Daily Graphic*, August 31, 1874, 427.

131. *Spirit of the Times Batavia*, December 25, 1880.

132. *New York Sun*, December 17, 1880.

133. Ibid.

134. City of Buffalo, *Directory for the City of Buffalo*, 1878.

135. *One Hundred Years of Brewing*, 232, 261.

136. City of Buffalo, *Directory for the City of Buffalo*, 1875.

137. Marthens, *Commerce, Manufactures and Resources*, 106.

138. *Buffalo Daily Courier*, November 12, 1874; City of Buffalo, *Directory for the City of Buffalo*, 1873; *Evening Republic*, August 3, 1880, 1.

139. Smith, *History of the City of Buffalo*, 249.

140. *Buffalo Courier*, March 15, 1891, 6.

141. *Evening Republic*, January 14, 1876, 1.

142. *Buffalo Courier and Republic*, April 21, 1879.

143. Smith, *History of the City of Buffalo*, 249.

144. *Buffalo Daily Courier*, January 24, 1877, 1; February 7, 1877, 1.

145. *One Hundred Years of Brewing*, 581.

146. Smith, *History of the City of Buffalo*, 248.

147. *Buffalo Times*, July 15, 1919.

148. *Buffalo Daily Courier*, January 13, 1879.

149. Smith, *History of the City of Buffalo*, 249.

150. *Men of New York*, vol. 1, 155.

151. Sullivan, "Buffalo's Gustav."

152. City of Buffalo, *Directory for the City of Buffalo*, 1860.

153. *Buffalo Evening News*, October 6, 1899, 7.

154. Smith, *History of the City of Buffalo*, 248.

155. Kriegbaum-Hanks, *History of the Germans*.

156. *Buffalo Daily Courier*, January 13, 1879.

157. Marthens, *Commerce, Manufactures and Resources*, 138.

158. Rizzo, *Through the Mayors' Eyes*, 138.

159. *American Brewers' Review*, April 1, 1908, 174 ; Smith, *History of the City of Buffalo*, 249.

160. *Buffalo Evening News*, June 16, 1931.

161. Michalak, "Short History of the Simon," 2.

162. Onlinebiographies.info, "Biography of William Simon"; Michalak, "Short History of the Simon," 2.

CHAPTER 10

163. Smith, *History of the City of Buffalo*, 248.

164. *Buffalo Courier*, May 8, 1910, 38; *Buffalo Express*, November 26, 1902, 9.

165. *Buffalo Courier*, May 8, 1910, 38.
166. *One Hundred Years of Brewing*, 234.
167. Marthens, *Commerce, Manufactures and Resources*, 116; Smith, *History of the City of Buffalo*, 251.
168. Smith, *History of the City of Buffalo*, 248.
169. Ibid., 250.
170. *Utica Morning Herald*, December 20, 1880, 1.
171. Smith, *History of the City of Buffalo*, 249, 251.
172. Powell, *Rushing the Growler*, 138.
173. *Buffalo Evening News*, May 17, 1881, 1.
174. *Buffalo Courier*, September 21, 1883.
175. *One Hundred Years of Brewing*, 582; City of Buffalo, *Directory for the City of Buffalo*, 1870–1880.
176. Smith, *History of the City of Buffalo*, 251.
177. Buffalo Brewers' Association. *Souvenir of Buffalo*.
178. Smith, *History of the City of Buffalo*, 249; White, *Our County and Its People*, 367.
179. *Buffalo Courier-Express*, October 11, 1938, 22.
180. Smith, *History of the City of Buffalo*, 248.
181. Ibid., 250.
182. *Buffalo Courier*, November 2, 1891, 5.
183. *Lowell Daily Courier*, November 11, 1883.
184. *Buffalo Express*, January 5, 1884.
185. City of Buffalo, *Directory for the City of Buffalo*, 1884.
186. Bailey, *Illustrated Buffalo*, 206.
187. *Western Brewer* November 1915, 176; Smith, *History of the City of Buffalo*, 248.
188. *Buffalo Evening News*, August 20, 1884.
189. *One Hundred Years of Brewing*, 252.
190. Smith, *History of the City of Buffalo*, 247.
191. Johnson, "History of Hormel Family."
192. Powell, *Rushing the Growler*, 44.
193. *Buffalo Evening News*, December 19, 1885, 1; *Memorial and Family History*, 412–13.
194. Buffalo Board of Trade, *City of Buffalo and Its Surroundings*.
195. Kriegbaum-Hanks, *History of the Germans*; *Erie County Independent*, August 7, 1885, 1.
196. *Buffalo Daily Courier*, January 9, 1886, 1.
197. *Buffalo Evening News*, June 19, 1886, 1.
198. *A History of the City of Buffalo*, 132.
199. *Men of New York*, vol. 1, 257–58.
200. NY State Bureau of Labor Statistics, *Annual Report, 1890*, 343; Powell, *Rushing the Growler*, 39.
201. *Buffalo Express*, March 6, 1886, 1.
202. *Buffalo Express*, Sunday, December 8, 1901.
203. Library of Congress, "Washburn Crosby Elevator."
204. Powell, *Rushing the Growler*, 44.
205. Buffalo Brewers' Association. *Souvenir of Buffalo*; Powell, *Rushing the Growler*, 115.
206. *Buffalo Evening News*, August 13, 1887, 1.

207. Buffalo Brewers' Association. *Souvenir of Buffalo.*

208. *Albany Times,* July 22, 1887, 1.

209. *Buffalo Evening News,* August 13, 1887, 1.

210. Ibid., September 9, 1887, 1.

211. Ibid.

212. *Buffalo Daily Courier,* March 6, 1887, 4; *Buffalo Evening News,* September 13, 1887, 1.

213. *Troy Daily Times,* November 16, 1887, 1; White, *Our County and Its People,* 142.

214. *Buffalo Evening News,* January 24, 1888, 1.

215. *One Hundred Years of Brewing,* 251.

216. *Buffalo Evening News,* May 1, 1888, 1.

217. Ibid.

218. NY State Bureau of Labor Statistics, *Annual Report,* 343.

219. Onlinebiographies.info, "Biography of William Simon."

220. Ibid.; Michalak, "Short History of the Simon," 3.

221. *Buffalo Express,* August 3, 1888.

222. Rizzo, *Through the Mayors' Eyes,* 138.

223. *Men of New York,* vol.1 , 228.

224. City of Buffalo, *Directory for the City of Buffalo,* 1870–1890; Carroll, "Buffalo Brewing Co. History."

225. *Buffalo Daily Courier,* December 7, 1888, 4.

226. Ibid., 5.

227. Ibid., December 10, 1888, 6.

228. *Buffalo Express,* January 12, 1889, 6.

229. *Albany Times,* August 17, 1889; *Buffalo Evening News,* November 7, 1890, 1; *Buffalo Courier,* January 12, 1892.

230. *Buffalo Daily Courier,* June 7, 1889, 6.

231. *One Hundred Years of Brewing,* 252; Onlinebiographies.info, "Biography of William Simon."

CHAPTER 11

232. *Buffalo Courier,* September 27, 1894, 7.

233. White, *Our County and Its People,* 135.

234. *Buffalo Express,* May 7, 1890, 6.

235. *Buffalo Courier,* April 18, 1890, 5, November 1, 1889, 6; NY State Legislature, *Documents of the Assembly.*

236. New York State Public Service Commission, *Annual Report.*

237. *Buffalo Courier,* April 1, 1890, 5; January 22, 1891, 6.

238. *Syracuse Weekly Express,* November 13, 1890, 3.

239. *Memorial and Family History,* 419–20.

240. *Buffalo Courier,* October 20, 1890, 5.

241. *Buffalo Evening News,* December 1, 1890, 1.

242. *Buffalo Courier,* February 1, 1891, 6.

243. *One Hundred Years of Brewing,* 251.

244. Rizzo, *Through the Mayors' Eyes,* 155.

245. *Buffalo Courier*, March 15, 1891, 6.
246. Buffalo Brewers' Association. *Souvenir of Buffalo.*
247. *Buffalo Courier*, September 12, 1891, 6.
248. Onlinebiographies.info, "Biography of Oscar P. Rochevot."
249. *Buffalo Daily Courier*, January 27, 1892, 6.
250. *History of the City of Buffalo: Its Men*, 140.
251. *One Hundred Years of Brewing*, 251.
252. *Buffalo Evening News*, July 14, 1892, 1.
253. Ibid., March 8, 1893, 1; *Buffalo Express*, April 17, 1893, 6.
254. *Buffalo Express*, Sunday, 1893.
255. *Buffalo Evening News*, January 18, 1893, 5.
256. White, *Our County and Its People*, 125.
257. Ibid.
258. *Buffalo Courier*, July 1, 1894, 11.
259. Ibid., September 7, 1893, 7.Sullivan, "Buffalo's Gustav."
260. Onlinebiograpohies.info, "Biography of Frank F. Illig"; White, *Our County and Its People*, 150.
261. *Memorial and Family History*, 121.
262. Michalak, "Short History of the Simon," 4; Onlinebiographies.info, "Biography of William Simon."
263. U.S. Census Bureau, "Federal Census," 1870.
264. *Western Brewer* July 1909, 368.
265. *Memorial and Family History*, 420.
266. *Buffalo Express*, 1911. ; *Buffalo Courier-Express*, October 8, 1967, 22.
267. Abel Trowbridge Blackmar, "'Our' Family Tree," http://trees.ancestry.com/tree/1101994/person/-1943381850/fact/200270335197.
268. *Buffalo Evening News*, March 18, 1896, 4; *Lewiston Daily Sun*, February 29, 1896, 1; *Syracuse Journal*, March 27, 1902, 10.
269. *Men of New York*, vol. 1, 420–21; *Buffalo Illustrated*, 110.
270. *History of the City of Buffalo: Its Men*, 141.
271. *Buffalo Evening News*, January 30, 1897, 5; *Buffalo Express*, September 14, 1916, 4.
272. *One Hundred Years of Brewing*, 261.
273. *Rome Daily Sentinel*, July 9, 1898, 5.
274. *Utica Daily Press*, October 1, 1897, 1.
275. *Buffalo Courier-Record*, November 20, 1897, 5.
276. *One Hundred Years of Brewing*, 583; *Buffalo Courier-Record*, November 20, 1897, 5.
277. *One Hundred Years of Brewing*, 261.
278. *Rome Daily Sentinel*, July 9, 1898, 5.
279. Michalak, "Short History of the Simon," 3–4.
280. *Buffalo Evening News*, July 15, 1898, 1, April 1, 1899, 1; *Batavia Daily News*, May 12, 1899, 4.
281. *Buffalo Evening News*, August 22, 1898, 1.
282. *American Brewers' Review*, September 20, 1898, 99.
283. *One Hundred Years of Brewing*, 580.

284. *Buffalo Courier,* July 11, 1899, 6.
285. *Buffalo Courier,* June 25, 1899, 24; *Buffalo Express,* June 25, 1899.
286. *Buffalo Evening News,* May 25, 1900, 5.
287. *Buffalo Courier,* June 21, 1899, 4.
288. *One Hundred Years of Brewing,* 251.
289. *Memorial and Family History,* vol I, 259.
290. *History of the City of Buffalo: Its Men,* 137.
291. *Buffalo Evening News,* August 30, 1899, 3.
292. *Western Brewer* October 1915, 112; German-American Historical and Biographical Society, *Buffalo and Its German Community.*
293. *Gambrinus v. Strangmann,* NY S. Ct. (1907); *Buffalo Courier,* February 27, 1902, 9.
294. *Buffalo Evening News,* January 27, 1899, 1.
295. Ibid., June 16, 1931.
296. Ibid., February 28, 1900, 8.
297. Ibid.

CHAPTER 12
298. Infoplease.com, "Population of the Twenty Largest."
299. *One Hundred Years of Brewing,* 580.
300. *Buffalo Evening News,* March 7, 1900, 7.
301. Ibid.
302. *Buffalo Courier,* September 13, 1900, 8.
303. Rizzo, *Through the Mayors' Eyes,* 235.
304. *History of the City of Buffalo: Its Men,* 129.
305. *Buffalo Evening News,* February 23, 1901, 9.
306. Ibid.; *Buffalo Courier,* March 25, 1902, 5.
307. *One Hundred Years of Brewing,* 580.
308. Ibid., 582.
309. Hubbell, Dolan and Jordan, *Our Police, Our City,* 611–613; Jacob Scheu, My Family Tree, http://trees.ancestry.com/tree/20146935/person/904934407.
310. *Gambrinus v. Strangmann,* NY S. Ct. (1907).
311. *Buffalo Courier,* August 17, 1902, 27; *Buffalo Courier-Express,* September 26, 1933.
312. *Western Brewer,* October 1915, 148; *American Brewers' Review,* September 20, 1903, 108.
313. Christian Zwickel, Beilmann Family Tree, http://trees.ancestry.com/tree/47100476/person/25103437930.
314. *Buffalo Evening News,* February 14, 1902, 1; Findagrave.com, "George Sandrock."
315. Rizzo, *Through the Mayors' Eyes,* 155.
316. *Syracuse Journal,* March 27, 1902, 10.
317. *Buffalo Courier,* June 18, 1906.
318. Ibid., August 2, 1902, 3.
319. Ibid., November 6, 1902, 7.
320. *Buffalo Express,* November 26, 1902, 9.
321. Powell, *Rushing the Growler,* 126; *History of the City of Buffalo: Its Men,* 133.

322. *Buffalo Courier,* July 19, 1903.

323. *American Brewers' Review,* May 20, 1903, 521; Findagrave.com, "Albert Ziegele Jr."

324. City of Buffalo, *Directory for the City of Buffalo,* 1903.

325. *Buffalo Courier,* July 30, 1903, 6.

326. *Buffalo Courier-Express,* April 2, 1933, 2.

327. Ibid.

328. *American Carbonator and American Bottler,* March 15, 1904, 80; December 15, 1904, 24.

329. *Syracuse Herald,* November 20, 1904, 6.

330. *Buffalo Express,* May 16, 1905, 6; September 14, 1916, 4.

331. *Buffalo Courier,* March 26, 1905, 24.

332. *Buffalo Express,* May 16, 1905, 6.

333. *American Brewers' Review,* June 1905, 237.

334. *Buffalo Courier,* July 23, 1905, 27.

335. *Buffalo Courier-Express,* December 7, 1932, 19.

336. Michael Schamel, Schamel Family Tree, http://trees.ancestry.com/tree/28288294/person/12025141886.

337. *Buffalo Courier,* February 12, 1906, 3; *Tonawanda Evening News,* February 12, 1906, 8.

338. *Memorial and Family History,* 413–14.

339. *Coopers International Journal,* August 1906, 488–94.

340. Witul, "Buffalo Beer."

341. U.S. Congress, Senate, *Brewing Interests,* 272.

342. *Buffalo Courier,* December 24, 1906, 9; *Buffalo Courier-Express,* June 13, 1933, 19.

343. *Grain Dealers Journal,* September 25, 1906, 412.

344. City of Buffalo, *Directory for the City of Buffalo,* 1903–1904.

345. *Buffalo Courier,* December 12, 1904, 7.

346. Powell, *Rushing the Growler,* 46.

347. *Buffalo Courier,* April 12, 1907, 7.

348. *Buffalo Courier-Express,* April 4, 1907, 2; *Buffalo Evening News,* April 24, 1925.

349. *Buffalo Courier,* September 4, 1907, 9.

350. *History of the City of Buffalo: Its Men,* 132.

351. Ibid., 139.

352. *American Brewers' Review,* April 1, 1908, 137.

353. *Buffalo Evening News,* October 22, 1884, 1; *Buffalo Courier,* March 8, 1905, 22, March 15, 1908, 17.

354. *American Brewers' Journal,* March 1, 1917, 215.

355. Rizzo, *Through the Mayors' Eyes,* 155.

356. Powell, *Rushing the Growler,* 44.

357. U.S. Census Bureau, "Federal Census," 1920. ; Zahm and Nagel Company Incorporated, "About Us."

358. Michalak, "Short History of the Simon," 6.

359. *Buffalo Courier,* February 17, 1909.

360. Ibid., May 10, 1908, 25.

361. Ibid., September 14, 1909, 3; Powell, *Rushing the Growler,* 138.

362. *Western Brewer* July 1909, 368.

363. *Buffalo Courier-Express*, October 11, 1938, 22; August 14, 1962, 6.

364. *Buffalo Courier*, September 16, 1909, 8.

365. *History of the City of Buffalo: Its Men*, 130.

366. *Post-Standard*, November 16, 1909, 5.

367. White, *Our County and Its People*, 459; *Buffalo Express*, November 29, 1909; *Ice and Refrigeration*, February 1910, 117; *Buffalo Courier*, April 15, 1911, 3.

CHAPTER 13

368. *Batavia Times*, November 24, 1912, 10.

369. *Buffalo Courier*, April 27, 1901, 6.

370. Ibid., May 22, 1911, 7.

371. Ibid., March 9, 1912, 6.

372. *Industrial Refrigeration*, Vol. 43, September, 1912, 101.

373. Ibid.

374. *Buffalo Courier-Express*, April 24, 1956, 9.

375. *Buffalo Courier*, December 5, 1912, 8; February 21, 1915, 67.

376. Ibid., July 14, 1919.

377. *Buffalo Evening News*, August 24, 1915, 13; *Buffalo Express*, December 20, 1912, 18.

378. *Buffalo Courier*, May 17, 1907, 12; June 17, 1911, 8

379. *Medina Journal-Register*, 1913, 1914.

380. *New York Times*, May 28, 1914, 15.

381. *Buffalo Courier*, January 26, 1915, 8.

382. Jacob F Kuhn, Kuhn Family Tree. http://trees.ancestry.com/tree/65326481/person/32148505037.

383. *Buffalo Evening News*, February 27, 1915, 8.

384. *Western Brewer*, October 1915, 112; Dennée, "Robert Portner."

385. *Western Brewer*, October 1915, 135,

386. Ibid., 148; *American Brewers' Journal*, October 1, 1916, 498.

387. *Western Brewer*, November 1915, 172; *American Brewers' Review*, January 1916, 16.

388. *Western Brewer*, November 1915, 176.

389. *Banking Law Journal*, January 1933, 1.

390. *Buffalo Express*, September 14, 1916, 4.

391. *American Brewers' Review*, November 1916, 318.

392. Ibid., September 1916, 245.

393. Ibid., December 1916, 368.

394. Ibid.

395. Ibid., August 1916, 220.

396. Ibid., 211.

397. Ibid., July 1916, 265; *Buffalo Evening News*, October 3, 1916, 2.

398. *Best's Insurance News*, October 10, 1921, 71.

399. *Buffalo Express*, December 18, 1916, 4.

400. *Western Brewer*, November 1917, 115.

401. *Buffalo Courier*, April 4, 1918, 8.

402. Ibid., June 14, 1917, 5.

403. Ibid., June 22, 1917, 2.
404. *Saratogian*, December 15, 1917, 3; *Buffalo Courier*, December 15, 1915, 5.
405. *Buffalo Courier*, February 27, 1918, 5.
406. *Western Brewer*, July 1918, 3.
407. *New York Sun*, March 18, 1918, 13.
408. *Buffalo Courier-Express*, October 11, 1938, 22.
409. *Buffalo Evening News*, June 16, 1931.
410. *Operative Miller*, October, 1918, 337.
411. Michalak, "Short History of the Simon," 5.
412. *Buffalo Courier*, May 10, 1919.
413. Ibid., May 20, 1919, 5; *Western Brewer* January 1918, 8; *American Brewers' Journal*, Vol. 50–51, 1918, 102.
414. *Buffalo Courier*, March 2, 1920, 4; May 30, 1919, 1.
415. *Buffalo Times*, July 14, 1919; July 15, 1919.
416. Fitch, *Encyclopedia of Biography*, 420; *Buffalo Times*, July 14, 1919; July 15, 1919.
417. *Buffalo Evening News*, June 25, 1919; *Oswego Daily Palladium*, June 26, 1919, 5.
418. *Buffalo Courier*, October 26, 1910, 14.
419. Ibid.
420. National Archives, "Teaching with Documents."
421. U.S. House of Representatives, "Historical Highlights."
422. *Buffalo Express*, September 10, 1919; *Buffalo Courier*, September 10, 1919, 2.
423. Official Gazette of the United States Patent Office, December13, 1910, 530.
424. *Oswego Daily Times*, November 11, 1919, 4.
425. *Buffalo Courier*, December 19, 1919, 11.

CHAPTER 14
426. *Rome Daily Sentinel*, February 14, 1920, 9.
427. New York State Department of Environmental Conservation, "1050–1088 Niagara Street."
428. *Buffalo Courier-Express*, July 17, 1932, 2.
429. Ibid., May 25, 1920, 11.
430. *Buffalo Courier*, May 25, 1920, 11; May 23, 1920, 53.
431. *Buffalo Express*, April 29, 1920.
432. Michalak, "Short History of the Simon," 4.
433. Brewers' Journal, Vol. 50–51, 1918, 102
434. Rizzo, *Through the Mayors' Eyes*, 236.
435. Ibid., 237.
436. Onlinebiographies.info, "Biography of Frank. J. Illig."
437. *Buffalo Courier*, March 2, 1923, 13.
438. Ibid., 5.
439. *Buffalo Evening News*, February 18, 1922, 11; *Buffalo Express*, May 23, 1922, 4; April 24, 1956, 9.
440. *Buffalo Courier-Express*, October 11, 1938, 22; City of Buffalo, *Directory for the City of Buffalo*, 1932.

441. *Buffalo Courier-Express*, September 11, 1959, 7.
442. Doug and Linda's Dairy Antique Site, "Colored Milk Bottles."
443. Michalak, "Short History of the Simon," 7.
444. *Buffalo Evening News*, June 8, 1926, 3.
445. Ibid., June 2, 1926, 18.
446. Ibid., June 10, 1926, 46.
447. *Buffalo Courier-Express*, October 1, 1926, 1; *Buffalo Evening News*, October 1, 1926, 20.
448. Library of Congress, "Kreiner Malting Grain Elevator."
449. *Niagara Falls Gazette*, May 6, 1927, 12.
450. *Buffalo Evening News*, June 2, 1926, 18; May 6, 1927; *Niagara Falls Gazette*, May 6, 1927, 12.
451. *Banking Law Journal*, January 1933, 1; *Buffalo Evening News*, March 24, 1927.
452. *Buffalo Courier-Express*, March 22, 1927.
453. *Banking Law Journal*, January 1933, 1.
454. *Buffalo Evening News*, August 23, 1927, 32.
455. Ibid., February 4, 1928, 1.
456. *Buffalo Courier-Express*, June 29, 1923.
457. *Buffalo Times*, July 3, 1927; *Buffalo Courier-Express*, February 23, 1929.
458. *Buffalo Courier-Express*, April 8, 1929, 18.
459. Ibid., June 22, 1929; June 30, 1929, 9; *Memorial and Family History*, 352.
460. *Buffalo Courier-Express*, October 17, 1929, 6; October 18, 1929, 10.

CHAPTER 15
461. *Lockport Union-Sun and Journal*, January 6, 1930, 2.
462. *Rochester Democrat and Chronicle*, January 3, 1930.
463. *Buffalo Courier-Express*, November 6, 1930, 11.
464. Ibid., February 28, 1932, 1.
465. Ibid., November 6, 1930, 1.
466. Ibid., February 9, 1931, 10.
467. *Buffalo Evening News*, June 16, 1931.
468. *Buffalo Courier-Express*, September 17, 1931, 1.
469. *Tonawanda Evening News*, December 18, 1931, 4; *Tonawanda News*, August 20, 1977, 21A.
470. *Buffalo Courier-Express*, December 7, 1932, 19; *Tonawanda News*, August 20, 1977, 21A.
471. *Buffalo Courier-Express*, October 11, 1938, 22.
472. *Buffalo Courier-Express*, May 16, 1932, 1; *Buffalo Courier*, February 7, 1926, 90.
473. *Buffalo Courier-Express*, June 7, 1932, 10; January 29, 1933, 1.
474. Ibid., December 7, 1932, 19.
475. Ibid., January 25, 1933.
476. *Tonawanda Evening News*, March 11, 1933, 2.
477. *Buffalo Courier-Express*, June 17, 1933, 9.
478. Ibid., April 20, 1933, 20.

479. *Erie County Independent*, 11, 1933, 9; City of Buffalo, *Directory for the City of Buffalo*, 1933.
480. *Buffalo Courier-Express*, October 11, 1938, 22.
481. Ibid., March 15, 1933, 1.
482. Ibid., April 7, 1933, 2; April 10, 1933, 10; May 7, 1933, 3.
483. Ibid., December 5, 1933, 20.
484. Ibid., June 13, 1933, 19.
485. Michalak, "Short History of the Simon," 8; *Buffalo Courier-Express*, May 11, 1933, 1.
486. Michalak, "Short History of the Simon," 9.
487. City of Buffalo, *Directory for the City of Buffalo*, 1933.
488. *Buffalo Courier-Express*, June 2, 1933, 24; July 21, 1933, 22.
489. Powell, *Rushing the Growler*, 52; *Buffalo Courier-Express*, March 19, 1935.
490. *Buffalo Courier-Express*, May 22, 1935, 12.
491. Michalak, "Short History of the Simon," 12.
492. *Buffalo Courier-Express*, April 22, 1934, 5.
493. Ibid., February 13, 1935, 15.
494. *Lockport Union-Sun and Journal*, June 25, 1935, 10; *Buffalo Courier-Express*, October 11, 1938, 22.
495. Kriegbaum-Hanks, *History of the Germans*.
496. *Buffalo Courier-Express*, May 18, 1935, 5.
497. *Tonawanda News*, August 20, 1977, 21A.
498. *Moffat v. Phoenix Brewery*, NY S. Ct. (1940); *Buffalo Courier-Express*, February 6, 1936, 7.
499. *Moffat v. Phoenix Brewery*, NY S. Ct. (1940).
500. *Buffalo Courier-Express*, May 26, 1936.
501. Ibid., May 26, 1936, 9.
502. *Buffalo Courier-Express*, June 30, 1936, 14.
503. Ibid., June 14, 1942, 6, 1.
504. *Buffalo Courier-Express*, September 22, 1937, 22; *Lockport Union-Sun and Journal*, April 7, 1939, 14.
505. *Buffalo Courier-Express*, April 28, 1937, 24.
506. Ibid., October 11, 1938, 22.
507. Witul, "Buffalo Beer"; *New York Post*, November 9, 1938, 13; Lilacs.
508. *Memorial and Family History*, 260.
509. Beercanhistory.com, "ABC's of Cans."
510. *Tonawanda News*, August 20, 1977, 21A.

CHAPTER 16

511. *Buffalo Courier-Express*, April 12, 1940, 28.
512. Ibid., May 30, 1940, 24.
513. Ibid., June 4, 1941, 24.
514. *Niagara Falls Gazette*, June 13, 1941, 1.
515. *Buffalo Courier-Express*, September 29, 1942, 20.
516. Ibid., June 14, 1942, 6, 1.
517. Ibid., November 4, 1942, 19.

518. *Tonawanda News*, August 20, 1977, 21A.
519. Ibid., September 17, 1977, 3A.
520. Beercanhistory.com, "ABC's of Cans."
521. *Buffalo Courier-Express*, July 15, 1944, 5.
522. Ibid.
523. Ibid., June 19, 1945, 5, June 20, 1945, 7.
524. *Lockport Union-Sun Journal*, May 4, 1939, 2; *Buffalo Courier-Express*, July 19, 1946, 9.
525. Ibid., January 21, 1947, 7.
526. Ibid., July 5, 1946.
527. *Tonawanda News*, September 17, 1977, 3A.
528. *Buffalo Courier-Express*, May 28, 1947, 23.
529. Ibid., June 16, 1947, 21; August 7, 1947, 23.
530. Library of Congress, "Kreiner Malting Grain Elevator."
531. *New York Sun*, April 19, 1948, 5.
532. *Buffalo Courier-Express*, March 25, 1948, 21.
533. Michalak, "Short History of the Simon," 8; *Buffalo Courier-Express*, January 14, 1958, 5.
534. *Buffalo Courier-Express*, January 18, 1949, 11A.
535. Ibid., April 1, 1949, 24.
536. Witul, "Buffalo Beer."
537. *Tonawanada Evening News*, April 42, 1949, 1.
538. *Buffalo Courier-Express*, November 22, 1950, 7.

CHAPTER 17
539. *Niagara Falls Gazette*, August 8, 1950, 4; *Buffalo Courier-Express*, October 5, 1950, 30.
540. *Buffalo Courier-Express*, December 15, 1968, 74.
541. Powell, *Rushing the Growler*, 97.
542. *Buffalo Courier-Express*, April 10, 1952, 13.
543. Kev's Cans, "Steins Brewery."
544. *Buffalo Courier-Express*, June 17, 1955, 3, May 14, 1955, 3.
545. *Buffalo*, "Beer & Buffalo," November 1964, 33.
546. *Buffalo Courier-Express*, April 24, 1956, 9.
547. Ibid., December 10, 1957, 42.
548. Ibid., May 15, 1957, 36.
549. Rustycans.com, "Tudor Ale."
550. *Buffalo Courier-Express*, January 14, 1958, 5.
551. Ibid., January 30, 1958, 30.
552. Ibid., April 8, 1960, 42D.
553. Ibid., June 1, 1959, 30, September 30, 1960, 5.
554. Ibid., September 12, 1959, 7.

CHAPTER 18
555. Library of Congress, "Kreiner Malting Grain Elevator."
556. *Tonawanda News*, March 24, 1962, 9; *Buffalo Courier-Express*, September 11, 1959, 7.

557. Ibid., August 14, 1962, 6.
558. Library of Congress, "Kreiner Malting Grain Elevator."
559. *Buffalo Courier-Express,* January 11, 1965, Deaths.
560. *Buffalo* magazine, November 1964, 34.
561. *Buffalo Courier-Express,* May 8, 1960, 42D.
562. *Findlay Republican-Courier,* March 8, 1966, 2; *Buffalo Courier-Express,* July 24, 1966, 11C; December 20, 1965, 19.
563. *Niagara Falls Gazette,* June 13, 1966, 12.
564. *Buffalo Courier-Express,* August 3, 1966, 34.
565. Ibid., November 20, 1966, 12A.
566. Ibid., March 12, 1967, 11C.
567. Ibid., February 28, 1968, 44.
568. *Buffalo Courier-Express,* February 28, 1968, 44.
569. Ibid., August 16, 1968, 16.
570. Michalak, "Short History of the Simon," 17.
571. *Buffalo Courier-Express,* March 16, 1969, 54.
572. *Hamburg Front Page,* May 12, 1966, 9; April 10, 1969, 6.
573. *Buffalo Courier-Express,* August 22, 1969, 8.

CHAPTER 19
574. *Niagara Falls Gazette,* July 23, 1970, 4.
575. *Geneva Times,* August 22, 1970, 3.
576. *Niagara Falls Gazette,* August 17, 1971, 14.
577. Pompa, "Iroquois Brewing History"; *Niagara Falls Gazette,* August 17, 1971, 14.
578. Michalak, "Short History of the Simon," 26; *Buffalo Evening News,* December 2, 1971.
579. *Buffalo Evening News,* December 2, 1971.
580. *Dunkirk (NY) Evening Observer,* December 1, 1971; November 25, 1974.
581. Ibid., August 12, 1972.
582. Ibid., November 25, 1974.

CHAPTER 20
583. *Medina Journal-Register* , September 8, 1988, 14.
584. E-mail correspondence with Jeff Ware, May 2014.
585. E-mail correspondence with Matt Kahn, June 2014.
586. Buffalo History Works, "Grain Elevators."
587. "Queen City Malting to operate at The Barrel Factory, Old First Ward!" http://wnycraftbeer.com/queen-city-malting-coming-to-old-first-ward (accessed October 26, 2014).
588. Vang, "Past, Present, and Yes."
589. *Buffalo Evening News,* September 22, 2014.

BIBLIOGRAPHY

BOOKS

Bailey, George M. *Illustrated Buffalo: The Queen City of the Lakes*. New York: Acme Publishing, 1896.

Buffalo Board of Trade. *The City of Buffalo and Its Surroundings, Its Business Facilities and Its Advantages as a Place of Residence and Summer Resort*. Buffalo, NY: Courier Printing Company, 1880.

Buffalo Brewers' Association. *Souvenir of Buffalo, On Occasion of the 37th Annual Convention at Buffalo, N.Y., June 1897*. Buffalo, NY: Matthews-Northrup Company, 1897.

Buffalo Chamber of Commerce. *Greater Buffalo & Niagara Frontier, Niagara Falls, the Tonawandas, Lockport and Depour*. Buffalo, NY: Buffalo Chamber of Commerce, 1914.

Buffalo Illustrated: Commerce, Trade and Industries of Buffalo. Buffalo, NY: Courier Printing Company, 1890.

Craemer, Josef Ludwig. *The Royal Bavarian Castles in Word and Picture*. Munich, Germany: self-published, 1900.

Dunn, Walter S., Jr., ed. *History of Erie County, 1870–1970*. Buffalo, NY: Buffalo and Erie County Historical Society, 1972.

Fitch, Charles Elliott. *Encyclopedia of Biography of New York: A Life Record of Men and Women Whose Sterling Character and Energy Have Made Them Preeminent in Their Own and Many States*. New York: American Historical Society, Incorporated, 1916.

Hill, Henry H. *The Municipality of Buffalo: A History*. 4 vols. New York: Lewis Historical Publishing Company, 1923.

Hill, Henry Wayland. *Men of Buffalo*. Chicago: A.N. Marquis and Company, 1902.

History of the City of Buffalo: It's Men and Institutions: Biographical Sketches of Leading Citizens, A. Buffalo, NY: Buffalo Evening News, 1908.

Horton, John Theodore. *History of Northwestern New York*. New York: Lewis Historical Publishing Company, 1947.

BIBLIOGRAPHY

Hubbell, Mark S., William H. Dolan and John A Jordan. *Our Police, Our City: The Official History of the Buffalo Police Department from the Earliest Days to the Present Time.* Buffalo, NY: Bensler and Wesley, 1893.

Larned, J.N. *History of Buffalo.* 2 vols. New York: Progress of the Empire State Company, 1911.

Mansfield, John Brandt, ed. *History of the Great Lakes.* 2 vols. Chicago: J.H. Beers and Company, 1899.

Mant, Richard, M.A. *Poetical Works of the Late Thomas Warton, B.D.* London, UK: Oxford, 1802.

Marthens, A.F., ed. *Commerce, Manufactures and Resources of Buffalo and Environs.* Buffalo, NY: General Publishing Company, 1880.

Memorial and Family History of Erie County, New York. Buffalo, NY: Genealogical Publishing Company, 1908.

Men of New York: A Collection of Biographies and Portraits of Citizens of the Empire State Prominent in Business, Professional, Social, and Political Life During the Last Decade of the Nineteenth Century, the. 2 vols. Buffalo, NY: Geo. E. Matthews and Company, 1898.

Mueller, Jacob E. *Buffalo and Its German Community Illustrated.* Buffalo, NY: German-American Historical and Biographical Society, 1912.

One Hundred Years of Brewing: A Complete History of the Progress Made in the Art, Science and Industry of Brewing in the World, Particularly During the Last Century. Chicago: H.S. Rich and Company, 1901.

Powell, Stephen R. *Rushing the Growler: A History of Brewing in Buffalo.* Buffalo, NY: Apogee Productions, 1999.

Rizzo, Michael F. *Through the Mayors' Eyes.* Buffalo, NY: Lulu Press, 2005.

Smith, H. Perry. *History of the City of Buffalo and Erie County.* 2 vols. Syracuse, NY: D. Mason and Company, 1884.

Warton, Thomas. *The Poetical Works of the Late Thomas Warton, B.D.* London, UK: University Press, 1802.

White, Truman C., ed. *Our County and Its People.* 2 vols. Boston, MA: Boston History Company, 1898.

NEWSPAPERS

Albany Times (Albany, NY), 1887–89.

Batavia Daily News (Batavia, NY), 1899.

Batavia Times (Batavia, NY), 1912.

Buffalo Courier (Buffalo, NY), 1890–1922.

Buffalo Courier and Republic (Buffalo, NY), 1879.

Buffalo Courier-Express (Buffalo, NY), 1926–82.

Buffalo Courier-Record (Buffalo, NY), 1897.

Buffalo Daily Courier (Buffalo, NY), 1842–1926.

Buffalo Evening News/Buffalo News (Buffalo, NY), 1881–present.

Buffalo Evening Republic (Buffalo, NY), 1876–80.

Buffalo Express (Buffalo, NY), 1846–1926.

Buffalo Times (Buffalo, NY), 1883–1939.

BIBLIOGRAPHY

Daily Graphic (New York, NY), 1874.
Erie County Independent (Hamburg, NY), 1885–1933.
Findlay Republican-Courier (Findlay, OH), 1966.
Geneva Times (Geneva, NY), 1970.
Hamburg Front Page (Hamburg, NY), 1966.
Lewiston Daily Sun (Lewiston, ME), 1896.
Lockport Union Sun and Journal (Lockport, NY), 1935–39.
Lowell Daily Courier (Lowell, MA), 1883.
Medina Journal-Register (Medina, NY), 1913–88.
New York Post, 1938.
New York Sun, 1880–1948.
New York Times, 1914.
Niagara Falls Gazette (Niagara Falls, NY), 1927–71.
Oswego Daily Palladium (Oswego, NY), 1919.
Oswego Daily Times (Oswego, NY), 1919.
Post-Standard (Syracuse, NY), 1909.
Rochester Democrat and Chronicle (Rochester, NY), 1930.
Rome Daily Sentinel (Rome, NY), 1898–1920.
Saratogian (Saratoga, NY), 1917.
Schenectady Cabinet (Schenectady, NY), 1820.
Spirit of the Times Batavia (New York, NY), 1880.
Syracuse Herald (Syracuse, NY), 1904.
Syracuse Journal (Syracuse, NY), 1902.
Syracuse Weekly Express (Syracuse, NY), 1890.
Tonawanda Evening News (Tonawanda, NY), 1906–33.
Tonawanda News (Tonawanda, NY), 1977.
Troy Daily Times (Troy, NY), 1887.
Utica Daily Press (Utica, NY), 1897.
Utica Morning Herald (Utica, NY), 1880.

OTHER SOURCES

Albright-Knox Art Gallery. "Buffalo Cotton Factory." Historypin.appspot.com. http://www.vs3-12.historypin.appspot.com/attach/uid31985/map/#!/geo:42.88793,-78.888254/zoom:15/dialog:167988/tab:details.
American Brewers' Review, September 1898–November 1916.
American Carbonator and American Bottler, March 1904–December 1904.
Banking Law Journal, January 1933
"Beer & Buffalo." *Buffalo*, November 1964.
Beercanhistory.com. "ABC's of Cans (A to D)." http://beercanhistory.com/abcs.htm.
Best's Insurance News, October 10, 1921.
Buffalo and Erie County Historical Society. *Niagara Frontier 1953–1983*.
Buffalo Historical Society. *Publications of the Buffalo Historical Society*. 34 vols. Buffalo, New York. 1879–1959.

BIBLIOGRAPHY

Buffalo History Works. "Grain Elevators: A History." http://buffalohistoryworks. com/grain/history/history.htm.

Carroll, Ed. "Buffalo Brewing Co. History." New Helvetia Brewing Company. http://newhelvetiabrew.com/history.

City of Buffalo. *Directory for the City of Buffalo*. 1828–present.

Coopers International Journal, August 1906.

Dennée, Timothy J. "Robert Portner and His Brewing Company." Revised. 2010. https://www.alexandriava.gov/uploadedFiles/historic/info/archaeology/ ARSiteReportHistoryPortnerBrewingCoAX196.pdf.

Doug and Linda's Dairy Antique Site. "Colored Milk Bottles." http://dairyantiques. com/Colored_Milk_Bottles.html.

Findagrave.com. "Albert Ziegele Jr." http://findagrave.com/cgi-bin/fg.cgi?page=p v&GRid=81322311&PIpi=52530922.

———. "George Sandrock." http://findagrave.com/cgi-bin/fg.cgi?page=pv&GRi d=128511896&PIpi=100223761.

———. "Valentine Blatz." http://www.findagrave.com/cgi-bin/ fg.cgi?page=gr&GRid=3498.

Gambrinus v. Strangmann. NY S. Ct. (1907).

German-American Historical and Biographical Society. *Buffalo and Its German Community: Illustrated*. Translated by Susan Kriegbaum-Hanks. N.p: Jacob E. Mueller, 1911–12. http://www.archivaria.com/BusDbios/BusDbios25.html.

"Grain Trade News." *Grain Dealers Journal*, September 25, 1906.

Ice and Refrigeration, February 1910.

Industrial Refrigeration, September 1912.

Industry in Buffalo. Buffalo, NY: Buffalo and Erie County Public Library, Buffalo, New York.

Infoplease.com. "Population of the Twenty Largest U.S. Cities, 1900–2012." http:// www.infoplease.com/ipa/A0922422.html.

Johnson, Holly. "History of Hormel Family." Hormelhistorichome.com. http:// hormelhistorichome.org/HiSTORY_OF_HORMEL_FAMILY.php.

Kev's Cans. "Steins Brewery." http://www.angelfire.com/ny/kevscans/steins.html.

Kiefer, David M. "Brewing: A Legacy of Ancient Times." *Today's Chemist*. http:// pubs.acs.org/subscribe/archive/tcaw/10/i12/html/12chemchron.html.

Kriegbaum-Hanks, Susan, trans. *History of the Germans in Buffalo and Erie County, N.Y. with Biographies and Illustrations of the Aforementioned German-Americans Who Have Influenced the Development of the City of Buffalo*. Buffalo, NY: Reinecke & Zesch, 1898. http://www.archivaria.com/GdDhistory/GdDhistory6.html.

Library of Congress. "Kreiner Malting Grain Elevator." http://lcweb2.loc.gov/ master/pnp/habshaer/ny/ny1600/ny1686/data/ny1686data.pdf.

———. "Washburn Crosby Elevator, 54 South Michigan Avenue, Buffalo, Erie County, NY." http://www.loc.gov/pictures/item/ny1672.

Lilacs, the. http://www.thelilacs.com.

Local Biographies Scrapbook. Buffalo: Buffalo and Erie County Public Library. Buffalo, New York.

BIBLIOGRAPHY

Local History Scrapbook. Buffalo, NY: Buffalo and Erie County Public Library.

Michalak, Andrew A. "A Short History of the Simon Brewery." Thesis, 1979.

Moffat v. Phoenix Brewery. NY S. Ct. (1940).

National Archives. "Teaching with Documents: The Volstead Act and Related Prohibition Documents." http://www.archives.gov/education/lessons/volstead-act.

New York State Bureau of Labor Statistics. *Annual Report*, 1890.

New York State Department of Environmental Conservation. "1050–1088 Niagara Street." http://www.dec.ny.gov/chemical/94915.html.

New York State Legislature. *Documents of the Assembly* 11.

New York State Public Service Commission. *Annual Report* 12, no. 1.

Onlinebiographies.info. "Biography of Anselm Hoefner." http://www.onlinebiographies.info/ny/erie/a-l/hoeftner-a.htm.

———. "Biography of William Simon." http://www.onlinebiographies.info/ny/erie/m-y/simon-w.htm.

Operative Miller, October 1918.

Pompa, J. Anthony. "Iroquois Brewing History." *Beer, Breweries, and Breweriana of Upstate New York*. http://heritage575.tripod.com/iroquois_history.html.

Rustycans.com. "Tudor Ale: Circa 1950s." http://www.rustycans.com/COM/month0108.html.

Sullivan, Jack. "Buffalo's Gustav Was the Other Fleischmann Brother." Those Pre-Pro Whiskey Men! http://pre-prowhiskeymen.blogspot.com/2012/07/buffalos-gustav-was-other-fleischmann.html.

U.S. Census Bureau. "Federal Census." 1860, 1870, 1920. Ancestry.com.

U.S. Congress. Senate. *Brewing and Liquor Interests and German and Bolshevik Propaganda*. 66th Cong., 1st sess., 1919. S. Doc. 62, serial 7597.

U.S. House of Representatives. "Historical Highlights: The Volstead Act." http://history.house.gov/Historical-Highlights/1901-1950/The-Volstead-Act.

U.S. Internal Revenue Service. "Products of Industry." Washington, D.C., 1863 and 1871.

Vang, Richard. "The Past, Present, and Yes, Future of the Hops Industry." *Upstate Alive Magazine* 1996. http://www.upstatechunk.com/beer/hops/nyhistory.htm.

Western Brewer: And Journal of the Barley, Malt and Hop Trades. Gibson Publishing Company, various years.

Williamson, Samuel H. "Five Ways to Compute the Relative Value of a U.S. Dollar Amount." MeasuringWorth.Com. 2006. http://www.measuringworth.com/calculators/ppowerus.

Witul, Gregory. "A Buffalo Beer Named for a Polish Opera." *Am-Pol Eagle*. http://ampoleagle.com/a-buffalo-beer-named-for-a-polish-opera-p6136-202.htm.

Zahm and Nagel Company Incorporated. "About Us." http://www.zahmnagel.com/AboutUs/tabid/56/Default.aspx.

INDEX

INDEX

INDEX

INDEX

INDEX

INDEX

N

Nagel, John F. 96, 112, 118, 124, 125, 128
Naisineth, John B. 80
nanobrewery 180
National Aniline and Chemical Company 107
National Association of Maltsters 112
National Fuel Gas 79
natural gas 69, 71, 79, 112
Newton, Charles 102
New York Central Railroad 60
New York State Brewers' Association 60, 121, 139
New York State Liquor Authority 155
Niagara College of Canada Brewing School 183
Niagara Falls 9, 55, 66, 89, 112, 134, 145
Niagara grain-elevator 46
Niagara Malt House 59
Niagara Malting Company 46, 65, 110
Niagara Stamping & Tool Works 87
Niagara Starch Works 87
Nichols Middle School 122
Niederpruner, J.W. 84
Nielsen, Johannes 152
Noble, Charles B. 56
Nomis Beverage Company, Incorporated 136
Nussbaumer, Newell 11

O

Old First Ward Brewing Company 182
Orpheus 87, 89, 105, 108, 125, 139
Oswego Milling Company 127

P

Pabst Brewing Company 88, 101, 154
Paderewski, Jan 110
Pan-American Exposition 98, 101, 122, 125
Pan-American Grill & Brewery 180

Pankow, Charles G. 65, 89, 98, 100
Parade House 106
Park Brewery 61
pasteurization 42, 119
Pasteur, Louis 42, 153
Patrzykowski, John 92
Patterson-Tanski, Gregory 180
Peace Bridge 141
Peacock, P. 19
Pearl Street Grill & Brewery 178, 180
People's Brewing Company 92
Persch, Gretchen 109
Persch, John P. 108
Peters, William C. 76
Phillips, Joseph 83, 99, 118, 124, 129, 135, 137
Phoenix Brewery 76, 97, 103, 105, 107, 110, 123, 127, 142, 149, 162
Phoenix Brewery Corporation 140, 149, 150, 151, 153, 155, 162, 165, 167, 171
Polish National Alliance 154
porter 44, 47, 67, 109, 111, 156
Portner, Robert 62, 95
Potter, Leo 158
Prohibition 15, 106, 108, 109, 110, 116, 117, 118, 123, 125, 127, 128, 129, 131, 132, 133, 134, 135, 136, 137, 138, 139, 140, 141, 142, 144, 145, 146, 149, 150, 151, 153, 154, 158, 160, 163, 164, 165, 167, 169, 170, 186
Pullman Palace Car Company 99

Q

Queen City Brewing Company 76, 83
Queen City Malt House 63, 93, 98, 100
Queen City Malting 185

R

Raines Excise Bill 89, 125
Ramsperger, Samuel J. 136
Ratcliffe, Stephen, Sr. 70
Rathskeller 171

INDEX

INDEX

INDEX

ABOUT THE AUTHORS

Michael F. Rizzo has been a network administrator, bike messenger, tour guide, school bus driver, historian, lecturer, father, brother, husband and son. He has written history, survived cancer and likes a good craft beer and loud music. A native of Buffalo, he lives in the Pacific Northwest with his family.

Ethan Andrew Cox is the president of Community Beer Works, a brewery he co-founded in 2010. He had a fifteen-year background as a homebrewer prior, as well as being a Beer Judge Certification Program–certified homebrewing competetion judge and a Certified CiceroneTM; currently, he is on the board of the New York State Brewers' Association. He lives in Buffalo with his wife, Jennifer, and their two sons, Phineas and Aleister.

Visit us at
www.historypress.net
....
This title is also available as an e-book